Materials, Specification and Detailing

Technical design in architecture is a vital function in the realisation of successful buildings. It ranges from the simple assembly of components to the fully integrated design of novel construction systems. Within the holistic philosophy introduced in Volume 1 of this series, this book is intended to develop students' understanding of the various layers of knowledge, skills and mechanisms that make up the many approaches to technical design.

Rather than offer a particular methodology, the writers draw on their experience in architectural education to provide a detailed description of the development process and to acknowledge traditional solutions while challenging designers to consider innovative alternatives. Attention is paid to materials choices, detail design and specification writing. The text is illustrated with the use of case studies. It aims to encourage students, as tomorrow's professionals, to take an enthusiastic approach to the development of the language of technical design and, above all, to fully embrace their environmental responsibilities as designers.

Norman Wienand is Head of the Architecture Subject Group at Sheffield Hallam University, where, as an academic and a Chartered Architectural Technologist, his focus is on the development of the pedagogy of architectural technology at undergraduate and postgraduate levels. Coupled with the pursuit of sustainable design through the application of sustainable technologies, he is engaged in the development of a theoretical approach to technical design in architecture.

Joan Zunde is an architect who has taught design subjects for many years. She is editor for the Technologies of Architecture series and co-author of Volume 1, *Integrated Strategies in Architecture*. She has a particular interest in communication between designers and clients and within the design and build team.

Technologies of Architecture
Editor: Joan Zunde

Technologies of Architecture is an introductory textbook series providing a coherent framework to the architectural design process in a practical and applied way. This series forms an essential suite of books for students of architectural technology, architecture, building surveying and construction.

Advisory board
Michael Ashley
Mark Kennett
Stephen Pretlove
Peter Smith
Norman Wienand

Other titles
Volume 1: *Integrated Strategies in Architecture*
Joan Zunde and Hocine Bougdah

Volume 2: *Environment, Technology and Sustainability*
Stephen Sharples and Hocine Bougdah

Volume 4: *Practice, Management and Responsibility*
John Hickey

Volume 5: *History, Performance and Conservation*
Barry Bridgwood and Lindsay Lennie

Technologies of Architecture
VOLUME 3

Materials, Specification and Detailing

Foundations of building design

Norman Wienand
with Joan Zunde

Illustrations by
Norman Wienand, Joan Zunde
and Sean Wienand

Taylor & Francis
Taylor & Francis Group

First published 2008 by Taylor & Francis
2 Park Square, Milton Park, Abingdon, OX14 4RN

Simultaneously published in the USA and Canada by Taylor & Francis
270 Madison Avenue, New York, NY10016

Taylor & Francis is an imprint of the Taylor & Francis Group, an informa business

Typeset in Univers by Integra Software Services Pvt. Ltd., Pondicherry, India
Printed and bound in Great Britain by TJ International Ltd, Padstow, Cornwall

British Library Cataloguing in Publication Data
A catalogue record for this book is available from the British Library

Library of Congress Cataloging in Publication Data
Wienand, Norman.
Materials, specification and detailing: foundations of building design / Norman Wienand.
p. cm. – (Technologies of architecture ; v. 3)
Includes bibliographical references and index.
ISBN 978-0-415-40358-0 (hbk : alk. paper) – ISBN 978-0-415-40359-7 (pbk : alk. paper)
1. Architectural design. 2. Building materials. 3. Buildings–Specifications. I. Title.

NA2750.W54 2007
721–dc22
2007020354

ISBN10: 0-415-40358-8 (hbk)
ISBN10: 0-415-40359-6 (pbk)
ISBN10: 0-203-94017-2 (ebk)

ISBN13: 978-0-415-40358-0 (hbk)
ISBN13: 978-0-415-40359-7 (pbk)
ISBN13: 978-0-203-94017-4 (ebk)

Acknowledgements

Appreciation is expressed to the following people and organisations without whom the book could not have been written:

- David Cheetham, who had the original idea
- the Advisory Panel
- the team at Taylor & Francis, whose patience has been significant
- CIAT for their continued interest and
  in particular,
- Joan Zunde, the series editor (who has also contributed a section to this book), whose support and encouragement throughout has been invaluable.

The following individuals and bodies who have permitted drawings of their buildings to be reproduced:

- the Chartered Institute of Architectural Technologists
- Ancon Building Products
- the Pilkington Group
- the Concrete Centre
- Sheffield Hallam University, Jonathan Arksey, Jake Rotherham and Rhys Edwards.

The colleagues and friends who have been supportive and especially my family for sacrificing yet another Christmas holiday.

Norman Wienand
JANUARY 2007

Contents

Foreword

As Vice President Education it gives me pleasure to support Volume 3 in the Technologies of Architecture series.

Materials, Specification and Detailing: Foundations of Building Design goes to the core of architectural technology.

This book provides for trainee or qualified Chartered Architectural Technologists (MCIAT) to understand their particular specialisms. To be recognised as competent, a Chartered Architectural Technologist must be able to analyse, synthesise and evaluate design factors in order to produce design solutions which will satisfy performance, production and procurement criteria.

This will be achieved through the design, selection and specification of material, components and assembly and the management, coordination, communication, presentation and monitoring of solutions, which perform to the agreed brief and standards in terms of time, cost and quality.

In this publication, the author carefully takes the reader through aspects of the technical design process from early stages right through to the detailed design. Any design has to be communicated to the end-user in a way they can understand so that the requirements of the designer are correctly implemented on site.

The book also explains the design process, methods of communication and the conventions in drawing and specification production. Communication of information is a vital section in this book as it is only through correct communication of designs that the designer can ensure that those carrying out the work on site can understand fully, as they need to, the ideas, thoughts and concerns of the designer.

Seemingly insignificant changes on site to a design can cause a design to fail and operatives need to be aware of the impact of these changes.

Wrong selection of materials can produce a failed design and the process to correctly select the right materials is very important. This book explains the process and establishes the selection criteria to enable a correct choice of materials.

The section on detailed design explains the process and presentation of the designer's ideas in a form that can be understood and used to ensure correct detailing on site. This section also includes important information on tolerances, joints and the sources of technical information.

With case studies included in sections of this publication, the author has helped to explain and demonstrate the importance of correct materials, their specification and detailing.

CIAT, in endorsing this publication, is aware of the need for books such as this as a support aid for both students and those practising within the discipline of architectural technology.

Working with the publishers, the writers and Advisory Board, CIAT considers that this book will become an essential tool for students on architectural technology degree programmes and associated courses.

Colin Orr MCIAT
Vice President Education
SEPT 2007

www.ciat.org.uk

Introduction to the series

Building, architecture and technology

The categories of building, architecture and technology often, and in many ways, overlap. They can properly be distinguished. A sensible distinction is to understand architecture as a philosophical consideration of the impact of buildings on peoples' consciousness, while technology is concerned with the application of scientific methods to their realisation. Building has more to do with the practicalities of creating the actual structures.

The professions cannot exist in isolation, and Building Manager, Technologist and Architect as well as all the other professions concerned with the built environment need a grounding in each other's concerns as well as empathy with one another's points of view.

Buildings are among the most substantial indicators we have of cultures other than our own. This is true whether we are considering varying geographical and climatic situations or taking an historical perspective. When we visit far countries or archaeological sites, our understanding of the values and aspirations of the people who made them is vividly enhanced by our experience of the buildings we find there. They speak of the patterns of life they were built to accommodate, of the conditions under which they were created and also of the skills deployed by their designers and builders.

The buildings created today are similarly evocative. Whilst they serve varied and complementary practical purposes, they are also markers for our sense of cultural identity. Whether we use a particular building or not, it may be a backdrop to our lives and a significant component of the environment in which we operate. It is an influential factor, whether consciously or not, in our sense of cultural identity. We should also be aware of the statement our buildings make to onlookers about our aspirations and values.

Buildings are not only the concern of those who commission and pay for them, nor of those who use them as places of work or as users of services. They are important to us all. A great hospital holds a different place in the consciousness of the Trust who owns it, the medical and administrative staff who run it, the patients who use it and the passers-by to whom it is just part of the urban scene. The same is true of the most elaborate governmental complex or of the simplest home or bus shelter. Each of these buildings contributes to a total environment.

The village or the city is a whole formed from the constituent parts. The coherence of the experience of people within depends not only on the excellence of those individual components in themselves, seen from the point of view of owners, users or onlookers, but on the total ambience they create. We are all, in this sense, consumers of the whole built environment.

It is the profession and art of architecture to empathise with these apprehensions of the significance of buildings, alongside ensuring that the buildings created are beautiful and practical. Buildings that are starkly functional without relationship to their age and their place cannot be described as architecture. Equally, edifices which simply crystallise an understanding of a culture, which stand only as features in a townscape or are merely sculptural, are follies, though possibly enjoyably decorative ones. Works of architecture serve practical purposes and do so well. They must suit the purposes of their users, must use resources wisely and must contribute positively to the visual environment. These considerations are the concern of architectural philosophy.

The technologies of architecture, as dealt with in this series, are the developed professional skills and techniques by which the needs of the consumers of buildings in all these senses can most efficiently be met through the use of available resources. They are in every case built upon an ability to assess need, including an appreciation of what is reasonable in terms of economic, energy and time constraints. They never assume that the most modern or high-tech solution is automatically to be preferred but always regard the low-tech and traditional as parts of the available armoury. Such technologies include aesthetics as well as acoustics, ergonomics as well as engineering and understanding both of communication and of construction.

They are, therefore, sophisticated tools that are necessary to the proper use of resources to provide an appropriate environment for the activities of society.

The expected audience

Understanding of such technologies is, of course, an essential component of the professional equipment of architects, surveyors and other practitioners, including structural, mechanical and electrical engineers as well as members of the newly emerged profession of architectural technology.

Members of all these professions need to be clearly aware of their interdependence and work in an atmosphere of mutual respect. In some cases, one or another specialist will lead the team involved in developing a design, whilst on other occasions, he or she will be a contributing member of that team. In yet other instances, a single professional may be involved.

In order to fulfil any of these roles, the practitioner needs a clear view of the following:

- the purpose of buildings
- the technology available to fulfil those requirements
- the specialisms that contribute to a satisfactory outcome
- how teams work
- the constraints upon the design process.

It is expected that this suite of books will be appropriate to an audience that includes students of architecture, they may be considered essential tools also for students of architectural technology, of surveying and of estate management and construction management in the UK, the Commonwealth and the USA.

Purpose

Volume 1, *Integrated Strategies in Architecture*, provides a preliminary examination of the knowledge, understanding and skills that the professional designer has to acquire. This text stands alone and is written for a student without prior technical knowledge. The theoretical topics covered are fundamental and basic and are introduced by way of material with which he or she may be expected to be familiar.

The present volume, *Materials, Specification and Detailing: Foundations of Building Design*, develops principles of effective communication introduced in Volume 1 to show how developed design solutions can best be conveyed to those assessing, valuing and constructing them. Care has been taken to show that the practices of selection of materials, of choice of methods of construction and of evocation of appropriate standards are integral parts of the single process which runs from the initial commission to the completed project.

The use of standardised elements is discussed alongside the development of innovative methods.

The programme

The specialised texts, Volumes 2–5, are to some degree time and culture specific and will be regularly reviewed so that they can be revised as necessary.

They are:

Volume 2   *Environment, Technology and Sustainability*
Stephen Sharples and Hocine Bougdah

Volume 3   *Materials, Specification and Detailing: Foundations of Building Design*
Norman Wienand

Volume 4   *Practice, Management and Responsibility*
John Hickey

Volume 5   *History, Performance and Conservation*
Barry Bridgwood and Lindsay Lennie

The whole suite of books is conceived as a set of course texts rather than as reference materials, since the breadth of data that would be necessary for such books is beyond the scope of student manuals.

It will be found that each section of each book is preceded by a brief summary of its contents and followed by a useful list of references. These references are those the authors believe will be most valuable to students, but their inclusion cannot preclude the need for individual library research. In the case of websites, the links to these have been confirmed as the texts were submitted, but it is important to be aware that websites and their addresses change frequently.

Introduction

This book comes as an integral part of a sequence, as explained in the preceding 'Introduction to the Series', and as such it has a defined area to cover. This area, encompassing the selection of materials, detailing and specification, forms the heart of the text and in so doing it also provides the primary elements of the process known as technical design in architecture. In many ways, this work could stand alone as a description of that process, but as with the many aspects of construction generally, it would be much poorer for doing so. The primary aim is therefore to explore the technical design process generally but with a specific regard to the fundamental aspects of the process as manifested by the discrete although highly interdependent areas of the selection of materials, detailing and specification.

Following the theme of **the understanding of technologies** being an essential professional tool to be developed by students of architectural technology, architecture, surveying and other related professional disciplines, it is expected that this book will build on the preceding volumes and be appropriate to an audience that includes those students above, having gained the background knowledge, who now wish to take the next step in developing their familiarity with the specific subject area of technical design in architecture.

Another fundamental feature of this book is the approach to sustainability, where the view has been taken that the need, desire and pursuit of environmentally sensitive and responsible design solutions is beyond debate. The case supporting global warming for instance is now so well documented that it does not require repetition here, but even though some of the arguments may well be proven incorrect in time, the general concept of sustainable design remains valid. The desire for sustainable solutions is therefore a constant theme that underpins the text without necessarily always breaking the surface.

Technical design

As we will see, technical design in architecture is on one level a process whereby conceptual designs are converted into 'buildable' schemes and on the other hand, the design of particular processes that form the foundations on which conceptual design can take place. This means that the process of technical design can be viewed as forming that essential link between concept and building, which it probably is in most cases but also can be seen as a distinct process in itself.

Technical design in architecture is not unlike many other forms of design in that it cannot stand alone as a discrete piece of work; in other words, it is highly dependent on the concepts or stimulation that precedes it and also greatly shaped by the processes that follow it. So while the detached practise of design can be studied, it cannot in this case be considered in isolation. Part 1 of this book, **Technical design**, is concerned with the key aspects of the technical design process but with its role in the context of building, paramount. The analysis therefore looks at both the response to initial influences such as the client's requirements, skills and knowledge available and also the eventual requirements of the design. A fundamental requirement of a successful design is the facility for manufacture, and this depends on how the idea is communicated.

Communication of information

Communication is so important to the technical design process that it forms a distinct section as Part 2, **Communication of information**, where the varied forms of communication introduced in Volume 1 are expanded on and explored in depth but with the specific mission of technical design always uppermost in the study. The rationale for this exploration is that it responds on one level to the logical sequence of tasks involved in taking a concept design with its very distinct aims and limitations and expands it to include all the additional information required to build whilst also acknowledging all the new strata of communication required; on another level, it also considers the existing structure of communication mechanisms currently available.

The aim is not simply to present a set of tools for the technical designer to use in effectively transmitting design concepts and technical information but to put forward an incentive to evaluate existing protocols based on a clear understanding of the primary requirements of the communication needed. In doing so, the process is taken back to first principles in order to identify the exact requirements prior to embarking on any specific method. The aims, styles and audiences all form an essential part in deciding on the most suitable mode of communication, but as with many aspects of technical design, the ability to compromise is usually necessary to achieve success.

Selecting materials

The relationship between technical design and knowledge of materials is fundamental to the production of sound solutions, whether they be evaluated as sustainable, economic or efficient in any other way. It is this relationship that is explored in this book. Aiming to avoid duplication of the many fine existing texts already available on building materials, Part 3 is much more about the process of **Selecting materials** and how this contributes to and, in many ways, defines the technical design process. The skills involved and the knowledge required to make informed and pertinent design decisions are as important in the approach to choosing materials as is the detailed information on any particular material.

The selection of appropriate materials depends on many aspects of a design requirement, and this book aims to examine some of the funda-mental approaches to this practice. It begins with an overview of the process before separating out aspects such as the actual procedures involved, selection criteria and methods for making choices. Three case studies finally aim to provide a realistic insight into the practise but with the proviso that a degree of relevant knowledge is required to fully appreciate the process. The case studies are examined again in the section on detail design because of the interdependence of these two aspects of technical design.

Detail design

In many ways, detailing is synonymous with technical design and as such forms another of the fundamental elements that this book aims to investigate. Part 4 examines the process of detailing or **Detail design** in a similar fashion to the sections preceding it, offering an insight into the process of pursuing detailed design solutions rather than presenting a formal methodology. This approach is aimed at providing a level of scrutiny leading to a capacity to critically evaluate current practices but without losing sight of the fundamental aims.

Detail design is the culmination of much preceding work, be it the initial conceptual thinking, the research needed to proceed or simply the requirement to translate concepts into processes. The image of an hourglass is a very strong simile with much information having to pass through a very narrow aperture. It is also different, however, in that the information going through the detail design process is trans-lated into a new form of information on exiting. The relevance of the image is in the amount of information that goes into the process and the degree to which the new information has to spread out again once prepared. The section on detail design aims to examine all three aspects: that is the preceding information, the actual design process and the requirements of the emerging production information.

The results of detail design work can be presented in many ways, but drawings and written specifications (discussed separately in Part 5) form the standard routes. The three case studies discussed in Part 3, **Selecting materials**, reappear in this section but with an altered yet complementary agenda.

Specifications

Technical design in architecture has been portrayed as a process that involves the assimilation of conceptual ideas and knowledge into a cerebral exercise called design. As part of the subsequent transfer of knowledge contained within the design, communication of detailed instructions and factual information have to be conveyed effectively. The process relies essentially on written instructions in the form of specifications to accompany drawn information, in most cases. The final section of this book, Part 5, examines the requirements of **Specifications** and in particular their integral role in the design process. Rather than a bolt-on optional extra, the specification can in fact provide a structure that enables a systematic approach to design. Starting from the simple act of keeping notes through the efficient communication between members of the design team to the final exact instructions to the production team, these written elements of the design can be developed into precise details in themselves. Case studies are also used to illustrate the use of specification systems.

Finally, it is intended that this book is used primarily to provide the inspiration to tackle technical design problems from a position of realistic self-knowledge and to gain confidence in the processes that enable efficient and therefore good design. Even for the most experienced designers, technical design can appear to have too many parameters floating around at any one time, but systematic approach and knowledge of limiting factors will allow these parameters to be identified, isolated and dealt with. Even if it is just to acknowledge that it is beyond the scope of the current expertise, it is still a step forward.

Part 1
Technical design

Part **1**

Introduction

In this introduction, the many facets that make up technical design will be described in an attempt to illustrate a complicated process when seen in isolation. In reality, however, it represents a series of skills that are acquired progressively by most designers in addition to those intuitive skills they are already blessed with.

Technical design in architecture is on one level a process whereby conceptual designs are converted into 'buildable' schemes and on the other hand, the design of particular processes that form the foundations on which conceptual design can take place. For example, a completely new conceptual design may require a completely new approach to the design of its individual elements, or alternatively, a new conceptual design may only become possible because of new developments in the design of the individual elements.

> Conceptual design can be, and often is, technology driven. However, it is during the detail design stage that the majority of decisions are taken to realise the design vision – a period during which technology is applied to abstract ideas and concepts.
>
> (Emmitt, 2002)

In this section, we will examine how the existing knowledge and skill level of designers will affect the detailed requirements of the process and the actual process itself.

Defining the task

The formal approach to arriving at design solutions starts with a definition of the task at hand. Although it is possible to keep this definition fairly vague in some circumstances, a clear definition does have a distinct role to play in reaching appropriate solutions. Clarity of definition identifies parameters that have a bearing on the particular task. This definition allows unrelated issues to be dismissed and relative degrees of importance to be allocated to the defined parameters.

An example of this process can be simply illustrated by the process of designing a handrail around the edge of a patio. By keeping the definition fairly vague, we can characterise the task as having to prevent people from falling off the edge. With this simple definition, a whole host of possibilities exist, such as:

* increasing the surrounding ground level so that there is no height difference to fall off; or
* ramping the edge of the patio to achieve the same solution; or
* building structures all around so that there is no longer an edge to fall off.

The number of ideas that follow this train of thought are numerous and may result in particularly novel solutions, but many of these are clearly not within the area that would normally be considered satisfactory.

By defining the task in more detail, however, we can for instance give more information on the size and strength required (by referring to appropriate legislation), and this can reduce the number of materials available. By deciding that the handrail should also allow light through, solid walls are also removed from the equation. The defining process then gets down to dictating the style, for instance is a modern design required or would a more traditional approach be more suitable.

To the experienced designer, a number of possible solutions based on precedents begin to formulate in their thinking. These can take the form of 'safe' options where precedent suggests that the solution will be

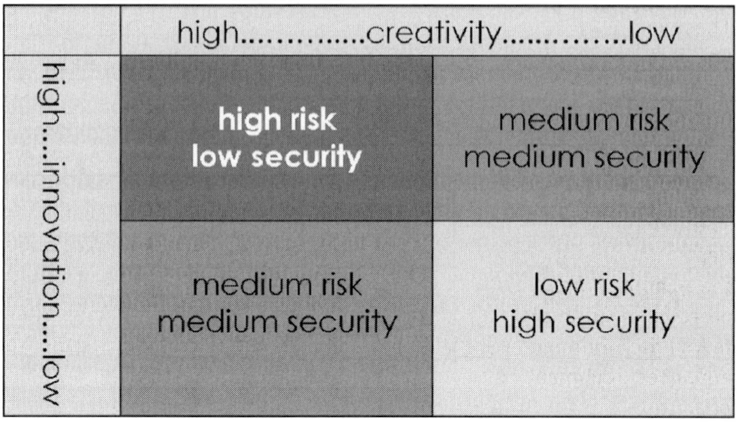

high............creativity............low	
high risk **low security**	medium risk medium security
medium risk medium security	low risk high security

(left vertical axis label: high...innovation...low)

1.01

acceptable to higher risk ideas where conceptual design skills can be demonstrated. Clear definition will decide whether these choices are possible. It may come down to a decision that only glass is possible, leaving the design decisions down to styling, technical and structural detailing. In other words, what the wall will look like, how will it be constructed and whether it will perform its function?

Controlling the design process

From the above description, we can see that there may be many solutions available and that two teams given the same task may come up with very different solutions depending on their approach. Controlling the process therefore becomes a relevant part of the process and is also directly related to the definition. An experienced designer will have an in-built idea of how much resource should be allocated to a particular task, within a range, allowing time for more innovation or keeping tight schedules with safer solutions.

The creativity of individual designers or the desire to strive for innovation are the forces that drive forward the realisation of design solutions. These are potentially among the most rewarding aspects of technical design but in most cases require careful control. Control of the process also has a major part to play in relation to responsibility. Conceptual responsibility (what will it finally look like?) is a major factor and so is economic responsibility (what will it finally cost?), but in particular, it is responsibility for safety that is paramount (will it perform its task safely and not present a risk to anyone near it?). There are other types as well, such as professional indemnity (PI) (can it be built?).

Dealing with risk

These last couple of paragraphs have highlighted some of the controlling factors in technical design, namely, the relationship with risk. Risk does not only involve issues of safety but includes a possible failure to provide the desired conceptual resolution or to provide a 'buildable' solution. There is therefore a relationship between degrees of risk and creativity or innovation and also security.

The relationship with risk in technical design is a variable notion depending on the degree of exposure of the final product. Returning to the example of the handrail above, the risk associated with a highly creative conceptual design can be repaid with recognition from clients, fellow designers, the public, etc., if successful. Whereas, even the most advanced technical solution, if it is not visually distinctive, will not provide the same rewards, therefore reducing the return on potential risk. The fear of failure becomes far more of potent driver in a purely technical design process than in most conceptual design.

The control and mastery of risk is a factor that tends to dictate another major decision required in technical design, whether to attempt a design from first principles or to adapt or adopt an existing solution. In reality, the choice is not so stark but presents itself in choosing in a range between the two extremes. In adopting existing solutions, providing no innovation and thus reducing risk, reputations can be protected and client's interests possibly best served. Most importantly, however, innovation and creativity can then be channelled in a controlled way to areas where it may see more appropriate returns. These risks and the required control of resources associated with designing from first principles can be controlled by adapting existing solutions to varying degrees.

Nurturing creativity

So far it could appear that there is little opportunity in technical design for creativity and innovation: this is not so. It is, however, valid to suggest that the consequences of failure are far more onerous and potentially fatal than in purely conceptual design. However, careful consideration of the task at hand and precise definition of the design parameters can free the designer from the constraints imposed by a fear of failure and allow truly innovative and creative solutions to emerge. Creativity can therefore be promoted and nurtured by the careful and responsible control of the design process. This process can also be extended to control the exposure of inexperienced designers to unnecessary risks by simplification of and guidance through the process.

Students, equally, can adopt this approach by careful definition and restriction of the project requirements and by consideration of their own ability range before launching into what can be a very daunting prospect for the inexperienced. Technical design therefore follows similar patterns, whether at the advanced levels of modern high-tech architecture or student project levels. The main criterion is to match the nature and complexity of the tasks to what can be handled by the skills of the designers available to complete the task.

The following chapters in Part 1 of this book will examine the stages that go into producing technical design solutions. This includes a look at registering the skills available to a particular project in defining proficiency levels. These skills are not static, they improve constantly with experience, they can be enhanced by study or the buying in of expertise or even by-passed by alternative design strategies. Following on from that, Part 1 then goes on to take a deeper look at the detailed requirements of technical design, delving deeper into the stages involved during the design process, looking at incorporating issues such as sustainability, health and safety and the assessment of success/failure. Part 1 finally concludes with a description of the various choices that go to make up the technical design process. These include choices such as high- or low-tech and aesthetic factors governing materials choice and finishes plus the difficult issue of quality control.

Many technical details are highly dependent on the quality of their production for success, and the designers cannot escape their responsibility to come up with designs that can be constructed within reasonable quality limitations. Keeping control of the overall design process allows degrees of reflection permitting feedback to be integrated into the evolution of new generation responses.

Chapter **1**

Proficiency levels: defining the skills available

The ability to design solutions to technical problems depends on the levels of experience, skill and knowledge already in existence. This then relates directly to the amount of resources available for any particular task. Although in theory it is possible for the most inexperienced individual to produce solutions to the most complex of problems, given adequate resources, in practice this is a luxury not generally available. Design solutions tend to come from an existing palette of knowledge with varying degrees of access to the acquisition of more information. Rarely does it come from a totally uninformed approach.

For this reason, expert consultants are frequently used to provide detailed knowledge where a particular shortage is recognised. This process is not without real risks, however, as an over-reliance on 'expert' opinion may fail to recognise that this higher level of knowledge may be based largely on current opinion, may be presented as fact and may also be only relatively superior to that already available in-house. Interpreting this type of advice can be difficult and overly dependent on the character of those employed. An example of this would be when an expert fails to see the project as whole but concentrates purely in their own area of skill and also with the added incentive to see their particular solutions adopted.

The tendency therefore to work within existing skills and knowledge ranges results in a reliance on safe solutions, thus avoiding risk but also recognising the higher responsibilities of designers. This last point refers to the professional responsibilities of the designer but also the legal responsibilities imposed by legislation in the UK such as the Construction Design and Management (CDM) regulations.

The scarcity of genuinely independent information is also a real constraint on truly innovative design where the designer takes on full responsibility for its success. How can one designer or even a team of designers manage to become sufficiently expert to fully evaluate all sources of information?

A fundamental element of technical design in architecture is the accurate definition of the skill levels available to the design team but vitally also the gaps in that knowledge.

Palette of skills

The skills that any designer brings to a particular problem will be varied depending on the levels of experience, the types of experience and the individual intuitive and academic skills acquired over their lifetime. These skills can be divided into subject-specific skills such as experience of design and detailing particular building elements and the ability to adapt to new situations such as the detailing of a particular element where no experience exists. This latter set of skills that could be termed general design skills are what make the designer able to deal with new situations in a controlled and systematic way but also include a recognition of the value of experience.

An example would be where a novice designer might spend hours going over and over a particular problem, always returning to same point but getting more and more frustrated. An experienced designer is more likely to understand their own limitations, acknowledging that their physical and mental stamina in limited, so returning to the problem after a good night's sleep often produces clarity of vision and thought. The next morning produces either a result or the acceptance that a new direction is required. An experienced designer is also more likely to recognise the limits of their own skill plus the limitations of those working alongside, be they novice or expert.

These general design skills that include a working knowledge of the design process alluded to in the example above exploit experience in a wholly productive way. The use of precedents to inform technical design is a profound process that can simply reproduce elements of a design or can inspire the development of new truly innovative variants. The study of precedents includes deliberate reading up of published working details, leafing through journals and picking up ideas or simply noticing a 'clever way of doing things' on a trip to another country.

Clearly, there are countless forms of exposure that could be termed precedents, and it is simply down to the individual designer as to how much is absorbed or understood. The clue to understanding this process is the inspiration it provides, which could be highly technical or simply aesthetic.

1.1 An open loft from the Southern French Alps

Subject-specific skills come in many forms and levels and also depend on the ability of the individual to comprehend the issues involved. This is not to suggest that there is a hierarchy of understanding but merely to acknowledge that individuals relate to different technical problems in different ways – an example being that of a simple domestic eaves detail where the individual designer may be concerned with the final appearance so will gain a greater understanding of proportion and the materials used, their characters, durability, etc., but rely on a standard text book technical solution.

Another approach could be where the appearance is of less importance but the environmental performance takes precedence. Here, it is possible to build up a detailed knowledge and particular understanding of the various alternative methods of roof-space ventilation including the potential drawbacks of their use in different circumstances such as exposure to high winds, spindrift, etc.

Yet another version of this particular skill could be based on the achievement of quality in the finish. Detailed knowledge of the construction processes, skills of operatives and the ease with which the systems can be constructed, maintained and repaired become valuable depending on the particular design to build process.

In reality, an experienced designer involved in the scenario above will have a degree of knowledge from all three aspects but to varying depths.

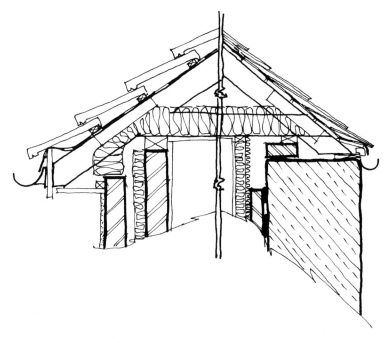

1.2 Two different eaves details

Self-knowledge

It would be foolish to suggest a universal approach to design, many books have been written on this subject, but a common view suggests that 'creative problem-solving' may be a good definition of the process. You will recall that this was described in detail in Volume 1, as it applies to the total building design. Enticing though it may be to assume that such an objective approach will always apply to the design of components, this definition does not necessarily consider the role of the individual designer and their relationship with the practice of design.

The suggestion here is that self-knowledge is a vital element in the approach to design without necessarily trying to dictate a particular method. Self-knowledge in this respect means an understanding of the individual's knowledge capacity but also an understanding of how they operate when confronted with design tasks. The section above discusses the advantages of experience, but there are also other cognitive

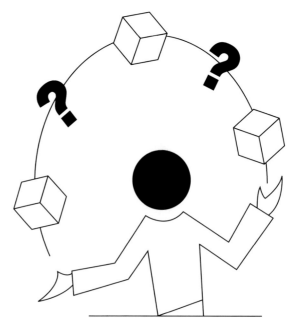

1.3 Juggling concepts

skills that allow designers to understand the problem they are trying to solve creatively. Chief among these is the ability to 'juggle' more than one or two concepts simultaneously. This would not appear to be directly related to experience, but significantly, experience can allow certain concepts to be dismissed and therefore the remaining ones to be dealt with more easily.

Experience with students has indicated that they struggle with too many design parameters at one time, suggesting perhaps that they are relatively poor designers based on their solutions. An alternative reflection, however, proposes that as the number of concepts new to them is actually very large and that they manage to produce relatively comprehensible results indicate a genuine capacity with a steep learning curve.

The general consensus, however, is that keeping the individual tasks limited to a manageable number of 'juggling' parameters is most likely to produce meaningful results. In other words, keep the tasks manageable by breaking down larger problems into their smaller constituent elements. As experience grows, more tasks can be handled and significantly more tasks can be discounted.

This has a particular relevance for designers working in isolation where the pressures can become insurmountable. Working in teams or design studios allows problems like this to be aired, shared and analysed before being broken down into manageable chunks.

Existing subject knowledge: experience profile

Although it is probably not an overtly common process in most circumstances to define existing knowledge, it is a practice that almost certainly happens subliminally. In other words, it happens without the participants necessarily being aware of it.

For students and inexperienced designers, it is a practice well worth considering. In future chapters, we will look at defining the task but here forming a picture of the total skills available to complete a task is the aim. In the same way as a joiner would approach a job with a selection of tools, adding and subtracting according to the nature of the task, so should a designer or design team approach a design task. Again just like the joiner, designers will have favourite tools or those with which they feel most in control but also need to branch out and attempt new skills where their level of expertise will be less in the initial stages. Design skills are therefore the designer's tools of the trade and can be acquired as necessary. Design teams have the added benefit of complementary members, where no one person has to have the full range of skills.

Defining the existing knowledge available to a designer or design team to complete a task should therefore take the form of a compilation of the relevant knowledge available plus a compilation of the gaps in that knowledge. This is not a precise art because as the previous description of subject-specific skills suggests, knowledge is a variable commodity. However, it is in these variations with different combinations that interesting breaks from the norm are possible. Careful design of design teams aimed at specific topics and effective design team management can be used to produce very high-quality results.

The experience profile cannot in reality be separated from the knowledge compilation, but it is a distinct element that can have a major bearing on the eventual outcome. Experience comes in many forms in addition to the cumulative effect of going through the process a number of times. It comes from many sources but in particular, learning from mistakes, learning from exposure to new environments, learning from other people and accepting, through self-knowledge and the current limits to individual ability.

Following the old cliché of the experienced old hand producing safe standard solutions against the young idealist producing innovative but highly risky solutions is tempting but the reality may well be very different. Each project should be evaluated independently in order to produce the best practicable results bearing in mind the price of failure in technical design.

Chapter review

- The ability to design solutions to technical problems depends on the levels of experience, skill and knowledge available.
- The tendency to work within existing skills and knowledge ranges results in a reliance on safe solutions.
- Subject-specific skills come in many forms and levels and also depend on the ability of the individual to comprehend the issues involved.
- General design skills are what make the designer able to deal with new situations in a controlled and systematic way, but it also includes a recognition of the value of experience.
- The use of precedents to inform technical design is a profound process that can simply reproduce elements of a design or can inspire the development of new truly innovative variants.
- Self-knowledge means an understanding of the individual's knowledge capacity but also an understanding of how they perform when confronted with design tasks.
- Keeping the individual tasks limited to a manageable number of 'juggling' parameters is most likely to produce meaningful results.

- Defining the existing knowledge and experience available to a designer or design team to complete a task should take the form of a compilation of the relevant knowledge available plus a recognition of the gaps in that knowledge.
- Each project should be evaluated independently in order to produce the best practicable results bearing in mind the high price of failure in technical design.

Chapter 2

Technical design process requirements

The art of arriving at design solutions can be seen on one level as a complicated process comprised of many distinctive stages but on another quite an instinctive and highly creative progression of thought processes. It can seem unwise to deconstruct this intuitive process, but architecture finds itself in a highly competitive and commercial, professional environment.

Buildings are not designed to hang on the walls of galleries but are required to perform at least adequately on many levels. The production of buildings not only involves a large number of professional designers, fabricators and builders, all working in a competitive and commercial environment, but the finished product will also have, in most circumstances, to provide the surroundings appropriate for the building's users. The technical design process should therefore be accurate in its response to these requirements in providing a professional service, and it should also be reproducible in order to survive in the commercial world. This chapter looks at the requirements of the process known as technical design.

Project definition

As we have seen previously, the formal approach to arriving at design solutions starts with a definition of the task at hand and that a clear definition can have a distinct role to play in reaching appropriate solutions. By defining the parameters that have a bearing on a particular task, unrelated issues can be dismissed and relative degrees of importance allocated to individual parameters. These parameters could be individual such as a particular health and safety requirement that radiology departments in hospitals have some degree of radiation protection. Others could be far more complicated and interrelated such as the aim to produce an environmentally friendly office building.

Understanding the client's requirements and deciphering the brief are fundamental to this process, and it is assumed for now that the brief is accurate in its interpretation of these requirements. The issue of the client's ability to fully comprehend a brief is a major topic of debate leading onto how the designer relates to what might appear as a lack of clarity. Unfortunately, it is beyond the scope of this particular book, but it does have impact on the definition of design parameters. (This topic is dealt with in Volume 1 of this series.)

In general, there is a suggestion that the technical design process works more effectively within a clear brief because it allows more specific definition of the overall project themes.

The brief supplied by a client is not definitive, it is an invitation to provide design solutions. These design solutions are, however, entirely related to the focus of the brief, and the ability to translate this focus into technical resolution depends on the skills of the designer. These skills, however, cannot work outside of the professional and commercial environment discussed in the opening to this chapter.

An example of this is a brief that asks for an environmentally responsible office building. The responsibility of the technical designer here cannot be divorced from the overall conceptual design as the concept will almost certainly be dependent on providing particular levels of environmental performance. This responsibility also involves providing the client with a level of performance that is intimated by the brief. This is where interpretation of the brief becomes a highly professional process, almost always involving compromise between ideal technical solutions and commercial reality.

Environmentally ambitious buildings can involve experimental, untested combinations of systems, products and concepts. They can therefore involve a degree of risk that the client may not be fully aware of. This risk coupled with the level of investment available often puts the designer in a difficult position. In this case, it means matching the client's budget to the required performance but with the control of risk being a constant guiding factor. The example of an office building brings in many more parameters, however, not least that of the particular requirements of the building's users. User requirements must be fully understood and matched to the commercial nature of the project and how it may evolve. So far, we have not even discussed legislative parameters, geographical and climatic influences or the responsibility to future generations, all of which will have to go into the definition of this particular design task.

Existing knowledge definition

In previous sections, we have now discussed, at some length, the need for a compilation of existing knowledge available to a designer or design team to complete a task that should include the gaps in that knowledge. This involves design team management and can be used to produce very high-quality results. Equally important is the experience profile that cannot be separated from the knowledge compilation, but experience comes in many forms in addition to the cumulative effect of going through the process a number of times. It comes from many sources but in particular, learning from mistakes and deliberate learning of new techniques and knowledge accumulation.

Each project should be evaluated independently in order to produce the best practicable results for the client, taking into account commercial reality. This process, although a separate function, is intractably linked to project definition and has a major bearing on the eventual solutions. It also invariably leads to one of two conclusions, either we have the knowledge and experience to complete a design or we do not. The latter conclusion may sometimes be the end of the matter but can also lead to a voyage of discovery that makes design such a particularly satisfying exercise for those involved with it.

Directing the search for knowledge focussed in a particular direction and the intellectual tools required to complete the process are among the specific skills bestowed by higher education. Clearly, this skill is not exclusive to higher education, but it does form a specific feature that provides a gateway to greater knowledge and experience of the diverse forms that it can involve. Research skills and experience therefore play a vital role in the definition of knowledge available to direct at a project.

Continuing with the example of the environmentally responsible office building, the skills palette available to the design team could include designers experienced in working within sustainable architecture, it could also include designers experienced in working at the cutting edge of current knowledge with the ability to assess risk accurately and deal with it accordingly. Of equal value to a team like this could be designers with experience of existing products available to perform identified tasks as this removes a great deal of risk, relying on the manufacturer's development processes. As mentioned above, however, the ability to research diverse sources of information can also add a valuable dimension to a design team by providing inspiration with various degrees of validity.

Using space heating as an example, the requirement might have been designed out altogether or reduced to particularly low levels. In doing so, underfloor heating may have been chosen to provide effective heating at lower temperatures, decreasing comparable heat losses and providing the ability to incorporate solar heat gains. Existing knowledge may be utilised to provide design solutions incorporating reliable existing products. However, research may provide the option of extending this system to include a cooling function, working in conjunction with the thermal mass of floor slabs and underground thermal water storage. The eventual decision will depend on the levels of risk involved versus the gains possible but more significantly, the client's brief and budget restrictions.

Project assessment: material choices, structural or performance requirements and quality

The definition of a project based on an interpretation of the client's brief, coupled with a compilation of the skills required, will lead to a stage of assessment that will eventually lead to specific design solutions. This stage of assessment provides a guide to types of solution required by matching factors such as budget, scale, prominence and risk. Although it is conceivable to vary these factors such as including an element of great daring and risk into a particularly safe design, the overall theme of the project will govern most aspects of technical design. This section looks at the aspects that make up a project assessment.

The project assessment essentially gives a form to the overall theme of a project by linking them together and providing boundaries to the variety of design solutions that may be applicable. In effect, the assessment is a description of the project by categorisation of the constituent parts. In its basic form, this includes such entities as roofs, walls and foundations but can clearly be magnified to include many further elements such as finishes, materials and structural calculations.

The difference between project definition and project assessment may not be apparent at this stage particularly as the two stages are very much interlinked. Project assessment in this case forms the prelude to the detailed design process by defining distinct elements whilst also providing a description of the expected quality. In all probability, each element will be subjected to further clarification such as choices of materials, structural and performance requirements and especially quality considerations.

Quality is a notoriously difficult concept to define and although a very interesting subject, detailed discussion is beyond the scope of this particular book. For the purposes of this section, however, we can take the description offered by the *Concise Oxford Dictionary of English* as a 'degree of excellence' as long as we have an agreed set of benchmarks to allow comparison with. In other words, we get around the concept of quality definition by providing examples of high, medium and low quality from existing models. The relationship between quality, cost and client expectation is discussed later in this section.

Definition of distinct project elements takes a particular scheme and in conjunction with the existing knowledge definition, identifies individual areas requiring particular responses. This process divides a project into individual fractions required to complete the process and responds to the knowledge definition by matching relative degrees of significance to each fraction. By doing this, it also sets up a probable sequence of events that will ultimately lead to detailed design decisions.

This time, using the example of an environmentally responsible dwelling, we may find that the local planning authorities dictate a pitched roof covered with a particular material. This provides a definition of the roof element and appears to restrict the possible solutions to a relatively small number. However, with the overall shape and materials finish restricted, the potential structural solutions are still numerous, including not only choices of materials but also the structural form. Timber solutions spring to mind due to the latent environmental credentials of timber and the vast amount of existing knowledge available to inform the design process. Many other materials could replace timber in the structural forms most likely to be chosen. For example, materials such as recycled metals and plastic can perform equally well, and although not common in the UK, concrete could also provide a pitched roof if required.

Project assessment will in this case make a decision on the appropriate response to the requirement of the planning authorities based on the availability of the apposite materials, skills and knowledge. This house set in a Nordic forest is likely to have ample supplies of sustainable high-quality timber available whereas in the middle of New York may find that recycled materials are more abundant.

This same house if set on a remote Scottish island, the local availability of stone has to be balanced against the environmental cost of transporting apparently sustainable materials over large distances. In this case, efficiently designed timber roofing structures utilising small section, lightweight timbers could reduce the overall transport expense but the structural potential of stone arches could also provide an even more sustainable solution. In this case, the knowledge definition should dictate whether the stone arch solution is possible or not. Either way, this process dictates the research required to produce solutions and as such sets up the sequence of events that will ultimately lead to a detailed design solution.

The example above deals only with the individual element requiring a solution. In reality, the quality question has to be superimposed onto the same process and would have a distinct bearing on the eventual outcome. Quality is not intrinsically directly related to cost but in the real world invariably it is. This rather sad reflection takes account of the fact that high-quality production either relies on high-quality materials (that generally cost more) or it relies on high-quality production methods that cost more in terms of labour time or development outlays. The quality

2.1 What is quality?

2.2

matter is not one to be avoided, however, as it plays a vital role in client satisfaction. Most projects to which this process relates involve a commission from a client. The client, in most cases, has to fund the process and expects a certain level of quality. This relationship between funding and expectation is one that is fraught with risk and can lead to much disagreement between client and designer. The client invariably expects maximum quality for the lowest outlay. Often these expectations are not reconcilable, and it is the designer's task to convey this information to the client. This may not become apparent, however, until some way into the design process, particularly if the design team have not prepared well by careful definition of the project, their skills and the assessment of the various elements involved.

The relationship between quality, cost and client expectation therefore provides a pivotal impact on project assessment. In other words, once a particular element is defined, the quality associated with the provision of a design solution will be directly linked to client expectation and financial resources.

Returning to the example of the roof to an environmentally responsible dwelling, quality expectation and client's budgets will play a particularly crucial role in the eventual choice of design solutions. Financial constraints can restrict the range of solutions and the control of risk even more so. The popularity of lightweight timber-framed house types on the Scottish islands could be explained in this way as it represents a fairly low risk and a cost predictable method. Other solutions that may appear more sustainable may carry the extra risk of unpredictable performance or unpredictable labour costs (builders will charge more to cover the unknown elements).

Project assessment will in this case makes a decision on the impact of the quality dimension including the eventual character of the building. For example, will the roof structure contribute to the internal aesthetic qualities of the house or will it contribute only to the environmental performance – are the clients after a grand design or an eco house or are they looking for a permanent home or a holiday retreat?

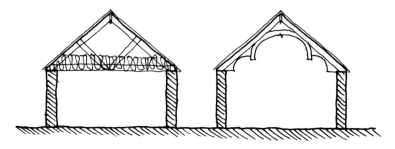

2.3 Alternative roof structures

As above, this process dictates the decisions required to produce solutions and as such sets up the sequence of events that lead to detailed design solutions.

Chapter review

- The production of buildings not only involves a large number of professional designers, fabricators and builders, all working in a competitive and commercial environment, but the finished product will also have, in most circumstances, to provide the environment appropriate for the building's users.
- The brief supplied by a client is not definitive, it is an invitation to provide design solutions.
- The definition of a project based on an interpretation of the client's brief, coupled with a compilation of the skills required, will lead to a stage of assessment that will eventually lead to specific design solutions.
- Each project should be evaluated independently in order to produce the best practicable results for the client, taking into account commercial reality.
- Project assessment forms the prelude to the detailed design process by defining distinct elements whilst also providing a description of the expected quality.
- By defining the parameters that have a bearing on a particular task, unrelated issues can be dismissed and relative degrees of importance allocated to individual parameters.
- Research skills and experience play a vital role in the definition of knowledge available to direct at a project.
- The relationship between quality, cost and client expectation provides a pivotal impact on project assessment.

Chapter **3**

Detail design process

As discussed in the last chapter, the production of design solutions can be a complicated process comprised of many distinctive stages but also an instinctive and highly creative progression of thought processes. In this chapter, the various stages and choices available to the design team will be examined in an attempt to provide an illustration of the process known commonly as **detail design** (or **construction details**). In reality, this process is often based on intuitive skills and not fully exposed to introspection.

It could be argued that this process should not be over analysed but recognised as a personal attribute of gifted designers, but this view is not sustainable in the modern world where the process of building design is evolving into an extremely complicated procedure, and it is no longer possible for individual designers to fully comprehend the entire process. Design teams are now the norm and increasingly this also extends to interdisciplinary teams. Efficient interaction of design teams requires knowledge and control of the process, particularly if clients' aims are to be fully realised. Perhaps, more importantly, however, the effective operation of design teams can also more fully exploit agenda such as sustainability and environmental design.

A construction detail is in most cases a scale drawing illustrating the finished piece of technology as it would appear in a finished project. Detailing (the production of construction details) is, however, essentially the process whereby an overall design concept is translated into a set of patterns that guide the reproduction of the concept into a built form.

This can take a number of forms from verbal instructions to the production of scale models. In practice, however, this process is normally confined to the production of drawings with accompanying explanatory specification notes. Detailing is not simply the production of drawn information; however, it provides solutions to the problems exposed during the process while providing methods to convert a conceptual design into the final

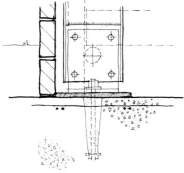

3.1

form. It becomes very much a design process when it is viewed as aiming to provide optimum solutions as discussed previously.

Historically, detailing has been viewed as less creative than the earlier conceptual design stage, but current thinking is beginning to realise that as material and technical choices become ever more complicated, this view is no longer tenable. Particularly when added to the performance requirements of a completed structure, the detail design stage is where the success or failure of a conceptual design is determined.

The prime requirement for successful detailing is therefore to recognise that optimum solution is being aimed for. This recognises that there may be many potential solutions, taking into account the many variables not directly related to the detailing process. There is a clear conflict when aiming for the ideal and therefore potentially novel solutions between the requirement to produce perfect solutions and the desire to innovate. Generally, there is a tendency to produce solutions with low-risk factors because the main requirement is to produce details that work in practice. The recognition, however, that what may appear as low risk today may turn out to be high risk when viewed retrospectively could be used to promote risk-taking.

We have already touched on the responsibility of designers beyond their relationship with individual clients. What requires some discussion in particular is their greater global responsibility and how that comes down to detail design decisions. This refers directly to the link between the development of technical design solutions and the adoption of sustainable technologies. The terminology involved here can give rise to some confusion, so it is important to clarify at an early stage that when the term 'sustainable' is used, it is concerned with sustainability in construction projects, i.e. building in a sustainable manner.

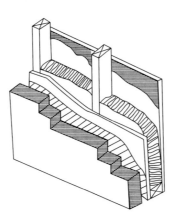
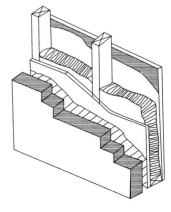

3.2 Sheep's wool insulation easily replaces fibreglass

As we have seen, the integration of sustainable and therefore novel solutions into mainstream detail design can rely on reproducing existing solutions (if they exist) or the development of new solutions (with all the attendant risk factors). Incentives to develop new ideas come from changes in legislation, the requirement to incorporate cost-saving materials or the insistence of strong-willed designers or clients after a particular theme. There is no doubt, a significant amount of development in technical design, but that which has occurred is limited in scale in global terms as low technical risk more often equates to proven cost-effectiveness.

Innovation or evolution: integrating feedback

Detailing is based on a permutation of choosing the requisite technology allied to the choice of appropriate materials. The source of this information is therefore of paramount importance in successful detailing.

Experience and habit form the basis for most detail design, relying on what has been accomplished previously by the individual designer, the design team or added expertise brought in to aid the design process. This experience, referred to previously as the skills palette, is extremely valuable as it amounts to the best risk reduction strategy available because workable solutions are known about and previous failures acknowledged. If it is assumed that real design cannot happen without some degree of risk, this risk is far more acceptable if diluted within a large pot of experience. Experience forms the standard method of integrating design feedback into the design process.

Beyond experience, there are many sources of information, each with particular levels of risk. This process cannot be viewed separately from the process of choosing materials, however, as each material type will have a selection of appropriate detailing technologies available to suit it. In addition, similar materials may allow the adaptation of their respective and similar technologies.

Conventional sources of information include literature concerned with construction technology where standard solutions will be explained. Regulatory authorities provide 'robust details' that can be adopted or adapted. Historical studies provide illustrations of previous methods that again can be used as the basis for adaptation. Published case studies can also provide actual details as well as inspiration to adapt. In addition there are now a whole host of publications where experimental alternative sustainable technologies are illustrated.

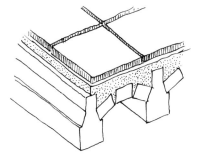

These sources unfortunately also fall into a range related to risk where the more detailed and useful information is associated with low-risk illustration of existing technologies. The more useful in terms of sustainable

3.3 The 'Barcelona' floor

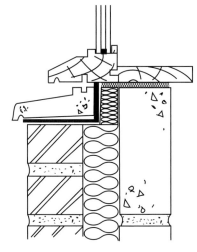

3.4

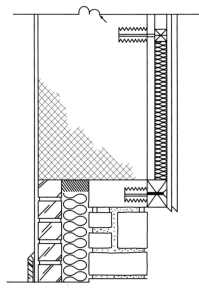

3.5

detailing and pushing the limits of design tend to be found in the more adventurous but clearly experimental technologies illustrated in the publications dealing with alternative technologies. The type of technology finally chosen will depend largely on the individual projects concerned, which in turn will dictate the process and choices available.

The concept that simple solutions are cost-effective particularly as they allow deep-seated learning by repetition is a difficult one to contest. Where buildability is paramount, it is the basis of good detailing. This is in itself an obstacle to the adoption of new solutions but need not always be so. It is at the problem definition stage that change can occur.

The process of finding possible solutions to a defined problem follows a number of different possible routes, but these can be grouped into three main categories:

1   *The adoption of standard solutions.* As outlined above, this is the safe route to successful detailing but tends to result in the repetition of existing non-sustainable solutions – for example, repeating a particular wall design in every respect.
2   *The adaptation of existing solutions.* Using new materials and/or regulations to improve on previous methods or using ideas from other areas and adapting them to fit – for example, taking the example of a roof structure where the individual requirements of insulation, structure and weather proofing are dealt with separately and applying this concept to the wall design. The integration of feedback in the form of experience is essential in making this method work.
3   *The production of completely new methods.* Brainstorming (see Volume 1) is a particularly useful method of developing new ideas as it uses the combined power of a group of individuals to juggle a greater number of concepts at any one time than each of the individuals could manage on their own. It also reduces the individual pressure to come up with a solution by sharing the responsibility and also allows individuals to concentrate on a minor portion of the problem without necessarily having to grasp the entire concept.

If the process of identifying optimum solutions is seen as the aim of detailing, then arriving at the optimum can also be described as the ability to juggle as many of the possible options as possible at any one time. More commonly these days, computer software allows mathematical calculations to be carried out very quickly and presented in graphic terms. This allows designers to play around with ideas and to quickly identify optimum solutions from a number of variables.

The choices available to a detail designer usually involve a balancing of risk, and it is governed by the fear of failure:

> the two basic questions to ask of a proposed solution are whether it can be built and whether it will fail . . .
>
> (Bryan, 2005)

This may seem particularly negative, but it can also be advocated as a fully responsible form of judgement. In conceptual forms of design, increased risk can be played off against the increased potential for glory.

Detail design is a specialist discipline that very few clients will have knowledge of, so they rely on the designer to make informed decisions on their behalf. Risky conceptual design can be conveyed to the client whereas risky detail design in most cases cannot.

High-tech or low-tech?

The terms 'high-tech' or 'low-tech' in architectural terms can be discussed at length, but for the sake of simplicity, **high-tech** has been assumed to mean new, cutting edge and usually complicated technologies that rely heavily on contemporary material science and credible product development.

Low-tech is assumed to be technologies based on well established, proven systems with relatively simple technology.

The choices here are very similar to those discussed in the preceding section in that they involve a relationship with subject knowledge and risk. There is more to it; however, in that the conceptual design theme will also have a direct bearing on whether a scheme is considered to be high- or low-tech (or somewhere between the two).

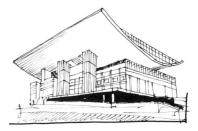

3.6 A high-tech steel building – Shanghai Opera House by Arte Charpentier and Associates

Mixing of the various styles is also possible where a very high-tech building may still incorporate areas of 'standard' brickwork for aesthetic, structural or environmental design rationale. Equally, an apparently low-tech straw bale building may involve a high degree of environmental design through detailed analysis of the design proposals and also incorporate high-tech features such as window systems, photo-voltaics or even building management systems. Essentially, however, high-tech would normally require the input of specialist knowledge from consultants or the product developer. This in turn either removes a degree of control from the design team or requires a more inclusive approach to the design process.

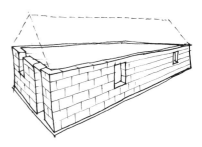

3.7 A low-tech straw bale building

There is also a direct correlation between the extent of high technology involved and cost. Development costs for particular products incorporate not only a degree of insurance but also a profit element to offset the research and development costs and risks. Technology development during the design of a scheme can be done in conjunction with a supplier to reduce risk but generally only very high-quality materials would be considered, again to reduce risk. It would be foolhardy to see a novel design fail simply because a cheaper material was used to save money. This again adds substantially to the build price but also significantly to the cost of failure.

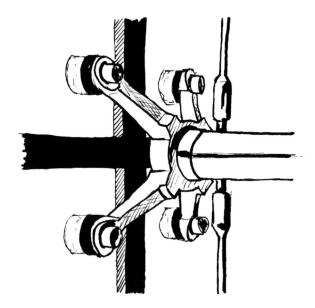

3.8 A proprietary planar glass connection

There are many examples of this process in operation but one of the most significant was the relationship between the glass manufacturers, Pilkingtons and the high-tech architects, Fosters and Partners in the development of the planar glazing system. The project was the Willis Faber & Dumas Headquarters in Ipswich, England (1971–5). The precise roles attributed to the architectural designer, engineer or product supplier/ developer are lost in the mists of time with each probably providing a different account of the process but what does remain clear is that an innovative new system was introduced that has gone to revolutionise the use of glass in building facades.

Adapting vernacular precedents

The more adventurous use of low-tech systems comes in the adaptation of traditional building systems. This process can take many forms but essentially falls into one of two categories: adaptation of an existing process in context as a result of a deeper understanding of the process itself and the performance requirements of the project; or the adoption of an existing process out of context by matching the performance requirements of the project to newly acquired knowledge.

The first of these two processes, adaptation of a system in context, works by retaining what may seem on the surface to be a tired, traditional method and through greater knowledge and understanding giving it a new relevance. An example of this process in operation is the use of draught lobbies. Originally valued for their ability to deal with leaky doors, they became less popular when high-performance doors and windows reduced draughts throughout. However, greater knowledge of airflow through buildings, ventilation and heat loss parameters introduced the value of buffer zones and airtightness, so draught lobbies came to the fore again for their ability to moderate the interface between internal and external environments.

The second process, adoption of a system out of context, involves taking a system used elsewhere under different conditions and making use of existing plus new knowledge, applies the existing method in new circumstances. An example of this process currently in vogue is the use of rammed earth. Rammed earth is an ancient building method using suitable subsoil rammed into place between formwork to produce load-bearing walls. Scientific study has revealed properties of moisture attenuation and thermal storage capacity (Houben & Guillard, 1994) that when coupled with the very low carbon dioxide production involved in its use makes it an extremely attractive material for sustainable solutions. Clearly, there is a very obvious limit to its use, but it can sit very comfortably alongside an unmistakeably high-tech approach.

Vernacular precedents exist throughout the world and are to be valued as sources of inspiration, because as the word suggests, these are ordinary buildings and as such typically demonstrate a maximum exploitation of local materials. This leads to high levels of economic and environmental efficiency as people generally attempt to get as comfortable and spacious internal environment as the local materials will provide.

This equates to the lowest possible cost as the transportation of building materials has always been a high-cost exercise and only used for products with high-performance values. Vernacular precedents therefore offer glimpses into highly refined, if somewhat, primitive building systems but with the major advantage of being tested over great lengths of time. In other words, the levels of risk when used in their original environment are substantially reduced.

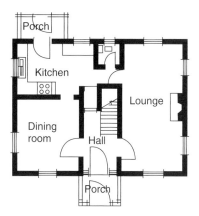

3.9 Draught lobbies

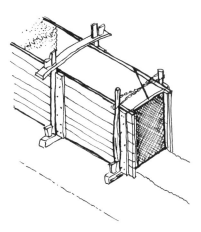

3.10 Formwork for rammed earth

3.11

Reflection: checking progress and accommodating change

Any form of design is a process that requires a high degree of personal involvement. It is difficult to become sufficiently detached from the process to permit a robotic response to situations without losing the element that makes design a creative enterprise. Design processes are therefore aimed at being a fulfilling exercise where the creative skills of the design team are harnessed to produce high-quality results.

There is a defined but variable pathway to each design process that ultimately leads to a feeling of achievement at the end. Like a mountaineer reaching the top of Mount Everest – the task is complete. Unlike the above example, however, there is seldom a defined end point – there is no summit, just a solution. As we have discussed previously, this solution is possibly the optimum under current conditions, but is it? The point here is that there is a clear feeling of having reached the summit when potential solutions are found and a clear reluctance to concede that this is just one possible solution among many.

This can and often does lead to the first solution being adopted as 'the only possible' solution. It is only with the benefit of experience that a more reflective approach can be used to inform the process by acknowledging that what might appear to be the summit is in fact a false summit and that a few more lie ahead.

This last paragraph has looked at the design process from the designers' personal perspective, but they also normally operate in an unmistakable commercial and professional environment. In this environment, reflection becomes a strict requirement, on one hand to avoid professional blunders but also to serve the best interests of the client. So reflection becomes a formal and commercial process aimed at regulating the creative aspect of the design process, checking for mistakes and optimising the eventual solution. It has to take account of the make up and personality of the design team plus the economic reality of the project.

Checking the progress of a particular scheme is a vital element of successful designing. Whether working individually or in a multi-disciplinary team, certain landmarks must be achieved in order to allow progress onto further phases. Good designers recognise this requirement intuitively, others need to be guided to avoid over emphasis on relatively minor elements. This process of design team management becomes an essential part of the successful operation of large design teams. This process of checking progress also tends to work against the natural creative enthusiasm of designers and must be handled sympathetically in the territory of design teams and objectively in individual circumstances.

We have just looked at what could be termed evolutionary change: another potential negative aspect to accommodate in the design process is the requirement for fundamental change. There are many reasons that such a change to a given solution may be required. These can range from a change in the client's plans, a development of consultant information or just poor communication along the line.

For those experienced in their particular design fields, this becomes a possibility to be lived with and accommodated as required. For those new to the process, it can be a very difficult encounter to deal with, sapping all the creative enthusiasm from the experience. So just as with reflection, accommodating change forms part of the formal and commercial reality of the design process.

A highly managed process, incorporating progress monitoring, can allow teams to refer back to periods in the process where the new version of the problem shares a commonality with the previous one; a bit like using a roadmap to retrace your route to a point where you could have adjusted to this new direction. This process becomes very difficult if the roadmap is not clearly defined and relies only on memory.

As with progress checking, dealing with change can be a difficult aspect for designers to deal with and must be handled sympathetically and objectively in most circumstances.

Aesthetic design factors: materials, finishes and quality control

It may seem strange to have left the discussion on the aesthetic aspect of detail design to the very end of the chapter, but this deliberate view assumes that, as discussed in Volume 1, good design will be aesthetically pleasing. Not only that but many of the aesthetic factors would also be covered in earlier parts of the process, particularly during the project definition and assessment stages where particular themes will largely dictate aesthetic factors. Also in purely technical design, the results are often hidden from view and do not directly contribute to aesthetic consideration.

There is often an indirect aesthetic requirement on detail design, however, in that certain details will be required to perform both technically and aesthetically. Exposed technical details are an example but more significantly are exposed surface finishes such as walls, floors and ceilings. Here, the choice of materials has a major aesthetic factor that must feed into the project development stages. At the detail design stage, practicality becomes of prime importance with questions such as 'will installation practices damage the surface?' or 'will we need new methods to provide the required quality of finish?'

The term 'buildability' should be confronted at many points in the detail design process but particularly at this stage. Not found in many dictionaries, it refers to the answer to a question that should be asked of any building design – **can it be accomplished within the terms of reference of the specific project?** It takes into account the degree of difficulty (the amount of expert skills required), the cost (the economic boundaries of the project) and the aesthetic limits of the scheme. However, if the design process is carefully planned and followed, questions such as this should be confronted and ironed out along the way.

Chapter review

- Design teams are now the norm, and efficient interaction of teams requires knowledge and control of the design process particularly if client's aims are to be maximised.
- The prime requirement for successful detailing is to recognise that optimum solution is being aimed for.
- Detailing is based on a permutation of identifying the requisite technology allied to the choice of appropriate materials.
- The process of finding possible solutions can be grouped into three main categories:
  1   the adoption of standard solutions
  2   the adaptation of existing solutions
  3   the invention of completely new methods.
- Detail design is a specialist discipline that very few clients will have knowledge of, so they rely on the designer to make informed decisions on their behalf.
- The term **high-tech** has been assumed to mean new cutting edge and usually complicated technologies that rely heavily on contemporary material science and credible product development.
- **Low-tech** is assumed to be technologies based on well established, proven systems with relatively simple technology such as vernacular precedents.
- Reflecting on and checking the progress of a particular scheme is a vital element of successful technical design.
- Accommodating change forms part of the formal and commercial reality of the design process. A highly managed process, incorporating progress monitoring, can allow teams to refer back to periods in the process where the new version of the problem shares a commonality with the previous one.
- At the detail design stage, practicality (buildability) is of prime importance.

Part **1**

Bibliography

Borer, P. and Harris, C. (1998) *The Whole House Book, Ecological Building Design & Materials*. Machynlleth: The Centre for Alternative Technology.

Bryan, T. (2005) *Construction Technology Analysis & Choice*. Oxford: Blackwell Publishing.

Building for a Future, Journal of the Association of Environment Conscious Building (AECB), published quarterly by Green Building Press.

Construction (Design and Management) Regulations (1994) London: Stationery Office.

Emmitt, S. (2002) *Architectural Technology*. Oxford: Blackwell Science.

Houben, H. and Guillard, H. (1994) *Earth Construction, A Comprehensive Guide*. London: Intermediate Technology Publications.

The Concise Oxford Dictionary of Current English (1977) 6th edn. Oxford: Oxford University Press.

Zunde, J. and Bougdah, H. (2006) *Integrated Strategies in Architecture*, Volume 1. Oxon: Taylor & Francis.

Webliography

Centre for Alternative Technology, www.cat.org.uk

Construction (Design and Management) Regulations 1994, www.opsi.gov.uk/SI/si1994/Uksi_19943140_en_1.htm

Foster and Partners, www.fosterandpartners.com/Projects/0102/Default.aspx

Part 2

Communication of information

Part **2**

Introduction

Communication may not need to be at the heart of the design process, but in most cases, it is an essential element that allows design teams to work together or that eventually transforms concepts into reality. The role of effective communication in the technical aspects of architecture, however, cannot be overemphasised. Unless the individual designer aims to conceive an entire scheme, produce the construction information and eventually construct the final product alone, communication of ideas in some form will be required between one individual and another. It is the dynamic process of sharing information through different forms of technical language in all its many forms that this section aims to explore. Refer also to the discussion of the theory of communication in Volume 1 of this series.

Essential role in translating conceptual design into built form

Conceptual design could be argued to be the beginning of the design process but even before that initial concept is allowed to form, a 'need' is required to give birth to the process. However, even at this stage, the provider of that need (the client) will hope to effectively inform the designer of these desires. This opens up a two-way channel of communication between the client and conceptual designer that is based on a common language that has to be adaptable enough to work with a range of clients from the totally uninformed domestic client to commercial clients with full professional backup.

These latter channels of communication can appear very complicated when viewed from the outside but are usually accomplished by building up relevant experience. Professional bodies tend to see 'professional practice' as a vital component in the development of their future members, providing confidence that they can act in a professional manner when dealing with members of the public – familiarity and eventual mastery of the relevant language is a major component of this process.

At the conceptual stage, the language involved will be mostly about ideas and potential costs and aim to be sufficiently accessible to all of those involved, but it does form the first stage in the process that can eventually lead to the finished project. The next important stage is the merging of the aesthetic design required during the conception of a scheme and the technical design required to build.

This process has many specific phases but has two distinct requirements, firstly the conversion of concept into the form of a technical design and secondly, the formation of technical information that can be used to create the finished product. The channels of communication involved in these phases range from conceptual to the purely technical and depend largely on the range of professional interests involved.

These channels can also take on many forms including basic verbal communication, written information, drawings with many customs and also physical models in many different modes. These various alternative forms of communication will be examined in further depth in this section but all tend to follow the rules of a language appropriate to each particular channel.

The overall language involved in the technical design of architecture follows these channels so it has to include knowledge of the language of architectural design, the ability to communicate effectively with a range of consultant professions and the ability to be fully understood by those responsible for the eventual manufacturing.

The language of architecture and building

Where the first stage of the process involving clients and conceptual designers will require familiarity with the language of architecture, the latter stages involving other professional disciplines and builders will require familiarity with the language of building. These two languages are not exclusive and involve a great deal of common elements, so the process of designing a building will in most cases move smoothly from one language through the other.

The language of architecture in this instance means the ability to convey ideas and concepts aimed primarily at communicating conceptual images with degrees of quality. Terms such as **modernism** and **classicism** or **minimalist** and **rococo** have very distinct meanings in architectural language but with a wide range of interpretations possible.

2.01 The language of architecture and building

The language of building, although having much in common with the language of architecture, cannot in most cases allow such a wide range of interpretation. Its main requirement is to accurately convey information with controlled degrees of uncertainty. The requirement for accuracy and clarity in the language of building forms a major aspect of the requirements of the language and one that calls for a great deal of further analysis.

This requirement for precision is particularly important as it is applicable to all the various channels of communication such as drawings, models, etc., but it should also be able to control the level of uncertainty (referring to the control of the impression gained by the recipient of information). If the designer is simply offering an idea for consideration, it must be presented and labelled in a form that makes this intention very clear. A good example of this intention is the labelling of initial rough drafts requiring feedback comments as 'sketch proposals'.

The demands of these channels of communication, relying on the language of building, can be very onerous. This section also aims to provide a description of the responsibilities associated with the production of technical design information.

Communication requirements: effective, concise and complete

Although the language of architectural design can allow a degree of openness in the communication of conceptual ideas, the language of building is a far more precise process and as such needs to communicate effectively. This is achieved by aiming to be both 'concise' and 'complete'.

The *Concise Oxford Dictionary* describes the word 'concise' as 'brief but comprehensive in expression'; in other words, this particular form of communication aims to be objective, clear, accurate, to the point and avoiding unnecessary narrative that may allow different forms of interpretation. 'Complete' is described as 'having all its parts' and this adds the requirement to include all the necessary pieces of information to allow a full understanding.

These two aspects of the language of building might at first seem impossible to reconcile – how can a description be concise and also complete? This is where the use of this common language comes into its own; by using expressions and conventions that have a specific technical meaning, effective communication can be achieved as long as both parties understand the language. The danger, however, lies in making assumptions about the levels of understanding and the use of jargon ('mode of speech familiar only to a group or profession').

The relevance of a technical language to professional practice was discussed earlier and its relationship with increasing levels of experience. The architectural professions in particular, have by the nature of their jobs to be able to communicate with a very wide range of individuals, from one-off clients to highly professional consultants. Knowledge of and the ability to effectively communicate within all these spheres is vital, but the emphasis must be on communication. Knowledge can be accrued as necessary, but communication must be achieved during its course, and unless this can be assumed, it involves an active awareness of feedback from the recipient.

It is important in any channel of technical communication, therefore, to make sure that your intended audience is capable of understanding not only the objective of the design but also the language in use.

Target audience identification: how people use information

Many forms of technical communication are taken for granted and accepted for historic reasons and in particular, because it is the way in which certain professionals were initially trained. Historically, these methods proved successful, and there is no reason to doubt their current significance. However, examining how these methods work will allow a deeper understanding of the process, enabling both more effective use of existing methods and the option of trying newer alternatives.

The first step as discussed previously is to identify the channel of communication involved as this also identifies the target audience. By also categorising how the information is likely to be used, a more specific form of information can be formatted, aimed directly at the recipient. However, technical information is in most cases required to be accessible to many different parties so the ideal language for one channel may not fit another. A degree of universality is therefore required which suggests why changes to this form of communication normally take the form of slow evolution rather than total revolution. The fact that it is still feasible (although increasingly difficult) to practice professionally without access to computer software is testament to this fact.

In other words, successful communication is far more important in design than the strict adherence to the specific rules of the technical language. The rules are there to aid effective communication.

Software compatibility

All of the communication discussed so far has been between people. Independent of the language, method or channel, it has always aimed to convey information from one individual or group of individuals to another. Among the various tools for communicating are the obvious human direct means such as speech and gestures plus those indirect devices involving the use of tools to depict ideas such as writing, drawing and model-making.

Tools used to help convey ideas still include pencil and paper for sketching, and although pen drawing is still around, it has largely now been replaced by the use of computers. Computer-aided design (CAD) will be scrutinised in more detail later in this section as its role as an active design tool as opposed to a drafting or calculation tool still gives rise to some controversy. The debate normally centres on the significance of hand–eye coordination between the designer's mind and the pencil or pen on paper.

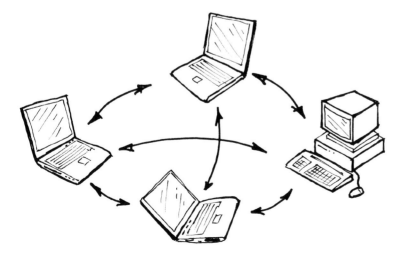

2.02 Talking computers

The truth remains, however, that a poor sketch in terms of artistic quality can convey information equally as accurately as any other. The value of computer systems in general communication is beyond doubt as is its role in the communication of technical information. The role of CAD in the technical design process is discussed in Part 4 – Detail design.

Computers and CAD are in most cases simply the current device of choice for communication in non-verbal, indirect ways. The language is therefore unchanged as it comes with the particular channel. What this does not address, however, is the possibility and now a genuine requirement that computers communicate between themselves.

In the early days of software developments, each new piece of software would have its own hidden language beneath the overt external presentation of information. Occasionally, one piece would become commonly accepted as the best and so take on the role of the 'industry standard'. This would set a common hidden language for others to follow, and the dominance of Microsoft Windows is a good example of this. In design terms, however, no such universal dominance has yet been achieved, and there are many alternatives available, each with its own particular highlights.

The requirement that different computer systems should be able to 'talk' to each other, **interoperability**, is at the time of writing becoming a major issue in the development of software packages. Once solved, however, the 'hidden' language of computer systems can return to the background and allow the overt language of communication to fully exploit this ever evolving and wonderful tool.

Chapter **4**

Communication methods

The introduction to this section looked at the central role of communication in the realisation of design concepts into a built form, it also suggested that many channels of communication exist, depending on the tasks involved and lastly that each channel would use a particular language suitable to its specific function. Moving on from the theoretical concept of communication and into the practical reality involves looking at the methods currently in use. This examination aims to be descriptive and evaluative, in other words critical when necessary but also approving as appropriate.

Four distinct methods of communication, drawings, models, writing and word of mouth, will be examined individually. This is for the sake of convenience only as it is fully recognised that these methods are seldom used in isolation. Drawings contain written elements, reports contain drawings, models and drawings accompany verbal presentations, etc.

A common weakness noted among those skilled in technical design, however, is a reluctance to fully engage in the use of the standard language of communication – in this case English. 'Words fail – see sketch' is a common mantra even if not articulated in exactly those terms, it does serve to illustrate the importance of acquiring skills in all the modes of communication commonly in use.

The procedure of creating buildings is a long process with many distinct and overlapping stages. In essence, however, there are three key phases: the initial conceptual design stage, the design of production information stage and finally the activities on-site stage. Communication practices in these phases use a combination of the methods outlined above but in differing degrees and with different emphasis.

For example, looking at the written requirements only – for the first phase, this may include letters to clients and planning authorities, feasibility

Communication required	Inception	Design	Construction
Client	yes	yes	sometimes
Authorities	yes	yes	yes
Consultants	sometimes	yes	yes
Contractors	sometimes	yes	yes

4.1 Design to construction

studies and design reports. The second phase may include letters to consultants and building control authorities and detailed construction information in the form of specification notes. The last phase may include letters to contractors involving contractual information, issuing of 'instructions' to site personnel and procedures for the project completion.

This chapter now goes on to examine the individual methods of communication used throughout the architectural process. These methods are examined in isolation whilst deliberately avoiding any direct association of a method with an individual phase of the design to construction process.

Drawings: developmental, presentation and production

Described by the *Concise Oxford Dictionary* as the 'art of representing by line', drawing in all its many forms still incorporates this major function. Although the main focus of this book, the process of technical design, has always had drawing at its heart, the aim here is to look more broadly at the intention of the various forms found in the practice of architecture, these being **developmental**, **presentation** and **production** drawings. The more distinct conventions applicable to the different phases will be discussed in Chapter 5.

Developmental drawings, normally called sketches, aim to explore concepts by illustrating initial ideas in some form, usually on paper. This exploration can take on many forms but the most pertinent tend to involve the individual working alone, keeping notes or the transfer of an idea from one individual to another.

1   Examples of this first practice include:
  • a record of a particular thought process
  • a rough scale drawing to see whether the idea fits together
  • a rough drawing to assemble the requisite elements in order.

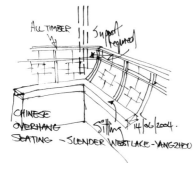

4.2 Sketch for self

2   Examples of the second practice include:
   - the depiction of a particular thought process for sharing
   - a rough scale drawing to show how the idea fits together
   - a rough drawing to show how an idea would work.

The above examples, by taking care not to identify any particular phase of the design process, serve to illustrate that this form of developmental drawing can apply to any of the phases. They also suggest that a crude definition of developmental drawing could be the use of simple lines only.

The second list, by involving the communication of information, raises the issue of drawing style. This subject was touched on in the introduction to this section and involves a combination of communication skills and time management. Taking the first example from list (b), if this idea was a new way of solving a particular problem, whether it be the conceptual design of an entrance, a site layout, a window component or a new wall construction, it would not make sense to provide a completed drawing for production prior to any discussion of the idea. This is because the idea is likely to evolve following feedback and further discussion. It also makes little sense in time management terms because of the clear waste of time. More significantly, a sketch design by its very appearance invites comment, whereas a production drawing tends to discourage comments because it appears complete, with all decisions made.

There are many ways to impart this 'sketchy' appearance to drawings, such as simply sketching the proposal in the first place. The prime consideration, however, is to separate out the drawing process from the communication process – if it is required. For example, if a sketchy feel is required but accurate, scaling information must also be contained, an accurate drawing can be produced but doctored to add the 'sketchiness' later. Formal scaled drawings, produced by hand or computer, can be traced over in pen/pencil or the effect specifically generated with appropriate computer software.

Presentation drawings fulfil a different function to developmental drawings but can include similar characteristics depending on the particular purpose. Generally, however, presentation drawings aim to present ideas for consideration, so the emphasis is on the effective communication of specific information. Presentation drawings also tend to be as persuasive as possible without being too overtly so as their task is to present information in the best possible light.

Conceptual ideas will be portrayed from the most advantageous angles, using colour to full effect, including added landscaping and resorting to a sketchy approach if harsh lines detract. However, a word of caution to consider: a particular design if presented too well may cause considerable disquiet when the finished scheme appears far less than the presentation drawings.

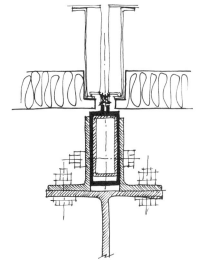

4.3 Sketch for others

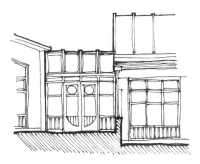

4.4 Sketchy sketch

4.5

Presentation drawings therefore introduce many aspects beyond simple lines to enhance the impression such as colour and shading in particular. A crude definition for presentation drawings would be **line drawings with rendering for added effect**.

The subject of architectural graphics is a complex area when studied at the psychological level but an immensely interesting subject when looked at for inspiration only. The use of perspective views and photo-montages can add greatly to the comprehension of conceptual ideas not only from the inexperienced client's viewpoint but also from the most hardened professional's. Architectural competitions create incentives to add further to the layers of rendering, raising questions of realistic imagery versus idealistic imagery or whether schemes are best viewed 'in context' or in isolation.

Depending on levels of skill, computer software now allows a great variety of choice in how a scheme is finally presented, and this introduces a major potential for conflict. Very realistic images can be perceived as an accurate view of how the proposed scheme will look on completion. Traditional 'artist's impressions' were always accepted as being only impressions, whereas photo-realistic images can easily be misinterpreted.

This book is not concerned directly with the conceptual design of buildings where the demands on presentation drawings are at their most onerous, but this area of graphic representation has many features that are directly transferable to the representation of technical details.

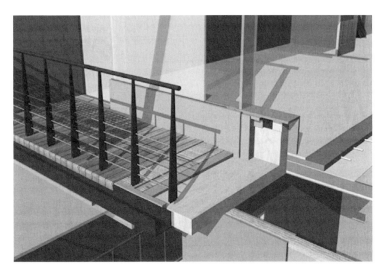

4.6 3D detail (Jake Rotherham)

Traditionally, the portrayal of technical details has concentrated on the factual, aiming primarily for successful communication of the technical content to a fully trained audience with use of two-dimensional (2D), black and white images with accompanying text. There is much scope for developing this model, however, as computers allow much freer use of three-dimensional (3D) imagery plus the advanced use of colour rendering.

Advanced architectural graphics therefore have a potential role in increasing the understanding of technical details. This is particularly valid for complicated, 3D objects that would traditionally require many 2D views and cut away sections. Computer software allows the object to be rotated in all three dimensions until the best views are obtained and rendered to maximise the transfer of information.

The production of paper-based drawings has much to offer in the transfer of information from the drawing office to production site where conditions can often be difficult, exposed and dirty. However, the increasing availability of portable computers means that interactive 3D information can now also be made available on site.

Production drawings as the name suggests are targeted at the production end of the process. No longer is there a need to appear open to feedback or to make an impression on the recipient; all that is required is effective transfer of information.

As discussed above, this does not exclude the use of any of the graphic techniques used for the other forms of drawing, it just means that any uncertainty must be removed. Traditionally based on scaled, black and white 2D views with added dimensions and explanatory text, these

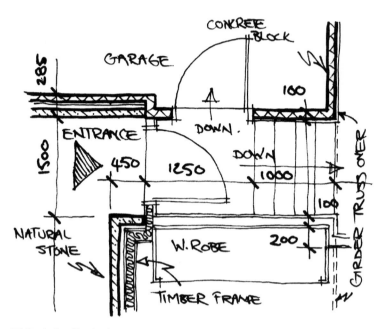

4.7 Standard working drawing

notions are open to challenge, provided they maintain the prime requisites of accuracy and clarity.

The possibility of interactive 3D production drawings is not a long way off and must not be viewed as a major step into the future. This is because the traditional 2D drawing in also a rudimentary interactive document. Although the document itself does not alter through the interaction with the reader, the 3D image it is attempting to portray does.

The more the reader engages with the drawing, taking dimensions, reading the text, returning for dimensions, the more complete the image is built up in the reader's mind. This is also what interactive 3D imagery would be aiming for in the first instance. What may indeed be a slightly longer way off is the equivalent of computer aided manufacture (CADCAM), where the computer software also controls the production of the individual components and assembly of parts as in the automotive industry.

The production of buildings is still currently a highly labour-intensive process dependent on the assembly of components on site. Increasingly, however, the benefits of factory production techniques are being recognised, particularly for individual components. The initial role of developments in this area may simply be in the ability of individual component manufacturers, designers and construction coordinators to communicate effectively on issues such as dimensions, tolerances, etc., but using a common digital language. The aim being that the interoperability of their respective software packages will allow automatic cross referencing and checking prior to production and on-site assembly.

The more precise requirements and variety of production drawings will be examined in the next chapter, but at this stage, it is imperative to differentiate this form of information from the developmental and presentation styles. Production drawings are not a style of drawing, they are vital documents in the design of buildings, often containing essential contractual information and obligations. Clearly, they may include stylistic techniques to aid comprehension, but their prime purpose is the accurate transfer of technical information.

Models: developmental, presentation and test (production)

The various forms of drawings found in the practice of architecture have just been discussed, including 3D drawings. These 'drawings' are not truly 3D, however, as they materialise as 2D images on sheets of paper. They only **represent** 3D images and require interpretation in the viewer's mind to become real.

Even interactive computer images manifest themselves as a 2D display although they are labelled 3D virtual models. These virtual models have much to offer and will be discussed further in Chapter 5. What physical models bring to the viewer, however, is a real 3D object to interact with. It can be moved around and viewed from different angles, distances and in different conditions. It can also be tested in 'real' ways such as its interaction with the physical world. Internal and external lighting studies can be carried out, including shading potential and scaled physical testing of its physical performance is also possible.

The three versions of drawings presented as **developmental, presentation** and **production** exist in response to specific requirements in the communication of conceptual and technical information. The requirements for physical models fall into similar categories with comparable limitations.

Developmental 'sketch' models can also be used to provide:

- a record of a particular thought process
- a rough scale model to see whether the idea fits together
- the depiction of a particular thought process for sharing
- a rough scale model to show how the idea fits together or would work.

Equally, the idea is likely to evolve following feedback and further discussion, so a sketch design, illustrated with a model, by its very appearance, should invite comment. Physical developmental models therefore form

4.8 Sketch model (Rhys Edwards)

an extension to the concept of developmental drawings and aim to incorporate a high level of 'sketchiness'.

Presentation models, as with presentation drawings, also aim to provide a physical manifestation of the proposed concept for consideration. Seeking to be as persuasive as possible, their task is to present information in the most advantageous manner. Computer software now allows incredibly realistic simulated 'fly-throughs' in the virtual world, but real physical models still have a significant role to play in persuading clients and take on a level of 'artistic interpretation' particularly when constructed in monochromatic forms.

This is a particularly valuable resource when attempting to convince a client that a high degree of professional competence is involved whilst simultaneously avoiding the preconception of a final product offered by over-realistic computer images. Presentation models therefore should be subject to the same precautions as presentation drawings.

Test models, as with production drawings, sit at the latter end of the design spectrum but can serve fundamentally different purposes. The main criteria for models at this stage is to provide feedback information to the designer. This can range from specific physical information such as the amount of daylight available through a window (although computer simulation is probably more effective) to a full scale model of a new window component to test either its long-term performance capability or its production and installation features. Increasingly, computer simulation will take on these roles because of the potential to include many more variables.

The case of the lighting study above allows different sun patterns, climate zones and site aspects to be tested easily and with little initial outlay. What this study does rely on, however, is confidence in the

4.9 Presentation model

results because the results tend to be in a range that the designer will be able to relate to, based on experience or intuition. Computer simulation becomes less trustworthy (in the short term) as it moves into areas where the quality of feedback information is more reliant on the accuracy of input information. In other words, there is a need for concern where there is a tendency to produce apparently very accurate information but based on vague early formative data.

Physical test models generally keep within the range of experience and intuition because the limits are more obvious. A test beam will be seen to break under load or the opacity of textured glass can be seen, directly compared with a clear example.

As a general rule, physical test models are only constructed if there is a clear need demonstrated, usually where a full-sized version already in use is not readily available.

Written: letters and instructions, reports and specification notes

The writing skills involved throughout the process of creating buildings are required to perform many distinct functions; however, a common theme is the necessity to be precise and accurate.

There is a distinct form of writing ancillary to this process, however, and that is the particular domain of architectural review. Although a notable form of descriptive writing and performing a genuine function alongside that of architectural history, the descriptive prose involved has little place in the day to day practice of creating buildings.

The range of the circumstances involving written communication in the more technically demanding world was briefly discussed at the beginning of this chapter. Situations where written requirements for three distinct phases were described as the initial design phase, the detailed design phase and the construction phase. The distinct forms of written communication to emerge, however, are **letter writing**, **report writing**, **specification notes** and **instructions**, and these will be considered individually.

The detailed study of the skill of **letter writing** and **instructions** is beyond the scope of this book and the specific analysis of the role of this form of correspondence in architecture will be dealt with in Volume 4. This book deals specifically with the practice of technical design in architecture and as such, the role of letters has a minimal but precise role to play in the communication process. Letters in this case can involve:

● the search for information on specific technical issues
● formal correspondence with consultants regarding the design development
● formal correspondence with contractors in the form of instructions and accompanying letters.

Instructions (more commonly referred to as architect's instructions) are a formal procedure for conveying decisions and alterations to contractors once a project has gone beyond to the signing of contracts. Standard forms are available from the relevant professional bodies (CIAT and RIBA) specifically for this purpose.

Letter writing seeking technical information does not require detailed study, they simply ask the question and wait for the reply. Correspondence with consultants can take the form of simple enquiry in which case letters are very similar to those above but can also take on a more formal role. In cases such as the initial appointment of consultants or the transmission of detailed design information with potential impact on profession indemnity (PI), care is required in the use of language.

PI insurance (PII) provides insurance cover for situations where a client suffers a financial loss as a result of alleged mistakes or omissions by someone offering professional services. It also provides cover from being sued by a client who is simply dissatisfied and has no valid claim, but which could still incur substantial legal costs.

Letters of appointment for consultants are documents with considerable potential legal significance, identifying specific positions of design responsibility. These letters need to be both concise and precise in the designation of specific accountability but will also be dealt with in much greater depth in Volume 4.

4.10 Sample 'instruction' sheet (CIAT)

Detailed correspondence with contractors is also mostly within the realms of Volume 4, but there are also elements that fall within the extent of the technical design process. The prime example here are changes and updates to the original design. These changes are a common occurrence in professional design, and detailed study of the consequences comes under the category of **controlling information** in Chapter 7.

As with formal letters to consultants, however, these are documents with considerable potential legal significance, so they need to be both precise and timely. In other words, contractors must be informed as soon as possible to allow them time to adjust their programmes, but the information must also be clear so that there is no doubt that there has been change and to what degree they are required to accommodate that change.

The significance of **report writing** is a component of the technical design process that is often overlooked. It is frequently seen as a requirement to produce a formal essay in a specifically non-visual format that is outside the standard expertise of the creative technical designer. In reality, however, this need not be so, in fact, 'standard essays' are normally crying out for the creative input of design professionals to aid their comprehension.

Although the presentation skills of the designer can add significantly to the readability of a report, the key divergence of note is that

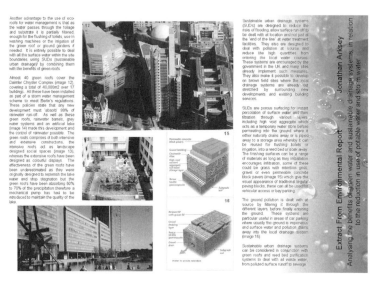

4.11 A good report layout (Jonathan Arksey)

reports contain elements of 'factual' research findings that require communication in specific ways. Clearly, they may also contain design information, but the essence of reports is the communication of 'factual' information.

The reason for stressing the word **factual** is to highlight the transitory nature of apparently truthful information. The history of science is littered with new discoveries proving previous hypotheses incorrect or perhaps more generally, only correct under certain circumstances. It makes sense therefore to always bear in mind when using factual information and particularly when formally referring to it in a report, for instance, that this information may well be superseded in the not too distant future.

In most cases, reports are required to transmit the findings of specific research. Whether it be a feasibility study or the performance potential of a particular material, its prime purpose is to convey new information to the receiver. The style of report is therefore pertinent to both the content and the prospective reader. There is very little requirement for inspiring prose although it is essential to convey the notion that the writer is in full command of the content. An example that combines this requirement with the earlier qualification on factual information would see a sentence starting with 'Current informed thinking suggests that ...' rather than 'The fact that ...'.

The first instance gives the impression that a wide range of sources have been investigated and also that the apparent 'fact' can possibly change. The second, although commanding, conveys the impression of a closed mind and therefore of limited value when research is aimed primarily at exploring the unknown.

As with the discussion regarding letter writing, the writing of reports benefits greatly from being concise and precise. This does present the writer with a dilemma, however, in ascertaining whether the information presented is understandable or not. Authors of fictional novels, for instance, will quite blatantly repeat a particular concept in many sentences to convey their ideas. In report writing, this simply adds a level of confusion so other methods are required, in particular graphic elements.

Rudimentary graphic design is usually well within the skills palette of most designers and can add considerably to the production of reader friendly documents. The writing of reports therefore becomes an amalgamation or merging of concise prose and complementary but specifically relevant graphic illustrations. The specific skills of the designer come to the fore in manipulating the layout of the assorted aspects of the report in a visually stimulating but above all, comprehensible form.

Specification notes are a fundamental component of the communication of technical design concepts. The subject area has produced many books and much research material and in recognition of its role in the communication of technical design, this book devotes a specific section (Part 5) to the system. The role of specification notes sitting alongside drawn material is one that has changed in its significance historically. The relationship between specification notes and drawings is fundamental, however, and although it is possible for each to exist in isolation, in most cases each is employed to aid the understanding of the other.

Drawings can be sufficiently simple to provide the necessary information for construction without the use of any words. Explanatory notes can also be sufficiently well written to avoid the need for diagrammatic illustration, but any graphic aids become drawings and similarly, any instructions or descriptions on a drawing become embryonic specification notes.

The typical production of specification notes as a practice, however, starts at one end of a scale that includes minimal further explanation of detailed drawn information, with the other end comprising meticulous written specifications that refer to drawn material as required. There are therefore many variations possible between these two ends of the scale but with the following being the most common forms:

- *Notes on their own with drawings simply arranging layouts.* This form allows detailed written information to be easily disseminated and reproduced; updating the information is also a simple process. Reproducing existing building systems is a prime example. An illustration of this form in effective use is when a house builder has a number of stock designs, all of which use identical construction methods with only the layouts changing from one house to another. Any changes are therefore easily included to cover all the

4.12 Drawing with separate specification notes

designs and involve minimal changes to the drawn material. The major disadvantage is the requirement for separate documents – written notes and drawings.

- *Standard working drawings.* In reality, there probably is no standard form of working drawing, but it is assumed here for the sake of convenience that this includes fairly detailed drawings that rely on further written explanation placed directly on the drawing and in most cases alongside the relevant information. Specification notes, in this case, form part of the overall graphic communication process, creating what is probably the most persuasive form of technical communication. This is particularly effective in aiding the comprehension of complex designs. Well-constructed working drawings become highly effective communication tools with an aesthetic appeal all of their own. The major disadvantage, however, is allied to its primary benefit and that is, all the information is contained on the one drawing. This makes it very easy to read but very difficult to update effectively.

- *Specification systems.* These systems are simply a form of words that have a predefined meaning. They therefore sit quite comfortably in both of the above forms of specification notes. The National Building Specification (NBS) is collection of specification clauses that are available on subscription and offer choices covering most aspects of technical design in building. The main advantage of the system is universal acceptance of its clauses by many professionals in the UK as part of an aim to coordinate the various disciplines and stages of the construction process. The main disadvantage is the tendency to adopt clauses because of their acceptance without due consideration for optimum alternatives.

4.13 Drawing including specification notes

The National Green Specification (NGS) is an attempt to provide a greener alternative, and the section on specifications will examine these alternatives in much greater detail.

Oral communication: meetings, reviews and presentations

It is tempting to say that oral communication has no part to play in the technical design of buildings, but this would be to diminish its role in the functioning of teams in particular. Personal confidence plays an integral role in the ability of individuals to communicate effectively in the presence of others, and it is also crucial to recognise that there is little correlation between this confidence and knowledge. Any discussion on oral communication in this field should therefore take full cognisance of the range of character types likely to be involved and the desire to make the most of all communication channels.

Many of the formal aspects of this portion of the communication process will be dealt with in Volume 4, but the general aspects of oral communication are worth a brief discussion at this point.

The constructive management of formal **meetings** is a skill that can contribute greatly to effective and open communication. It will always be difficult to avoid the potential domination of meetings by confident and strong-willed individuals, particularly if they are also very knowledgeable. The aim should, however, be to be as inclusive as possible with a structure to the process that allows the views of all concerned to be aired fairly. One way is to assume that the most reluctant to speak are those with most to offer. Clearly, this is not a fundamental truth but it is a way of ensuring examination of all possibilities. Volume 1 includes some helpful guidance on group dynamics, which may be found relevant.

Continuous **review** of work and reflection is a difficult but totally necessary routine to incorporate into the design process. This is because of the highly personalised aspects of design having to operate in a very competitive professional environment. It is therefore necessary to keep a formal check on progress to keep it in line with the economic reality of the project.

The handling of reviews has very many similarities to running meetings but with the added complication of potentially having to deal with more negative aspects. Considerable skills are required to maintain enthusiasm for a design scheme when significant achievements must be aborted due to client's revisions or mistakes of the team.

On occasion, formal **presentations** are required to convince an audience of a particular design process. Good team organisation would see the best talkers handling the verbal elements with the graphic

4.14 Addressing an audience

designers handling the visuals, etc., but this is not always possible. The act of standing up in front of an audience can be very difficult for some, but it is something that can be made easier by practice. One of the best methods of gaining confidence is to be fully conversant with all aspects of the subject. The knowledge that the audience is eager to hear what is on offer is very comforting if that information is readily available. What tends to be more daunting is talking to an audience whose knowledge is perceived to be greater than that of the speaker. This can only be overcome by self-delusion (persuading oneself otherwise) or by gaining sufficient knowledge to be at least equal to the audience.

Practice, particularly to ensure that all audio visual aids are working efficiently, is often helpful. The reality, however, is that in most cases, the audience are genuinely interested in the presentation and not only eager to learn more but also willing the presenter to be comfortable with the process.

Chapter review

- Developmental drawings, normally called sketches, aim to explore concepts by illustrating initial ideas in some form, usually on paper.
- Presentation drawings also tend to be as persuasive as possible without being too overtly so as their task is to present information in the best possible light.
- Production drawings are traditionally based on scaled, black and white 2D views with added dimensions and explanatory text, these notions are open to challenge, provided they maintain the prime requisites of accuracy and clarity.
- Physical models bring a real 3D object to interact with. It can be moved around and viewed from different angles, distances and in different conditions. It can also be tested in 'real' ways such as its interaction with the physical world.
- Presentation models, as with presentation drawings also aim to provide a physical manifestation of the proposed concept for consideration.
- Test models provide feedback information to the designer although computer simulation is probably more effective because of the potential to include many more variables.
- Letters to consultants and contractors including instructions are documents with considerable potential legal significance, identifying specific positions of design responsibility.
- Reports are required to transmit the findings of specific research, such as feasibility studies or the performance potential of a particular material, their prime purpose is to convey new information to the receiver.

- Specification notes are a fundamental component of the communication of technical design concepts.
- Personal confidence plays an integral role in the ability of individuals to communicate effectively in the presence of others, and it is crucial to recognise that there is little correlation between this confidence and knowledge.

Chapter **5**

Drawing conventions

The communication process in technical design has been built and developed into a fairly efficient process but is based on a mutual understanding and acceptance of underlying rules. A fresh approach starts from first principles asking basic questions such as:

- Who needs to know?
- Why do they need to know?
- What do they need to know?

Traditional methods approach this process by providing accurate drawings, specification notes and/or specification systems such as the NBS. These are particularly suitable in most circumstances and have the added advantage of being understood by most commercial organisations. An alternative approach that is perhaps appropriate to the development of new concepts is to question the fundamental culture of the entire traditional process.

The traditional process relies, in principle, on the concept of an expert instructing an operative on how to complete a task. By defining the giver/receiver pathway and opening this up as a two-way developmental practice, it allows both sides to value the process and potentially combines both theoretical and practical advancement. What this does is allow dynamic feedback loops, ultimately reducing risk and can mean the difference between success and failure.

An example would be asking a joiner on site for expert opinion on how to manage the proposed solution in a way that recognises their skills as equal to those of the designer in finding a successful new way forwards.

This approach is in stark contrast to the scenario where the designer issues instructions. This alternative approach requires non-standard methods planned to fit each application individually but needs to take account and fully appreciate the current conventions in order to build on their present achievements.

This chapter intends to examine some of the standard drawing conventions with a view to gaining an appreciation of their current value but also with the aim of allowing the reader to take this understanding into the development of new variations. In other words, this discussion is aimed at moving forward current conventions rather than simply describing standard practice.

Hand sketching

The role of drawings in technical design is widespread and takes on many forms. Initial sketch ideas can be on the back of an envelope to aid design development; instructions on site can also be conveyed in a similar fashion. At the other end of the scale are detailed production drawings produced with considerable care and skill.

The philosophy behind the choice of communication methods was discussed in Chapter 4, particularly in the developmental stages of a project, but what is worth looking at in more depth is the role of hand sketching specifically. Sketching here is seen very much as a process that achieves what no other function can.

As a method of communication, it provides the communicator with an added dimension to spoken or written language. It can also be adaptable and dynamic so that if one view fails, another can be tried immediately. It becomes part of the technical language between designers, and although quality sketching can be striking, it is not normally essential, it is the concept behind the sketch that matters.

5.1

Hand sketching also allows concepts to be worked through prior to the communication process, it is quick and potentially permanent if kept in a sketch book. Individuals vary in their approach to hand sketching and the process of technical design, but what is very impressive to observe is a collection of technical design thoughts evolving through the pages of sketch book. It allows both the designer and the observer to return in a systematic way to earlier phases of the process and contemplate different directions to that taken. It also provides a record of what may appear to be a casual conversation on site but may turn out to be far more significant at a later date.

Elemental drawing conventions

This section aims to classify the conventional systems that have evolved to serve particular functions in the transfer of technical information. The design process that aims to produce finished buildings starts with design development, and the drawing conventions reflect the developmental nature of the process. The initial design process requires regular reworking of concepts so the drawing conventions reflect this need. They are necessarily 'sketchy' and easily produced and altered. The process for detailed technical design is no different, where initial ideas can be explained or simply ordered to see if they work.

At some point in the design of buildings, however, the concepts must be presented for consideration by parties other than the design team. This could be the client, the planning authorities or even the public. At this stage, the requirements of the drawings change as discussed in Chapter 4.

A word about drawing to scale at this point: scale drawings came about to allow the creation of images that are proportionately the same as the object being drawn. Using relatively normal-sized paper and a scale rule, very accurate drawings of very large objects can be created. Essentially, 1:1 (pronounced 'one to one') is full size with 10 mm of the object equalling 10 mm on paper, 1:2 (pronounced 'one to two') is half size with 10 mm of the object equalling 5 mm on paper and so on.

Presentation drawings

Location drawings sometimes called sketch plans, form a distinct stage in the development of building projects and not necessarily part of the technical design process. They are, however, a formal drawing convention and warrant some discussion, particularly as they often form the launch pad for the technical design process by presenting the desired finish that is being aimed for.

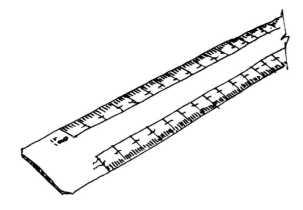

5.2

The scale chosen for presentation drawings is normally aimed at controlling information transfer, i.e. attempting to persuade but without giving too much away. An example of this would be illustrating the overall style, position and scale of a window or door opening but without providing information on the finer construction details such as joints and hardware.

Colour is important at this stage, however, so information will be included to explain the proposed finish and materials. This information would normally be in the form of coloured details followed up with a written account. So, for example, the doors and windows above could be coloured brown to indicate timber construction, but explanation would be required in the form of a written account to differentiate the materials from other possibilities, such as PVC or colour-coated aluminium.

The aim of these drawings is to present the viewer with an image of the proposed scheme as it may appear on completion. It is important therefore that the drawings include a realistic view as much as possible so surrounding buildings, people and landscaping would normally be appropriate in these drawings. A common scale for domestic-sized projects would therefore be 1:100 with the scale reducing to 1:200 or even 1:500 for larger projects where consideration of the overall massing is required within the scope of individual drawings.

5.3

The stage that follows presentation drawings in the conventional process is that of **production drawings**. These drawings are aimed at controlling and directing the production process so they have evolved into a fairly rigid set of conventions that although restrictive in some respects do have the notable advantage of being tried and tested, and more importantly, they are universally understood by the building industry.

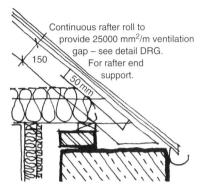

5.4

Great skill is required in the production of these drawings as they contain vast amounts of information, usually in the form of a common technical language but also form the main method of communicating with the contractor on site. This then puts an onus on the drawing to be technically correct but also to take account of the contractual, regulatory and legal framework of the proposed scheme.

Because of the many different requirements of production drawings, four further classifications have developed. These are location drawings, assembly drawings, component drawings and schedules. These classifications are now categorised formally in the CI/SfB classification system, the most widely used and the industry standard. CI/SfB stands for **Construction Index/Samarbetkommitten for Byggnadsfragor** – a Scandinavian system of classification set up in 1959 and aimed specifically at the construction process.

Location drawings

Location drawings provide an overall reference guide for the supporting information, assembly and component drawings plus schedules. Their primary task is to provide information on the overall layout of a scheme so they include information on the location of services and also basic setting out dimensions. They come in the standard forms of plans, elevations and sections. As they are not restricted to the building itself, they also include site location plans and site layouts as well as the building floor plans. Because of this, they are also sometimes known as layout drawings.

The scale of location drawings reflects their purpose, so **site location plans** could be 1:1250 in most cases and sometimes 1:2500 for country areas. The reason for this scale is that identification of the site in relation to its surroundings is the primary requirement as well as pinpointing matters such as access routes, neighbouring properties, etc.

Site layout plans are generally 1:200 or 1:100, because the primary function here is to accurately locate the proposed building within the site as well as access points and other site-related activities such as service connections and storage compounds.

Floor plans and **elevations** are generally 1:50 or 1:100 in order to identify areas of particular importance and so point to further detailed drawings or to clearly and accurately locate significant elements such as walls,

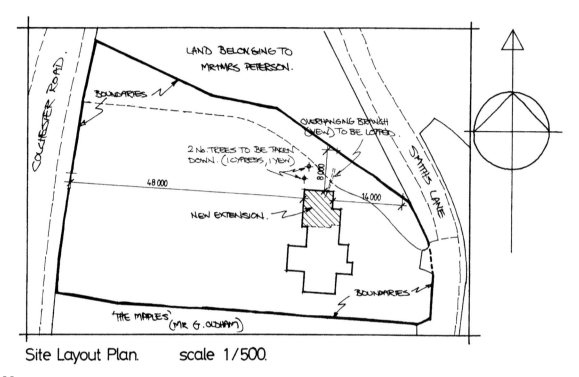

Site Layout Plan.   scale 1/500.

5.5

openings and servicing positions. In other words, it defines the position or location of individual elements without necessarily giving any more detail.

Dimensions are a vital element, and the general rule is that dimensions should never be scaled off a drawing and the written dimensions always taken. The reason for this is that traditionally, dimensions may alter slightly when finally computed and amended without requiring a change to the drawing, so an accurately scaled dimension would in fact be incorrect. It is also vitally important to clarify precisely the points to which dimensions are taken.

There are two schools of thought, one suggesting that only finished sizes should be given, i.e. to the finally plastered wall, with the builder making all the necessary subtractions to arrive at the 'hard' size. The other school of thought says that 'finished' dimensions belong to pre-sentation drawings so that clients and planning authorities can judge the final product but that these need to be computed into 'hard' sizes so that the builder can have real sizes to work to that take account of real building materials such as modular brick or block sizes. It also means that dimensions can be calculated calmly and accurately in the office and

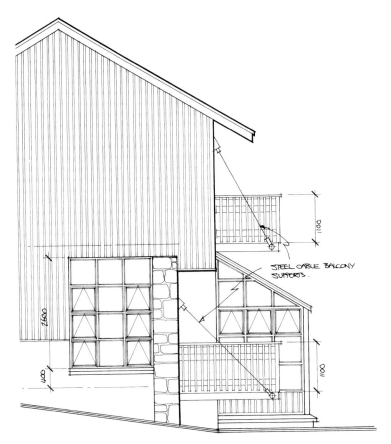

STEEL CABLE BALCONY SUPPORTS.

5.6

any consequences dealt with as opposed to having to manage these sorts of issues on site and under pressure.

Lastly, in the line of location drawings are sections and these tend to be found scaled as 1:50 or 1:20 for the simple reason that they tend to contain slightly more significant dimensional information such as floor and ceiling levels that in turn affect the design of elements such as staircases and floor finishes.

A good example of why the vertical location is more significant than horizontal positioning is in the cases of a staircase. A staircase that is 5 mm too high will have major bearing on the subsequent flooring system whereas 5 mm too wide will probably only affect one wall (stair-cases are normally constructed to fit with a tolerance of 5 mm either side anyway so this would not be a problem). Tolerances are a very important issue and will be discussed in further depth in Part 4.

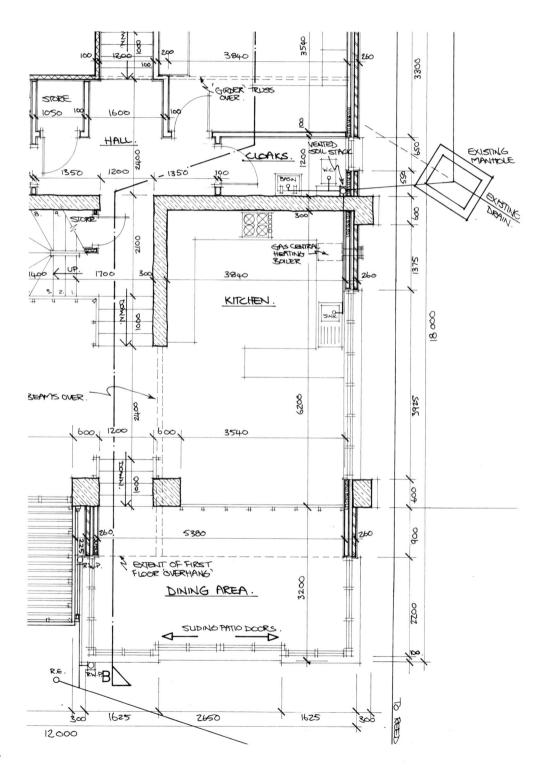

STORE

HALL.

'GIRDER' TRUSS OVER.

CLOAKS.

VENTED SOIL STACK

W.C.

BASIN

EXISTING MANHOLE

EXISTING DRAIN.

STORE

UP.

GAS CENTRAL HEATING BOILER

KITCHEN.

SINK

DOWN

BEAMS OVER.

DOWN

DOWN

EXTENT OF FIRST FLOOR 'OVERHANG'

DINING AREA.

R.W.P.

SLIDING PATIO DOORS.

R.E.

R.W.P.

B

FEED TO REED

5.7

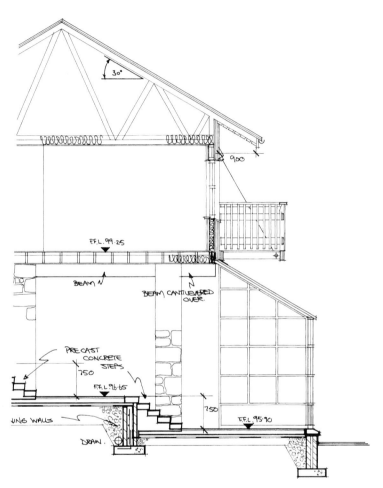

30°

900

F.F.L.99·25

BEAM

BEAM CANTILEVERED OVER.

PRE CAST
CONCRETE
STEPS
750

F.F.L 96·65

750

F.F.L 95·90

JING WALLS

DRAIN.

5.8

Because sections are generally drawn at a larger scale than floor plans to accurately locate vertical elements, it also provides the opportunity to provide additional information. Information on elements that may not have been possible on the plan such as lintels, insulation, etc. can be more readily identified on a 1:20 section drawing.

Assembly drawings

Assembly drawings indicate how different parts of a building come together; in other words, how they are assembled. They show the shape of a particular part and its relationship with the rest of the building, so include important dimensional information as well the location and placement of particular materials. The scale required will be chosen to fit the level of detail required and will include 1:20, 1:10 and 1:5. Occasionally, 1:50 may be appropriate.

A good example of an assembly drawing would be the wall/roof junction illustrated by an eaves detail. This drawing typically would identify the wall construction (including the wall head detail) plus the roof construction and all of the additional aspects such as insulation positioning, ventilation and rainwater drainage systems. It will also include details of finishes and dimensions.

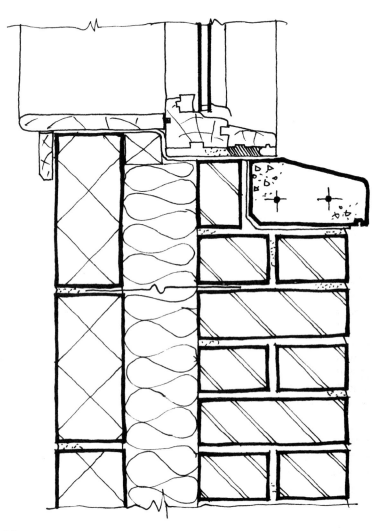

5.9

Assembly drawings will be referenced on the main location drawings, and because of the complex nature form a fundamental part of the technical design of buildings.

Standard 'details' are very common where an office uses previous examples repeated from scheme to scheme. The advantage of a standard detail is that builders may have used them previously, they are tried and tested, and if alterations are required, they are generally minor so that the integrity of the detail is not compromised.

They also mean little time, and therefore cost is associated with reinventing solutions to problems that have already been solved.

The disadvantage, however, is that inherent flaws can be repeated and one of the more satisfying parts of the technical design process bypassed. The reality, however, is that most of these standard details are regularly revisited as regulations change or new or more sustainable materials and construction practices are introduced.

Component drawings

Component drawings are frequently supplied by specialist contractors to illustrate the construction and dimensions of components manufactured off site. These can be incorporated into a scheme to aid understanding and identified on the location drawings. However, the intention is that these drawings illustrate how certain components such as doors and windows should be constructed, including the particular 3D shape and finished size. Scales such as 1:5 and 1:2 are common with 1:1 (full size) less so.

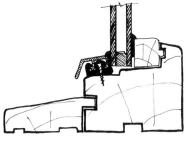

5.10

Schedules

Schedules form the last in this list and are not strictly drawings but generally a table or list of components with additional information. Schedules form the bane of an office junior's life as they are generally where most are first introduced to the technical design process. Schedules are important, however, as they contain large amounts of information that cannot be placed elsewhere without overcomplicating assembly or location drawings. Basically, they provide information in the form of a code that can be conveniently placed on location drawings.

The standard example is that of a door schedule where the piece of information may contain a component drawing, i.e. a detailed drawing of the particular door construction. The schedule will also include additional information, however, such as ironmongery, finishes, special requirements (e.g. fire doors), handing (opening information), etc. The location plan would then have only this code reference written against the door opening.

The schedule has other benefits in that it can be used to count up the number of similar doors required and cross referenced with other specification documentation. Window schedules, ironmongery, sanitary fittings and even a schedule of finishes are all common.

Line drawing forms

The essence of technical drawing is to provide drawn information in a form that can be readily understood by the reader. As Ching (1996) suggests, we are in fact using an abstract method to represent reality. The following information on technical drawing systems may appear to repeat that discussed in various other sources, but the aim here is to recognise the terminology involved and the amount that this can vary.

To provide a complete range of information, we can either use various views of an object in two dimensions, attempting to give as comprehensive a view as possible or rely on a single 3D simulation of the object. The route that provides a series of 2D views has been channelled into a format with universal acceptance which of course aids understanding. Commonly termed **orthographic projection**, it provides a rationale for plans, elevations and sections.

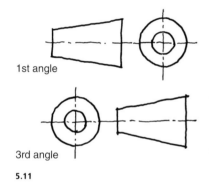

1st angle

3rd angle

5.11

The projection is the route by which the view is generated, and although it is worth a few words here simply in order to introduce the terminology, it does not affect the final drawn elements.

First angle and **third angle** projections both place the front elevation above the plan view but then differ in where the side elevations are placed. The symbols used to indicate the views also explain the projection.

In first angle projection (more common in Europe), the view of the object from the right-hand side is 'projected' on to the left-hand side of the drawing. In third angle drawing, the view of the object from the right-hand side is drawn on the right-hand side.

Another more generic term for orthographic projection is multi-view drawing where the information is transferred using a number of views. This allows each of the individual views to be expanded further. Views such as reflected ceiling plans, horizontal sections, site plans and detailed floor plans all take the basic plan view and expand on it.

The plan view of a basic domestic house would initially be the view of the roof from above, but clearly, although a genuine view, there is also a lot more information to be incorporated in other forms of this plan.

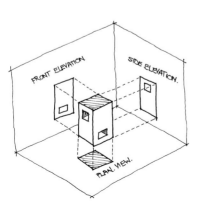

5.12

Essentially, however, multi-view (orthographic) drawings use parallel lines and 'real' angles to portray images (90° = 90° on paper). 3D views, unlike multi-view or orthographic projections, attempt to convey information with one view only.

2D drawings that attempt to illustrate impressions in three dimensions are commonly termed 3D drawings. Clearly, they are not 3D when

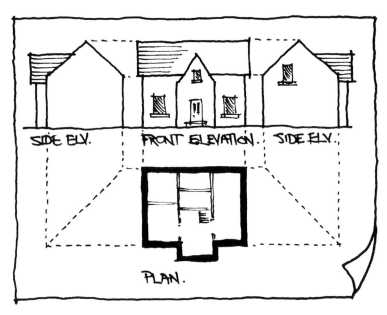

5.13

illustrated on a 2D sheet of paper or computer monitor (computer mod-elling is slightly different concept however) but endeavour to use the intelligence of the reader to form a 3D concept in their imagination.

The aim is to transfer more information than would be possible with a 2D image alone, but it must be remembered that the reader's brain is essentially being tricked into forming the image. This trickery does not always work, so care should be taken to choose the right view and rendering/hatching to avoid confusion. There are some classic exam-ples of how the process of reading 3D drawings can be manipulated such as the work of Escher (1898 to 1972).

This form of drawing is also termed **paraline drawing** because of the process where each of the three dimensions is depicted using parallel lines (as for orthographic views) but using different angles to create the 3D effect. These angles vary according to the convention used and these will be considered further.

Paraline drawings, because of the parallel lines, exclude perspective views which although offering a far more realistic view, cannot be scaled. Paraline drawings are therefore limited to smaller views but include the fundamental technical advantage of being to scale and there-fore contain considerably more useable technical information.

The term paraline drawing is not commonly used in the UK but has been chosen to provide a generic term that describes 2D abstract views of 3D objects prior to further discussion of the various forms.

The reason for this is because some confusion surrounds the terms in normal everyday use. The term **axonometric** means all paraline drawing and comes from a development of the axes used to create the 3D effect. However, axonometric is also commonly used for one particular view more correctly termed 'planometric' or 'plan oblique'.

The most common views available as paraline (axonometric) drawings are based on one common feature – the vertical elements remain depicted as vertical lines on the drawing. The parallel sides of the object then radiate off at a specific angle along the relevant axis, according to the view chosen.

Oblique drawing is a simplistic method of creating a 3D image in that it requires the least amount of new drawing. This is not to condemn it however as there is a valuable use for it in the form of the planometric view. For simple objects, however, the elevation or plan is drawn flat and facing the viewer as in orthographic projection. The other dimensional views are then radiated off with 45° lines. This produces a distorted view and it is common to half the radiated dimension to create a more realistic view. Oblique treatments of elevations appear naive at the scale of small technical details but can work effectively at the larger scale of buildings.

The most effective use of the oblique view is the **planometric** or **plan oblique** where a plan is drawn to full orthographic detail but rotated through 45°, i.e. with one corner facing the viewer. Vertical elements can then be drawn out vertically producing the 3D image. This view is particularly valuable in the depiction of internal floor layouts in 3D as it can be drawn from an existing orthographic floor plan.

In architectural layout design, this is the most common form of paraline drawing so the term axonometric, strictly covering all paraline drawing, is commonly used to describe this single format, i.e. planometric or plan oblique.

Isometric projection is based on 30° angles and produces the most realistic of paraline drawings. It is also claimed to be a mathematical drawing method in that all the dimensions are drawn using the correct scaled sizes. This still creates a 'realistic' image without the adaptations required by oblique views. Isometric can be adapted by altering the angles to create different views but essentially they all have one corner of the object facing the viewer.

Computer-aided design

There is no doubt that computer technology and software has transformed the way architectural practices operate. Very few now have

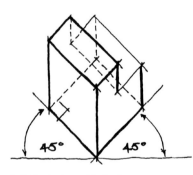

5.14 Simple oblique drawing

5.15 Simple planometric drawing

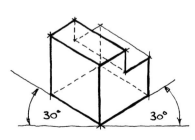

5.16 Simple isometric drawing

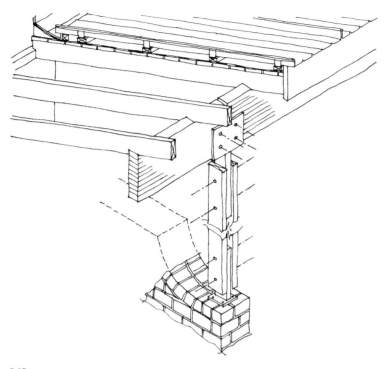

5.17

drawing boards with the PC terminal or laptop now the norm for most designers. In the representation of conceptual architecture, there is no limit to use of visualisations and 'walk through' simulations; however, in the realm of technical design, the integration of computer technology has been very much as a drafting tool. Clearly, this is a very powerful tool and presents much potential in the transfer of information as the information is stored digitally in electronic form instead of on paper in large drawing banks. The final product of this immense development is, however, still commonly a black and white drawing.

Little development has occurred in the way technical information is portrayed using this powerful medium. All of the lined drawing conventions referred to previously still apply to digitally produced information.

There are developments in this area, however, and it is to be found in the university departments specialising in architectural technology. Many young graduates in this discipline have grown up with computer technology, have learnt to design and find the presentation styles commonly used in practice, stuck in another age. Consequently, there is rapid, if experimental, development of the depiction of highly technical details in

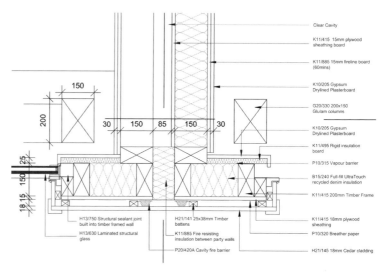

Clear Cavity

K11/415 15mm plywood
sheathing board

K11/885 15mm fireline board
(60mins)

K10/205 Gypsum
Drylined Plasterboard

G20/330 200x150
Glulam columns

K10/205 Gypsum
Drylined Plasterboard

K11/495 Rigid insulation
board

P10/315 Vapour barrier

B15/240 Full-fill UltraTouch
recycled denim insulation

K11/415 200mm Timber Frame

K11/415 18mm plywood
sheathing

P10/320 Breather paper

H21/145 18mm Cedar cladding

H13/750 Structural sealant joint
built into timber framed wall

H13/630 Laminated structural
glass

H21/141 25x38mm Timber
battens

K11/885 Fire resisting
insulation between party walls

P20/420A Cavity fire barrier

5.18 2D CAD detail (Jonathan Arksey)

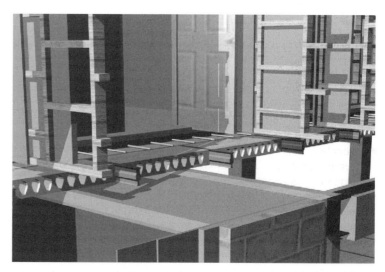

5.19 3D CAD detail (Jake Rotherham)

3D with full colour rendering. The advantage to this new way of presenting technical information in that it goes directly to the core of the original
intentions, that is, to convey information accurately.

By making this information more accessible, in 3D and with the use of
colour, more information can be transmitted or made accessible to
those with less knowledge of drawing conventions. Interactive drawings
can allow the user to move the image around until they find the piece of
information they are looking for.

Imagine a simple eaves detail drawn in this fashion with all of the materials depicted as in real life so the timber looks like timber and the insulation like the particular material chosen. The reader could then investigate the drawing to find further details such as fixing systems or the ventilation system. A major burden on the designer, however, is the need to put all this information into the drawing, a task not commonly carried out in the present system.

There are risks involved in venturing outside of the common conventions, but there is also much potential gain. A whole new realm of possibilities is opening up for architectural technologists and technical architects. There are no new rules to follow as yet so it can be alarming but also very exciting for those involved. In order to make a meaningful leap forwards, however, it is important that students still maintain a good working knowledge of the existing systems and why they are there in the first place as this will almost certainly be the point at which they begin the development of their careers.

Chapter review

- Sketching is a method of communication that provides the communicator with an added dimension to spoken or written language.
- Scale drawings allow the creation of images that are proportionately the same as the object being drawn.
- Presentation drawings, sometimes called sketch plans, form a distinct stage, aiming to present the viewer with an image of the proposed scheme as it may appear on completion.
- Location drawings provide information on the overall layout of a scheme so they include information on the location of services and also basic setting out dimensions.
- Assembly drawings indicate how different parts of a building come together, including the shape of particular parts and their relationship with the rest of the building.
- Schedules are not strictly drawings but generally a table or list of components with large amounts of information in the form of a code that can be conveniently placed on location drawings.
- Orthographic projection (multi-view) is the basic 2D drawing convention consisting of plans, elevations and sections.
- Paraline drawing (axonometric) is depicted using parallel lines and different angles to create a 3D effect.
- Oblique drawing is a simplistic method of creating a 3D image with the elevation or plan drawn flat and the other dimensional views radiated off with 45° lines.
- Planometric or plan oblique (axonometric) is where a plan is drawn to full orthographic detail but offset to 45°, i.e. with one corner facing the viewer and vertical elements extended upwards.

- Isometric projection is based on 30° angles and produces the most realistic of paraline drawings with all the dimensions drawn using the correct scaled sizes.
- CAD has not led to much development in the way technical information is portrayed but much is possible including interactive 3D visualisation.

Chapter **6**

Specification writing conventions

As we have seen, the conventional communication process in technical design is based on a fairly efficient process. Traditionally, this process provides accurate drawings with accompanying written information in the form of specification notes. These notes can be found on the drawing itself or in a separate document, and they may also rely on formal specification systems such as the NBS.

This chapter will examine the aims of specifications and the ways in which they attempt to convey information by describing the performance required or by the exact description of a product or detail. The value and difficulties in writing specifications from first principles will be contrasted with those associated with the use of standardised systems. Part 5 will examine all aspects of specification writing in detail, but this section aims to look at it primarily as a communication tool.

It has been acknowledged that drawings have limits to the amount of information they can convey and that some form of words can aid the process of communication. This is particularly true in the area of quality. The drawing of a high-quality object can look identical to a poorer version. This is not always the case, however, as high-quality elements would normally be apparent by the extent of the detailed drawn information provided. In practice, however, it is the added text that defines the quality required.

Types: performance or prescriptive

Performance specifications

Performance specifications characterise the requirements of a particular element of the design scheme by defining and listing a series of characteristics to be met. Without naming a particular product, they provide the technical specifications that could be achieved by a number of products. They can also vary in the amount of information given. The essential value of a performance specification is that it allows contractors to use their knowledge of the market to obtain best value returns.

Simple performance specification: Supply and construct a roof system based on trussed rafters in full compliance with current building regulations to provide the roof profile and slate finish as indicated on design drawings.

6.1

An example would be the specification of 'high-performance timber windows'. Simply put, this offers the contractor much choice, but the designer should assume that the cheapest possible would be installed. This specification could and should be worked on, however, to include information on glazing systems (double, triple glazed, low-e, etc.), the species of timber and the sourcing of that timber.

This specification could therefore be improved to state, 'triple glazed (with low-e glass) high-performance timber windows constructed with softwood from certificated sources and finished in a factory applied low VOC preservative stain'. More specific information could be included or left out while still giving the contractor the opportunity to shop around or use a supplier whose components they are familiar with. The specification that products comply with particular performance certification criteria such as kitemarks or British Agrément Certificates adds to the control of the process.

Performance specifications are perceived as being difficult to write because of the requirement to cover any potential loopholes. The example above, for instance, has not mentioned colour or the type of finish (gloss, matt, etc.), the opening style or hardware (handles, hinges, etc.) although these may well be mentioned elsewhere in elevations or window schedules.

Performance specifications become much more useful when they are describing elements where the designer does not have too much concern over the final appearance and where the in-use performance will be guaranteed by other parties. An example of this would be the installation of services that are normally hidden, so as long as they provide the servicing required and fit into the space provided, the designer can feel content with a performance specification. This example can be complicated if there is desire to reduce the energy demands of the servicing system, so the specification would work in conjunction with an overall environmental design strategy.

Performance specifications can be valuable where the procurement route provides the contractor with an incentive to reduce costs of an overall scheme. This is particularly relevant in the outlay of public money where there is responsibility to achieve value for money. However, experience has led many to feel dissatisfied with the results, where the final appearance can be very different to that initially perceived and the control of quality can be particularly difficult to achieve. As long as the performance specification is well written, however, the responsibility to provide a satisfactory solution lies with the contractor. Another option, however, is for the designer to state exactly what product they require – a prescriptive specification.

Prescriptive specifications

Prescriptive specifications describe components as products and commonly provide their brand names. This has many advantages for the designer in that the final appearance is extremely predictable but has two major disadvantages. One is the requirement to be knowledgeable about the product prior to specification, which involves research or the reliance on established knowledge because the responsibility for eventual performance lies with the designer.

The second disadvantage is that there is little scope for cost saving on behalf of the client particularly if the product can only come from one source. The major advantage of prescriptive specification is that it allows the designer more control of the process.

A compromise between these two apparent extremes is to insert the clause 'or similar'. This is thought by some to be bad practice, and it certainly can be abused if used indiscriminately, particularly on larger projects. However, on smaller projects, it can offer the client the opportunity to make genuine improvements in quality and cost, particularly if the overall specification system presents an overriding instruction that 'or similar' can only be used with the agreement of the designer. This allows for an enhanced relationship between the designers and those working on site helping to develop a genuine dialogue in the client's best interest.

> Simple perscriptive specification: Construct hipped roof system with trussed rafters, designed and supplied by nominated specialist contractor. Roof pitch to be 35°. Roof covering to consist of reclaimed natural slates as approved, on 50 x 25 mm softwood battens ... etc.

6.2

Writing from first principles

For the technical designer, there can be no more valuable way of gaining a full understanding of their proposed design, particularly the areas where there are gaps in that understanding. Essentially, writing from first principles is providing a list of specific instructions to accompany the drawn information to allow operatives on site to construct the scheme. In addition, however, as for all specification systems, it also allows contractors to provide cost estimates and plan the construction sequence.

An example of this process is to be found in the specification of a standard brick/block cavity wall. Normally, this might start with a list of the elements in order of their occurrence in the wall preceded with the opening words, 'construct external wall with...'. It could start with the internal finish and end with the external finish or vice versa.

When writing this specification from first principles, i.e. not using stock solutions, the designer will think about each part of the construction, including how it is fixed, when it is fixed and what it is fixed to. Elements such as the wall ties will need thinking about, how many, what spacing and what else is involved. This example was chosen deliberately to illustrate a problem that could arise without using this staged approach.

The control of interstitial condensation in external walls is an important aspect of wall construction, it is particularly important in timber-framed walls where it is controlled with a vapour barrier fixed to the sheathing layer. This is possible because timber-framed walls are built timber frame first and then the outer elements are added later.

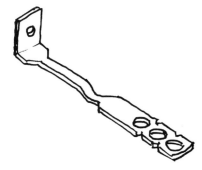

6.3 An Ancon timber frame wall tie

It may seem sensible to apply this same concept to a brick/block cavity wall; however, by thinking through the building process as the specification is being written will highlight the fact that most brick/block cavity walls are built with both leaves progressing at virtually the same rate. This does not therefore provide a flat surface for fixing a vapour barrier to as it does in timber frame. Another aspect is that wall ties fixed to timber frames are 'L' shaped with the flat foot of the 'L' provided with screw holes through which screws fix the flat foot onto the timber frame. This can penetrate the vapour barrier with little effect because the tightening of the screws seals the vapour barrier by squeezing it tight against the sheathing layer.

Conversely, in brick/block build, the wall ties are laid into the mortar of joints between the courses so offering no prospect of sealing any holes made in the vapour barrier. Locating a vapour barrier in the cavity is therefore a very difficult task and one that certainly would cause great difficulty on site.

The solution comes from a deeper understanding of the science of cavity walls and their construction. A vapour barrier could be installed by building in manner similar to timber frame, i.e. building the inner leaf first; alternatively, it could be argued that by making careful choice in materials and detailing an effective ventilated cavity, the condensation is allowed to form but the damage limited by using waterproof materials and allowing effective evaporation. Another option would be to consider impermeable wall construction, but that needs careful consideration as it alters the performance characteristics of the internal environment.

All of these ideas and judgements, particularly a consideration of 'buildability', would be made while writing the specification, thereby reducing the risk of producing an inappropriate specification but also allowing further development of new concepts that resorting to stock solutions would miss.

Clearly, it would be an arduous undertaking to begin each piece of specification writing from first principles, making the process extremely uneconomic in most circumstances. However, there are times when it is also an integral part of design and the way that technical design in particular develops. This is particularly true in the development of sustainable solutions where it may be appropriate to question all aspects of a design.

Standard forms of specification

In this section, we have looked at the types of specification and writing from first principles. The need for brevity, efficiency in time management and the desire to communicate in a standard form has led to the development of standard forms of specification like the NBS. Essentially, these prewritten and fully referenced clauses provide a stock of ready-made phrases for the designer to choose from. They cover most areas of building in an extensive and very useable form, allowing most scenarios to be written up and referenced in standardised form, thereby removing much of the tedium of having to write standard specifications from scratch.

These systems also have the added value of being kept up to date with current developments in materials and regulations in particular. Also available over the Internet (although access is not free), this now removes the need to keep the catalogue of clauses in hard copy form and fits in well with the contemporary move to the digital, paperless office.

In purely communication terms, they are extremely efficient at cutting down misinterpretation of intentions, but they can have the effect of restricting the development of technical design. They also form part of a much larger attempt to coordinate the flow of communication throughout the life of a construction project. This process will be examined in depth in Chapter 20. However, at this point, it is worth noting that their role is one that will vary depending on the nature of the project.

F30 Accessories/sundry items for brick/block/stone walling
270 Joint reinforcement for ...
Ancon SMR 60
    Bed joint reinforcement with 4 mm diameter outer wires and 2.5 mm diameter cross wires.
    SMR 60 has an overall width of 60 mm.
    Consult Ancon Building Products technical literature for details. Ancon Building Products can also provide a design and specfication service and it is recommended that they are consulted early in the design process.

Material: Austenitic stainless steel.

6.4 An NBS clause (Ancon Building Products)

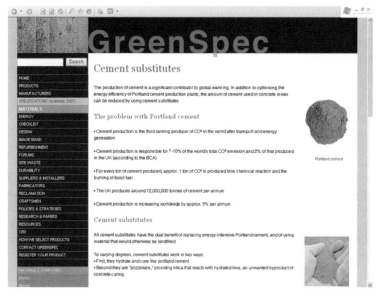

6.5 An NGS web page (GreenSpec)

Alternative forms exist, particularly the NGS, aimed at providing simple off-the-shelf solutions but with the knowledge that the clauses have been well researched to provide sustainable alternatives. The advantage lies in the knowledge that the NGS is a system dedicated to the pursuance of sustainable design solutions and is therefore continuously seeking improvements. The disadvantage is that in the relatively new discipline of sustainable design, opinions can vary significantly, so some degree of discretion is required in the adoption of standard 'green' solutions.

The responsibility of the designer to specify appropriately is not removed with these clauses as the requirement is to control the transference of information. The next chapter will address these particular issues.

Chapter review

- Specification notes provide the added text to drawn information that defines the quality required.
- Performance specifications characterise the requirements of a particular element of the design scheme by defining and listing a series of characteristics to be met.
- Prescriptive specifications describe components as products and commonly provide their brand names.

- For the technical designer, there can be no more valuable way of gaining a full understanding of their proposed design than writing specification notes from first principles.
- Standard forms of specification in the shape of prewritten and fully referenced clauses provide a stock of ready-made phrases for the designer to choose from.

Chapter **7**

Controlling information

This chapter is concerned primarily with the communication of information in the practice of technical design in architecture. As we have seen, there are many aspects to this process and all hold the capability to increase the levels of information transfer, but equally they also harbour the potential to disrupt that process by containing conflicting information. This capacity for confusion is potentially disastrous, and it is in most cases the responsibility of the technical designer to manage the confluence of information at this vital point.

This point in the design process is where the conceptual design makes way for the input of various technical design components. So where there may be one conceptual designer, this could then open up to include input from a technical designer (architectural technologist or technical architect), structural engineers, services engineers, landscape architects, interior designers, etc., the list could go on. It is, however, commonly the responsibility of the technical designer (also the conceptual designer in smaller projects) to coordinate this input as it relates directly to the further development of the project into the phase when decisions are made concerning how the project will actually be built.

Imagine if you will the difficulty in resolving the following situation. A client is persuaded to change the external cladding of a building from brick to timber boarding, and the planning authorities accept the amendment. However, the initial feasibility sketches that went out to the various other designers were the brick-based version. A simple matter of not issuing up-to-date information to any one of those designers could have major repercussions if the incorrect base information continues throughout the project, and this potential for misinformation repeats every time any part of the initial design or drawing is altered.

Controlling this process becomes far more complicated as the scale of the project increases. There is a point where the control of information becomes such an onerous task that it has to be handed to specific professionals to deal with. This then falls into the scope of **design team management** or **project management**. Many technical designers may still be held ultimately responsible, however, with only the coordination role being removed.

Responsibility: avoiding conflicting information

Taking on the responsibility for providing consistent information streams may seem to be a particularly burdensome liability for the technical designer but for most it is also where the great rewards can be found. The learning experienced in real professional practice is much about the formal office practices that deal with the risk aspects of this responsibility.

This involves defined levels of responsibility apportioned to individual staff according to experience and skills, formal practices for amending designs, recording the process and issuing new instructions resulting from the amendments. The formal processes for dealing with the risk can be documented, but individual offices usually have their own customised version. Ultimately, it is a system that formally records all amendments and provides a method for disseminating that new information to the required recipients.

Digitally produced information makes this a much simpler task in one respect, as it does not necessarily require new paper-based drawings to be sent out but can be done using electronic means and simply 'saving' the new version. This does not remove the obligation to keep control of the dissemination process and includes a further potential for error. A new paper-based drawing arriving by post will be opened and read in most cases, a large bundle of drawings, less so – but with digital information, there is strong need to make the recipient engage with the changes to avoid it being 'saved' for later.

This whole process can be seen as tedious when there is exciting design to be involved with, but it is vital for designers in this sensitive area to be very mindful of their responsibility. This is so important that professional bodies representing the designers of buildings (CIAT or RIBA) insist on their qualified members taking out insurance to cover this responsibility.

PI insurance as discussed in Chapter 4 is a cover-all type of insurance policy that essentially aims to provide design professionals with a form of cover that will protect them from the consequences of their design going wrong. The reality, however, is that this insurance is seldom called on because very few design professionals would enter into a situation where

Members are to return evidence confirming that they hold current professional indemnity insurance in compliance with the Code of Conduct. This is monitored on an annual basis and the Institute's Conduct Committee will take disciplinary action against those members not in compliance or have not demonstrated compliance. Members that have been found, by the Conduct Committee, to be in breach of the Institute's Code of Conduct Clause 6 have been expelled.

PII is there to protect not only the client but of equal importance the member against an act of negligence.

7.1 The relevant clause (CIAT)

problems of this magnitude become likely. This is because the adverse publicity would itself become ruinous. Also, the professional bodies make the process of achieving full membership sufficiently onerous to ensure that those fully qualified have sufficient knowledge and experience to avoid these pitfalls.

There are, however, situations beyond the control of individual designers that can result in claims on their insurance and also errors do occur. With the most stringent of quality control systems, mistakes can happen, and it is in these circumstances that the eventual costs of remedial action can run into millions. Even the most understanding of clients will claim when large sums of their money are at stake.

The issue here is to recognise the potential for disaster and then deal with this potential by organising sufficiently robust systems to protect your method. First in this process is recognising the relationship that exists between the various drawings and other project documentation.

The advent of the CDMT regulations in the UK has now added extra emphasis to the responsibilities of designers. The CDM regulations place a formal responsibility on designers to produce safe buildings, and this requires clear communication of information. An added degree of responsibility comes from the fact that the CDM regulations create a criminal and not a civil liability.

Relation to other documents/drawings

As a general rule, the timeline of the design of a building tends to follow a standard path. It starts with the conceptual design and is followed by development of the design into the regulatory approval stage before the start of detailed production design and information. At the production information stage, the various other design inputs come together before it moves onto the tendering stage with possible bills of quantities (BoQ). Finally, it will go to site for assembly.

There are clearly many opportunities for change and particularly gaining feedback information. This means that the process that checks for

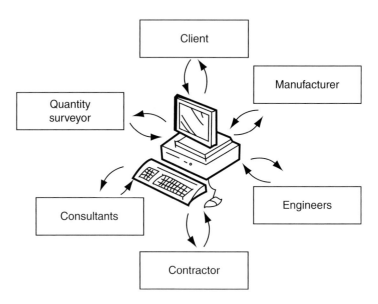

7.2 Data exchange

mistakes and maintains the quality control system can also be used constructively to incorporate modifications brought about due to new learning further down the line.

The documents involved in the quality control system may include the presentation drawings if there is a distinct need for them to accurately represent the finished scheme; however, this is not normally required. All other drawings and documentation will require updating across the board to accommodate alterations if they are affected by the changes.

These will include all the production drawings, location, assembly and possibly component drawings, plus all schedules, specifications and tender documentation. Another form of documentation not referred to as yet is the 'schedule of works' that represents a description of work to be done, particularly common in repairs and alterations where it will accompany drawings and other information.

An especially critical aspect of technical detailing that requires specific attention in the maintenance of consistent information is the matter of dimensions. There is a generally accepted rule, referred to in Chapter 5, that dimensions should not be scaled from technical drawings, and most drawings will actually specifically state this at some point. The chief reason for this is to make the dimensions over-rule the drawn information, allowing minor alterations to be made without altering the drawing.

This is essentially only true for hand drawn material, however, as amendments to digital information can include both the drawn elements and

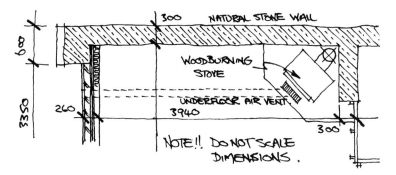

300 NATURAL STONE WALL

WOODBURNING
STOVE

UNDERFLOOR AIR VENT
3940
260

300

NOTE!! DO NOT SCALE
DIMENSIONS.

68o

3350

7.3

dimensions. Current software allows the amendments to go much deeper by also including all of the subsidiary drawings as well. This new
development, although extremely valuable, does also require some caution in its use in that what might appear to be a reasonable and simple
alteration on one drawing may actually have a major impact, unseen on
another detail.

Dealing with changes in the design of a building has to be expected as
part of the normal process of design. How it is accommodated, controlled
and approved is what really matters. Changes may require the approval
of the client, and it is worth considering keeping the client aware of all
changes, regardless of their nature. Changes may and usually do have
cost implications, but they might also have consequences affecting legal
issues, planning approval and building regulations.

Drawing registers

The first step to keeping a control of technical information is a robust
process for the recording and collating of drawings. It includes both drawings produced in-house and also those coming in from other sources. This
process requires responsibility and management as it will need to provide
a system that will give each drawing a reference number initially but also
record the history of its development. So dates of initial production and
subsequent amendments are required plus the dates of its issue and to
whom it has been distributed. The same requirement also extends to new
information coming in or the return of previously sent out work.

Historically, this process involved the storage of copies of all the versions and the hard copy register itself, so simple systems worked best to
accommodate the large amount of information. With the advent of
digital information systems, the process can handle far more information and automation providing much more control over the management of the drawing register.

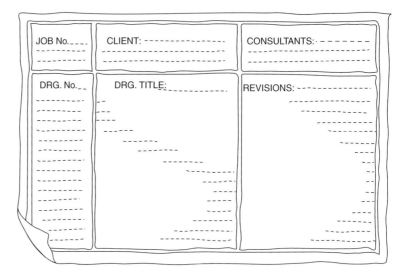

7.4 A simple drawing register

As discussed earlier, the control and coordination of information involves a two-way flow as design teams require information input from external sources to develop designs and they themselves produce design work. The need to check for errors is paramount, and it is worth working on the assumption that mistakes have been made as they are a frequent occurrence. This can take the form of staged checks and approvals signed off formally.

What this discussion points to is the complexity of the process in quality control terms, that starts at the initial concept stage and ends with on-site production. The complexity is much reduced, however, by the use of standard information protocols considered in this section. The deliberation has looked at the technical design process in isolation, however, but the reality is that, this is just one element of a much larger construction industry.

The necessity for information to flow freely from one stage to another requires a system that coordinates production information throughout the process that creates new buildings.

Coordinated project information

The need to manage the production of information becomes very important as the construction process becomes more complex and more inclusive. This not only includes the design component of the process but also those beyond, where production information moves into specifications and bills of quantities.

A multi-disciplinary organisation, the Coordinating Committee for Project Information (CCPI), now the Construction Project Information Committee (CPIC), was set up with the aim of generating guidelines to provide a consistent method for the production of design documentation. This committee (originally the Project Information Group) published a sequence of Construction Project Information (CPI) documents aimed at promoting enhanced production information.

There are three documents produced under the auspices of CPI: one on Production Information, another on a Common Arrangement of Work Sections (CAWS) and a third, Uniclass that aims to organise library materials and the structure of project and product information.

There is no doubt, a great deal of value to be had from CPI in the effective coordination of this type of information in the more complex projects. For smaller practices, it is less obvious and an efficient office-based system can work successfully. It is in the communication between practices and professions in particular that it becomes increasingly valuable.

A similar dilemma is found in the apparent difficulties caused by the use of different CAD software packages. The concept of 'interoperability' examines different software systems being able to transfer information directly so that a particular package could read and assimilate information produced on another. CPI aims to provide a similar notion of interoperability between office information production systems. The main concern in the current climate of IT dominance is that it is founded on an outdated paper-based system of communication. The concept, however, remains pertinent in the modern construction industry.

Chapter review

- There are many aspects to the process of information transfer that harbour the potential to disrupt that process by containing conflicting information.
- Responsibility for providing consistent information streams commonly falls into the remit of the technical designer.
- A change to one drawing may require all other drawings and documentation to be updated to accommodate alterations if they are affected by the changes.
- Dealing with changes in the design of a building has to be expected as part of the normal process of design. How it is accommodated, controlled and approved is what really matters.
- The control of technical information requires responsibility and management and a robust process for the recording and collating

of drawings. It includes both drawings produced in-house and also those coming in from other sources.

- CPI provides a formal mechanism for management of the design components of the process and also those beyond, where production information moves into specifications and bills of quantities.

Part 2

Bibliography

Ching, D. K. (1996) *Architectural Graphics*, 3rd edn. New York: Van Nostrand Reinhold.

The Concise Oxford Dictionary of Current English (1977) 6th edn. Oxford: Oxford University Press.

Construction (Design and Management) Regulations (1994) London: Stationery Office.

National Building Specification (1972) London: National Building Specification.

Zunde, J. and Bougdah, H. (2006) *Integrated Strategies in Architecture*, Volume 1. Oxon: Taylor & Francis.

Webliography

Autodesk – computer aided drawing software, http://usa.autodesk.com/adsk/servlet/home?siteID=123112&id=129446

British Board of Agrément, www.bbacerts.co.uk/bba.html

Chartered Institute of Architectural Technologists, www.ciat.org.uk

CI/SfB classification site, www.ascinfo.co.uk/index.html

Construction (Design and Management) Regulations 1994, www.opsi.gov.uk/SI/si1994/Uksi_19943140_en_1.htm

Construction Project Information Committee (CPIC), www.productioninformation.org

Foster & Partners, www.fosterandpartners.com/Projects/0102/Default.aspx

M. C. Escher website, www.mcescher.com

National Building Specification, www.thenbs.com

National Green Specification, www.greenspec.co.uk

Royal Institute of British Architects, www.riba.org/go/RIBA/Home.html

Square One – environmental software, www.squ1.com/products

Part 3
Selecting materials

Part **3**

Introduction

This section aims to explore the process of choosing materials during the technical design process. It is pertinent because the detailed knowledge required to fully understand and appreciate even the most mundane of building materials is in fact well beyond most designers. This is not to suggest that designers cannot become expert in the field of materials and indeed, they require a substantial knowledge of particular materials in order to design effectively but simply to acknowledge that there are too many parameters to consider in all the materials involved in technical design.

To illustrate this point, consider the humble brick: how many designers have sufficient knowledge of the bricks they specify to fully understand the sourcing of the clay, the energy supply used in firing, the chemistry of firing or the process of crushing as part of the eventual demolition for any particular type of brick?

By looking at defining the requirements of materials, selection criteria and the methods used, it is intended to highlight some of the issues that

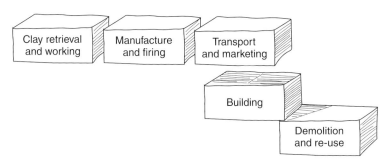

3.01 The life of a brick

confront design teams when making these choices. This section is not intended to be a comprehensive guide to materials; however, it would be beyond the scope of this book. For comprehensive and definitive information on building materials, three existing works stand out for the breadth of information they offer:

- *Materials for Architects and Builders* by Arthur Lyons.
- *Ecology of Building Materials* by Bjorn Berge.
- *Materials in Construction: An Introduction* by G.D. Taylor.

Chapter **8**

Summary of requirements

Materials generally form one of the most important variables in the process of technical design. There are many parameters involved in the choice of materials, but they fall into three main categories, initially availability and suitability are the primary variables, but the familiarity of the designers with these two issues is also paramount. This defines the 'comfort zone' for most designers and also represents the primary obstacle to innovation and a subsequent move to more sustainable design practices.

Suitability and availability have a major impact in the process of selecting materials. The definition of suitability will depend on many factors, however, including other materials involved, assembly processes, skills availability and budgets. This will include having to make decisions on whether a particular material is available as a refined component, perhaps factory finished within strict quality control standards or whether the choice will require the education of design and site staff in order to fully understand the performance variables of something new.

This process becomes far more complicated when a more holistic and sustainable design approach is chosen because the performance criteria itself becomes a variable. The availability of a material is, however, a real constraint on selection. It includes the:

- physical availability (can it be acquired?)
- financial availability (is it affordable?)
- environmental availability (is it a good and safe material to use?) (Wienand and Watson, 2006).

The method of choosing materials will generally reflect the approach taken to the design process. The safer the chosen route the more limited and therefore less potential for innovation with the more risky approach allowing considerably more potential in the choice of materials. The safe approach does allow for a degree of innovation but would see choices limited to those with fully accredited and proved backgrounds, in other words, materials where the performance is highly predictable.

The other end of the scale involves the selection of materials with little or no proved performance standards although other forms of data may be available. Clearly, the risk increases dramatically but so does the potential for genuinely innovative design. Unfortunately, the effect of failure or the fear of failure also represents a major obstacle.

The choice of materials comes from a definition of the problem requiring a solution, knowledge of what has worked previously and what is available. Moving outside of the 'comfort zone' requires the acceptance of additional risk although this can be controlled by looking to prototype examples where some performance issues have been considered.

The definition of performance requirements will therefore have a major part to play in the selection and eventual specification of a material. By defining the performance criteria, the overall choice of materials able to satisfy those criteria reduces and so do the number of alternatives available.

Performance: functional, structural, insulation, etc.

The selection of a material to perform a task starts with a definition of the problem requiring a solution. In most cases, this is done intuitively, as in roofing, materials are 'assumed' to be water resistant. This practice can often represent obstacles to design innovation because there are many ways of dealing with the requirement for roofing materials to effectively 'handle' water. It could be by soaking it up until it evaporates or by shedding it quickly.

Both experienced and novice technical designers should consider every problem from first principles although the time is not always available to do so. Returning to the example of the roofing material, a better definition of the problem requiring solution would be 'keeping rainwater out' and not 'provide a waterproof roof', and so a functional performance criteria is established.

Buildings comprise many different components, some made up and assembled on site and others bought in as manufactured items. All will be expected to provide a certain performance that in turn relies on the materials of its manufacture. The definition of performance criteria should come before the choice of materials although in reality, experience in most cases means that these happen simultaneously. Performance criteria can also be numerous with different degrees of magnitude.

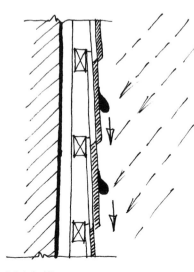

8.1 A shedding system

On the first level of importance are basic requirements such as:

- **Structural stability** – will the material stand up to the imposed gravitational loadings, wind and thermal movements, etc.?
- **Durability** – will the material be able to perform its function long enough?
- **Health and Safety** – can the material be guaranteed not to present a health risk during construction and subsequent use?
- **Fire** – will the material behave acceptably in the advent of fire?

These first four criteria are of such importance that it requires more than the opinion of the designer to verify their suitability. Building regulations primarily aim to ensure safe buildings so will lay very heavy emphasis on these issues and will require evidence in the form of independent certification that these requirements can be met.

The next level of performance criteria is more likely to fall outside the realm of legislation and includes requirements normally considered to be 'design' decisions. These include:

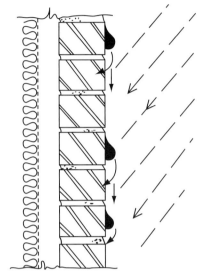

8.2 A partial soaking system

- **Appearance** – will the material provide the finish required?
- **Weathering performance** – will the material behave as expected when exposed to local weather conditions?
- **Serviceability** – can the material be maintained and repaired?

As we have seen previously, there are other issues as well, availability, cost, buildability and of prime importance – environmental features.

Environmental accountability

The levels of responsibility directly attributable to designers should be no more than to any other member of society: we are all responsible. The difference, however, lies in accountability. Designers plan the creation of **things** in most cases and whether these things are designed to be transitory or everlasting, they are usually constructed with materials of some kind.

The designers therefore have a choice in whether to partake in the design exercise and in the materials that are used in making the thing. The materials chosen could have little environmental impact such as the sand in a sandcastle or they may have a profound environmental impact such as the ultra-dense concrete used in a nuclear reactor. In the first case, there is little for the designer to account for, but in the second, the accountability stretches far beyond a simple choice of materials.

8.3

Technical design in architecture involves the production of buildings that mostly will be around for a good number of years, be in direct contact with people and include materials extracted and produced in processes totally outside the control of the designer. Designers do therefore have the capacity to make decisions that matter in the longer term and should be held accountable for those decisions.

This is clearly recognised in the sphere of health and safety by clients and designers so it is a simple extension of this same concept to expect designers to produce buildings that are also ecologically healthy and safe. It is a sad reflection on the construction industry, however, that for both health and safety and environmental design issues, the prime driving force is legislation. That is not to say that there has been no progress, as many advances in both spheres have been developed but they are not generally found in mainstream construction.

The primary responsibility of designers is to the client, but this responsibility also carries with it a greater accountability to society in general. This is already recognised without much debate when the design process follows formal codes and regulations.

There is therefore a sound argument to suggest that designers should seek to persuade their clients to take the more environmental options whenever possible, including the extra cost that sometimes accompanies the choice. This book has no specific section dealing with sustainable design practices because it is assumed throughout that it is inherent in the motivation of the designer as part of the process of 'seeking the optimum solution'. The issue here is to make the point that the responsibility to produce sustainable design solutions carries with it a degree of accountability beyond the legislative.

Quality: cost, maintenance and sustainability

Another important factor governing the choice of materials is the relationship to the quality expected of the finished object. This comes down to providing an appropriate definition of quality and the vagaries that surround this apparently simple process.

An example of what may normally be accepted as a quality object is a Mercedes car, because it has reputation for being reliable, expensive and a good performer. This is all very good if that is what it is being asked to provide. What if a potential owner, wanting the performance and reliability, does not have the money to afford a new Mercedes? Is the reliability and performance still available in an older Mercedes? What if the prospective car buyer favours low-cost and particularly low environmental cost? Is the Mercedes's quality reputation still relevant to this particular client?

The point of this example is to illustrate that a Mercedes may be universally viewed as a quality product but that view is only relevant to a client if it falls within the remit of their particular project requirement.

An uncomplicated definition appropriate to the construction industry is offered by Oakland and Marosszeky (2006) when they suggest that achieving quality is simply 'meeting the customer requirements'. This goes beyond the perceived quality of materials and includes a degree of reliability but most importantly it also includes the notion of quality of design. In other words, simply choosing materials of the appropriate quality is not the end of the process; is it suitable for the design, does the design make good use of the quality and will it continue to perform as expected for the duration of the project are important factors to be taken into account. Oakland and Marosszeky (2006) also go on to relate the concept of quality to professional reputation and suggest that the label of excellence comes from routinely exceeding basic quality requirements.

8.4

As indicated in the Mercedes example above, cost is a major element in the choice of materials and its association with quality. It is also important to differentiate between the various forms in which the term cost can be found. Cost relates directly to the price paid for something but that price need not only be measured in economic terms. It is essential for designers to consider all aspects of cost that relate to the construction of buildings in this case, be they environmental or human as well the purely financial. Health and safety issues are related to both environmental and human costs and will also directly affect economic costing.

In the first place, economic cost is a major factor that will ultimately dictate the quality of the finished product. Not only must the client's requirements be reflected in the most appropriate choice of materials but consideration should also be given to the overall planned life expectancy of the building. This therefore relates to potential maintenance programmes and sustainability values equally.

An example to illustrate this point is the choice of materials for the timber cladding of a building. Oak may seem to be the most appropriate material to provide the longevity required in addition to its relatively low-maintenance requirements. This material is financially expensive (sourcing is rarely local) but can be justified with the low maintenance and the overall environmentally friendly nature of untreated timber. An alternative cladding system may be the choice of a locally produced softwood where the maintenance regime assumes regular renewal of failing timbers. The latter example scores well environmentally by reducing transport costs and encouraging the new growth of timber where CO_2 uptake is at its highest. It also scores well in human terms in that it provides regular skilled employment.

The quality issue then comes down to accurately defining the client's requirements – do they require a building that looks good and durable or do they want to maximise their environmental credentials?

Maintenance has now raised its head as another major factor involved in the choice of materials although current thinking suggests that Western society ultimately aims for low-maintenance regimes. Being too tied to this form of thinking can, however, have very negative consequences.

Firstly, it tends to discount the concept of potentially very sustainable sacrificial coverings as described above.

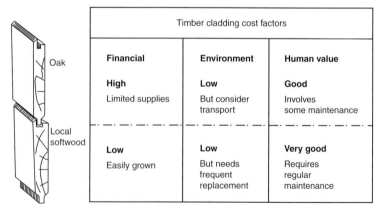

	Timber cladding cost factors		
Oak	**Financial** **High** Limited supplies	**Environment** **Low** But consider transport	**Human value** **Good** Involves some maintenance
Local softwood	**Low** Easily grown	**Low** But needs frequent replacement	**Very good** Requires regular maintenance

8.5

Secondly, it tends to hand the initiative to systems that promote low maintenance above all else, and the current vogue for PVC external cladding and window systems is proof of this pressure.

This last point raises a fundamental dilemma facing technical designers when choosing materials and it is one that warrants much further discussion – how can informed decisions be made? PVC is assumed by many to be impossible to recycle, but the truth is that (at the time of writing) PVC is recyclable but it involves a very expensive process (the vinyl loop process). A rating of the environmental performance of PVC is therefore a variable that relies on economic factors and scientific knowledge.

The benefits of high-quality timber alternatives are well known as are the drawbacks of low-quality versions. The dilemma can easily be illustrated by the case of an old age pensioner living off the UK state pension in their own home with failing windows.

The high winds experienced in the British Isles means that air-tightness can achieve large reductions in heat losses from buildings. High-performance window systems can play a major part in providing increased air-tightness. What decision will a designer make when confronted with the possibility of affordable PVC windows against the unaffordable high quality but more sustainable timber systems. No definitive solutions are available, but what can be achieved is a process that ensures that as far as practicable, the best return on investment (time, research and the client's resource) is achieved.

Chapter review

- There are many parameters involved in the choice of materials but they fall into three main categories, initially availability and suitability are the primary variables but the familiarity of the designers with these two issues is also paramount.
- The choice of materials comes from a definition of the problem requiring a solution, knowledge of what has worked previously and what is available.
- The definition of performance criteria should come before the choice of materials although in reality, experience in most cases means that these happen simultaneously.
- The basic requirements of performance criteria include:
  - **Structural stability** – will the material stand up to the imposed gravitational loadings, wind and thermal movements, etc.?
  - **Durability** – will the material be able to perform its function long enough?
  - **Health and safety** – can the material be guaranteed not to present a health risk during construction and subsequent use?
  - **Fire** – will the material behave acceptably in the advent of fire?

- Technical design in architecture involves the production of buildings that can be around for a good number of years and be in direct contact with people, so design decisions matter in the longer term and designers should be held accountable for these decisions.
- The quality of a product is only relevant to a client if it falls within the remit of their particular project. This goes beyond the perceived quality of materials and includes a degree of reliability, but most importantly, it also includes the notion of quality of design.
- Economic cost is a major factor that will ultimately dictate the quality of the finished product. Not only must the client's requirements be reflected in the most appropriate choice of materials but consideration should also be given to the overall planned life expectancy of the building.

Chapter **9**

Process

The process of selecting suitable materials for a given project is complex when viewed from the outside, but as with the process of technical design, it becomes second nature to the experienced designer. The palette of skills discussed in Chapter 1 is in fact inextricably linked to a similar palette of materials knowledge. Successful designers develop a deep understanding of the resources they use, whether it is based on a narrow or a wide range of materials.

Unlike the designer/builders of the past, described so admirably in Volume 1, designers today have far more materials at their disposal than they can possibly come to terms with. Even within living memory, most designers would normally work with materials that they effectively grew up with. Their practical knowledge would be deep with few alternatives and also less concern over global issues.

These days, due to cheap forms of transport and many technical advances, a far greater assortment of materials is available than ever before, but this is not without consequences. The sustainability of global transportation must be questioned together with the tendency for smaller local production units to be put out of business by cheaper imports.

We looked at the humble brick in the introduction to this section, and again, it could be used to illustrate this change in our relationship to materials. Until relatively modern times, bricks were only available if a source of clay and energy to fire the brick was close by. Even the industrial revolution did not change this concept drastically for the majority of buildings. Now, however, we have the choice of bricks in almost any form and from any source around the world for even the most routine of projects. Not only has the choice grown exponentially but so has the pressure to discriminate between environmental merits and client satisfaction.

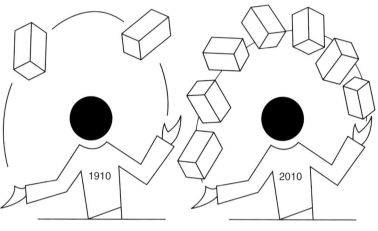

9.1

Realistically, our grand parents probably had a handful of brick types to choose from, whereas we might have at least ten times as many with the added responsibility of being accountable for that choice. If we then add in the multitude of new materials that were not available back then, a true view of the magnitude of the problem facing modern designers can be put into perspective. The process of selecting materials is as much about acknowledging this situation as it is with working with an existing palette of knowledge.

Materials palette: range or depth of knowledge

Designers can have different relationships with the materials they specify and this depends very much on their initial depth of knowledge and experience. This relationship not only depends on the depth of knowledge but on a number of different methods in which a material can be assessed. It is not possible to assess one property of a material without being aware of most of the other properties because they all tend to be interdependent. For example:

- **scientific properties** – will affect its relationship with other materials, its durability and its behaviour in fire
- **structural properties** – will affect issues such as the durability, its behaviour in use and therefore its limitations
- **durability** – will affect maintenance programmes and therefore building cost
- **behaviour in use** – will affect its relationship with other materials and health and safety issues

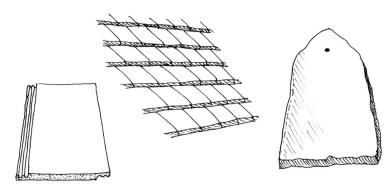

9.2 Concrete versus stone

- **all of the above** – will affect the cost assessment including the purely economic supply cost plus the potential for recycling and embodied energy.

Appearance is probably the only property that can be subtracted from the list as it can be subjective and also easily faked in some circumstances. A concrete roofing tile, manufactured to imitate a traditional original stone roofing slate, may only be apparent to experienced professionals. The properties of concrete will be very different to the original stone, however, as will its environmental assessment. An added complication to this example occurs when strict requirements for historical accuracy result in a significant rise in value of the original genuine slates and the destruction of historic properties results in order to free up slate stocks.

For many common building materials, most of this knowledge can be easily learnt and is almost intuitive: the properties of timber and stone, for example, being fairly easy to assess and compare.

For newer materials, this may require a targeted learning campaign and assessment of all the factors outlined above. In reality, however, very few new products using materials in a new way are launched without a high degree of background research and development, so most of the assessment required is already in place.

This can raise further issues, however, related to a manufacturer's desire to recoup developments costs. Manufacturers and their sales staff will be charged with and trained to maximise sales to recover the investment costs but also to generate many 'on-site trials' for further assessment.

Designers should enter this arena with care as they will be held responsible for ultimate performance by the client. It is possible to shift responsibility to manufacturers in some circumstances, but the negative implications of failure will be difficult to escape.

When using traditional materials in new circumstances, care should also be taken to gain sufficient knowledge to be confident of performance under all the likely conditions. Assessment should follow all of the factors outlined above but in response to the individual situation. These assessment factors will then be further developed according to the situation.

An example to illustrate this process would be the use of rammed earth or compressed earth blocks for building walls. The assessment factors would be very different if the wall was exposed to the external

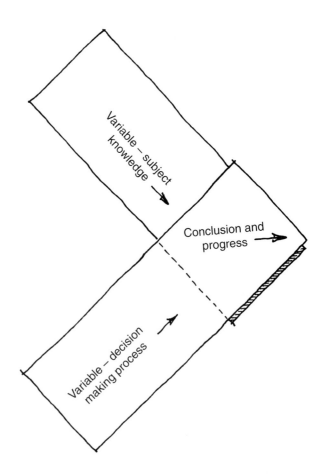

9.3

environment rather than simply used for internal partitions. Similarly, if the walls were load bearing or forming the internal leaf of an external wall, different understanding of the material's likely performance would be required.

This research and targeted learning can be immensely rewarding particularly if it then leads to a successful conclusion because often hidden properties can come to the fore. The unfired earth systems referred above can possess an especially favourable and useful relationship with the control of internal atmospheric moisture (humidity control) levels.

The process of coming to conclusions is therefore a very complicated one, with many layers of significance in one direction and levels of awareness of the decisions made laying across in another direction. A simplified view of the process splits it into two distinct parts:

1   the clear and conscious making of decisions
2   the knowledge that informs the decision.

Decision making process: environmental, human or economic efficiency, the client's role and resources

The conscious decision making process involved in choosing materials takes on many forms depending on the circumstances in each individual project. Efficiency will be a prime quality that the design process aims for in its endeavour to produce **optimum solutions**, but it is important to consider what is meant by the word. In its most common form, it is meant to be economic efficiency and aims to produce the maximum output for the least financial cost. This simple aim has led to many advances in the construction process, and the vast majority of modern buildings would not be possible without this progress.

However, this apparent progress is not without significant costs in other areas. An example that on first viewing may appear simple is the issue of hand tools being used on site. In very recent memory, wheel barrows were a common sight on building sites as was the use of hammers and cold-chisels for cutting concrete blocks. Hammers and nails also were common as was the use of screwdrivers for inserting screws.

These are now becoming much more rare as power tools replace them. Blocks are cut with petrol-powered, diamond-tipped saws, nails are punched into timber using compressed air machines and even wheel barrows are replaced with highly manoeuvrable site trucks. The main drawback of all this magnificent evidence of technical progress is the total reliance on external sources of energy. The result is a highly

	Hand tools	Power tools
Time/cost	High	Lower
Health + safety	Can be both	Can be both
Environmental	Low	High

9.4

efficient process in economic terms in that each task takes considerably less time to complete and fewer people are employed.

Another major factor is the possible improvements in the health and safety aspects of construction sites; no more back problems from carrying heavy weights, broken fingers and fewer people to fall off scaffolding. Modern tools are not without their potential for accidents, however, as power tools can be very dangerous and also produce potentially very hazardous dusts.

Environmentally, however, most of these advances are very costly but also considered to be 'essential' to the modern construction industry and assumed therefore to lie outside of the remit of the designer.

Addressing these assumptions can be difficult but not impossible, and the choice of materials can have a significant impact on certain practices. Choosing materials and systems that require less work on site or that require more manual labour could both reduce the environmental impact of design decisions. The first example includes the acceptance of construction methods that make maximum use of modular materials and components, for instance, a method that has economical benefits as well.

Methods that require more manual labour, however, tend to fall outside of the standard forms of construction but potentially have a major part to play. This concept is clearly more relevant to underdeveloped regions of the world and in terms of energy use can be a valuable learning resource.

The concept is not without precedent in modern construction in developed parts of the world, however, with the prominence of self-build and its reliance on high-labour involvement. Materials can therefore be chosen for their suitability to be easily worked and safe. Efficiency in this case comes down to an assessment of its contribution to the 'human' cost or experience. Generally, in self-build, however, the human or labour costs are assumed to be contributed freely and is therefore a different concept to that found in underdeveloped areas where labour is simply cheap. The working of materials and use of tools may be very similar, but the ethics surrounding the choice of materials becomes very different.

The self-build route is normally a freely made philosophical decision by the client. In underdeveloped parts of the world, one may legitimately respond to the pressure to maximise employment opportunities by employing labour-rich practices but at the same time denying those communities of the genuine development associated with some aspects of modernisation.

Environmental and human efficiency cannot be separated from economical efficiency, however, as both are defined by the problems associated with the drive for profit making, the essence of economical efficiency. Economic efficiency cannot and must not be relegated to a negative drive for profits: it is the inspiration for most of the modern advances in construction referred to earlier, but it is also a highly relevant motivator for change to more sustainable solutions.

Earlier in this section, we discussed the situation of a pensioner on a limited income; here the motivation to produce sustainable solutions and the consequent choice of materials is intimately tied up with economic reality and the philosophy of the designer.

The client therefore is highly influential in the process of choosing materials although they may have very little direct involvement. This influence relates to both the character of the client and their resources. Commercial clients will almost certainly wish to project or simply protect their corporate image and the palette of suitable materials will relate directly to this desire and to the resources available. Consider and compare the materials likely to be found in the design of a new Mercedes showroom to those likely in a new museum of vernacular design.

The ability of individual designers and design teams to respond to such requirements will depend very much on their experience or their ability to make up for shortfalls with robust information-gathering procedures. This brings us back to the other significant part of the decision process, the relationship with knowledge and information gathering.

Information sources: reliability, evaluation and certification

Knowledge of materials comes in many forms, from the experience of living to the detailed study of new research. Most designers grow up with the same capacity to learn from their experiences, so the fact that stone is hard and heavy comes as little surprise. This initial palette of materials knowledge is added, through the process of learning and experience that most designers go through from their very first attempts to the most experienced. This information is picked up in an uncontrolled way but with the natural inquisitiveness of designers being a prevailing factor. This almost accidental process of accumulating knowledge is not of much use when confronted with the demands of a new project requiring new information.

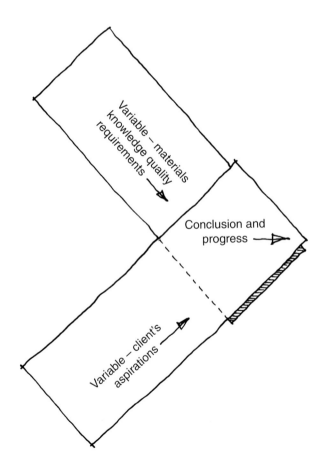

Variable – materials knowledge quality requirements

Conclusion and progress

Variable – client's aspirations

9.5

The ability to carry out research channelled in a well-informed direction is one of the hallmark traits of the discipline of architectural technology. This process, based on finding and evaluating information relevant to the technical design of buildings is clearly not restricted to architectural technologists, but it does form a vital and major element of their normal role. This skill is one that should be learnt and valued as an attribute that reflects the level of professionalism attained by individual designers. In other words, it is proof that you are working in the client's best interests to produce design solutions that not only work on the conceptual level

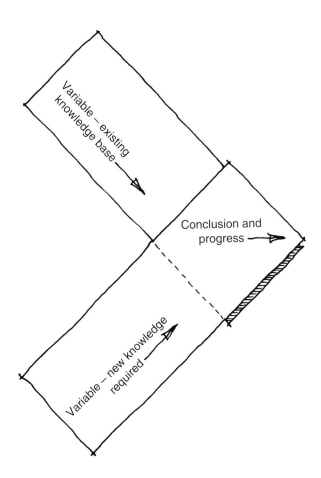

9.6

but also in terms of the required efficiencies and its buildability. This skill allies existing knowledge to the ability to identify and fill any gaps in that knowledge in a professional manner.

The model of knowledge currently in use tends to focus on the concept of **facts**. This model is not without some concern, however, as facts do have a rather disturbing habit of being replaced with new facts from time to time. So firstly, facts can become outdated and therefore possibly completely wrong or just not entirely correct.

A prime example of this is the **Physics** of Isaac Newton (1643–1727). Once thought to be the ultimate, it was developed and to some degree replaced by Albert Einstein's (1879–1955) **Theory of Relativity**, which has now also evolved into **Quantum Physics**.

Newton's rules still work and can be accepted as **fact** under some circumstances, but they also fail under other more demanding circumstances. It is probably worth putting the word fact into inverted commas, 'fact', to acknowledge this qualification of the term.

If we assume therefore that all 'fact' will someday be upgraded, it gives us a healthy circumspectness with which to treat all information. In other words, do not always assume that single sources of information are correct, so double check and, in particular, be certain that the conditions prescribed are similar to those in which the claims were originally made, i.e. relevant.

The example of the pensioner on low income, requiring new windows is again useful here. The example quoted was based in the windy British Isles; transport the same person to the climate of Northern Australia and the information so vital in Britain becomes useless as it is not relevant although still 'fact'.

Research to find more information will have to locate the information source initially before attempting to evaluate the source and the content. The first aspect of this is identifying sources of information and there are many. As a general rule, however, one can assume that information published in established forms such as this book is possibly already out of date, a bit like Newton's Laws.

Information published in journals is likely to be more up to date and to reflect current standard practice. Information accessed from the Internet is likely to be state-of-the-art but with a high degree of uncertainty. In fact, a general rule of thumb would suggest that information published in book form is the most reliable (subject to the 'fact' test) but the most out of date with the exact opposite true for web-based information, it being very current but likely to also be very unreliable. Journal-sourced information, sitting somewhere between the two.

	Books	Journals	Internet
Reliability	Yes	Yes	Sometimes
Currency	Low	Yes	Very much
Conclusion	Good for basic info	Sound base	Innovative but risky

9.7

The second aspect of information evaluation is the motivation of the provider. Again, as a general rule, this type of information comes from three sources: manufacturer supplied information, scientific publications and that supplied by campaign groups. All three can be highly reputable but also flawed sources of information:

- Manufacturers will want you to use their products so will aim to persuade you in that direction. It is amazing just how many building products with little environmental advantage now have well-produced brochures espousing their 'greenness' with quite persuasive 'factual' references.
- Well-meaning but biased campaign groups will also aim to persuade you in their direction. Their study of environmental issues can be in-depth and based on empirical research, but again, it may represent information used out of context although with very persuasive 'factual' references.
- Lastly, independent scientific information will tend to be based on experimentation conducted in very narrow fields and as such is not always relevant to the wider world. The interpretation of sponsored research must be examined carefully and the old 'fact' problem still exists.

Evaluation of information therefore needs to consider all of these variables and the risks associated with them. Manufacturer's information can come with high levels of certification attached, giving the designer a useful tool to significantly reduce risk, the input from campaign groups, although not risk free, can help to interpret the material supplied by manufacturers and finally, empirical scientific research may well support all of the other sources.

The role of certification can be very useful in the evaluation of materials, and it is now a common way to demonstrate compliance with many regulatory requirements. The number of different agencies offering levels of certification can be daunting, however. In Britain, the British Standards Institute (BSI) takes responsibility for defining relevant standards and is also the leading organisation in the move to align standards definition across Europe as the European Standards where they receive the distinctive **CE** logo. They produce codes and standards covering most of the common building materials including assessment on performance and health and safety issues.

In addition to the British and European versions, there is the International Organisation for Standardisation (ISO) that attempts similar definitions on a global scale.

Of equal value to designers, however, is the product-specific certification scheme, the British Board of Agrément, where new products or techniques not covered by the other standards are tested, usually in context and come with approved installation methodologies.

These are product specific, so the manufacturers will arrange for the testing process to be carried out, but the BBA conduct the assessment and produce the independent information. It includes laboratory testing, on-site assessment and production controls. They also relate their information directly to the building regulations and can train installers.

Chapter review

- Designers today have far more materials at their disposal than they can possibly come to terms with.
- Designers can have different relationships with the materials they specify, and this depends very much on their initial depth of knowledge and experience.
- The conscious decision making process involved in choosing materials takes on many forms depending on the circumstances in each individual project. Efficiency will be a prime quality that the design process aims for in its endeavour to produce **optimum solutions**.
- Environmental and human efficiency cannot be separated from economical efficiency, however, as both are defined by the problems associated with the drive for profit making, the essence of economic efficiency.
- The ability to carry out research channelled in a clearly defined direction is one of the hallmark traits of the discipline of architectural technology. This process, based on finding and evaluating

information relevant to each project, forms a vital and major element of their normal role.

- The model of knowledge currently in use tends to focus on the concept of **facts**. This model is not without some concern, however, as facts do have a rather disturbing habit of being replaced with new facts from time to time.
- The role of certification can be very useful in the evaluation of materials, and it is now a common way to demonstrate compliance with many regulatory requirements.

Chapter **10**

Selection criteria

The discussion on materials in the previous two chapters has examined the requirements and the process of decision making. This chapter aims to consider the criteria that decisions are based on. Earlier, we established that designers should be held accountable for their decisions, but what was not discussed was how designers can work effectively in an atmosphere of liability and potential blame. There are safeguards that do not aim specifically to protect individual designers and design teams from the consequences of poor decisions but to guide and aid the decision making process. Although safeguards do not in themselves provide decision making criteria, the forms in which they are found can contribute significantly to the process.

The greatest impact on decision making, however, comes from the results of evaluation exercises. This is because the process of evaluation itself provides comparable information on suitability and investigates likely sources and availability, etc.

The evaluation process can take many forms and as such is well beyond the scope of this book, but it is worth identifying some of the more discernible factors involved. The growing prominence of environmental evaluation and the associated fundamental requirements make it one aspect worth examining in isolation and more depth.

Initially, however, the relationship between risk and innovation and how this relates to materials choice is one that can have major consequences for individual designers.

The choices do not just relate to the materials themselves but also to the related methods of their inclusion into technical design solutions. A brick can be laid in mortar structurally or decoratively, formed into precast concrete panels or hung from soffits using specialist hangers. The brick remains the same but the methods can vary considerably.

Professional liability: certification, standardisation, R&D

The creativity of individual designers and the desire to strive for innovation are the forces that drive forwards the realisation of most new design solutions. These are potentially among the most rewarding aspects of technical design but in most cases require careful control at the level of the individual designer. The culture of the design organisation will have a major bearing on this control, influencing the individual designer's propensity for taking risks and influenced in turn by the client's aspirations and aims (Emmitt, 2002).

The risks associated with technical design are numerous, and there is therefore a relationship between degrees of risk, creativity and also security. This relationship does not immediately appear to fit neatly into most models of risk management current in the construction industry.

Loosemore et. al. (2006) suggest that dealing with risk can have

> an aura of achievement and those who deal successfully with risky situations are held in high regard. Risk management is as much about developing a positive reputation in the long term as it is about making money in the short term.

Although wholly applicable to mainstream construction activities, these concepts do not reach down to the level of individual design teams or designers dealing with the minutiae of technical details destined to be hidden from view for a lifetime unless, for some reason, they fail to perform the tasks asked of them.

So how do designers deal with this risk and provide an atmosphere conducive to good design? One answer is PI insurance as discussed in Chapters 4 and 7. This does not allow designers to design bad buildings or even to take unnecessary risks but what it does do is provide some level of protection for professional liability.

Professional bodies such as CIAT insist that all full members are fully covered so that the reputation of the Professional body is also protected to some degree. CIAT suggests:

> Professional Indemnity Insurance (PII) is a cover against allegations of breach of duty of care. Should legal liabilities be established against a professional, this will, subject to terms and conditions, pay for the damages together with any costs awarded against the defendant.

PI insurance only covers potential mistakes, however, so how can these mistakes be avoided?

Firstly, there is the process of certification as discussed in Chapter 9. The use of any material in new or unusual circumstances or the use of new materials has a higher probability of going wrong than the more commonplace situations. This process is also the essence of creative and innovative design so should not be avoided for fear of failing. One solution is to provide adequate insurance against possible failure by passing the load to the supplier. Reliable certification provides this protection and can be used as proof that you as a designer had taken reasonable steps to ensure that your design solution was feasible.

Following on from the use of certification to protect your risks is the concept of avoiding risk by sticking to standard solutions. Although this may seem to restrict innovation, it can also act to focus innovation into areas where it may be more appropriate. An example of this goes back to the earth wall where the choice of compressed earth bricks provides an innovative solution but the use of a standard method of construction, i.e. bricklaying (although clay mortars may require further research) serves to reduce the risks associated with a completely new methodology and material.

Standardisation is therefore available in varying degrees and can be used to offer a degree of risk protection by providing fewer opportunities for things to go wrong.

If a material has limited standard forms of construction available to draw from or certification available for your proposed use, it is still possible to provide some degree of protection by engaging in adequate research. Research may not be sufficient, however, and some development may also be required. This process is not as daunting as it may at first appear.

Returning to the compressed earth bricks referred to above and in particular the subject of the appropriate mortar, it may simply involve finding out what clay is available, how it is best presented (i.e. mixed with sand, water content, etc.) plus some development through practice. Building a small sample wall, experimenting with mortars and most importantly, involving the potential site operatives will provide invaluable information on the proposed system.

The finished wall can be tested structurally, it could be used to ascertain the time taken to build compared with standard methods and it could be used to illustrate a novel concept to those unfamiliar with it.

Research and development is not therefore only available to those with large research budgets but has a real potential for all aspects of technical innovation.

Environmental evaluation: ecology, embodied energy, lifespan and recyclability

The case for environmental evaluation has already been made in the introduction to this chapter, but what is not yet clear is the degree to which this evaluation should be undertaken.

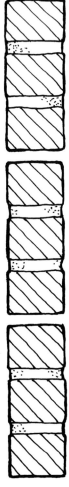

1. Use manufacturer's advice, instructions and certification.

or

2. Use a standard method with low cement or lime mortar.

or

3. Try building a sample using different clay mortar mixes, including feedback from bricklayers to make final choice.

10.1 Range of solutions for compressed blocks

The suggestion was also made that the evaluation process would in itself make some of the initial decisions in selecting materials. In other words, making the decision whether a material was suitable or not prior to the decision as to whether it was acceptable or lastly desirable.

Environmental evaluation is a complex procedure, however, and we have already seen the example of the standard brick in the introduction to Chapter 9. There, we discussed the breadth of knowledge now required to fully understand materials in common use. Evaluating a material for its environmental credentials goes beyond the material itself, however, and has to also include assessment of the alternatives.

Concrete as a material illustrates this issue well. In most forms of environmental assessment, concrete performs badly because of the very high levels of embodied energy, the high levels of energy involved in its transport and placement and limited potential for recycling in any form. The difficulty comes in finding acceptable alternatives and in its structural capabilities, its fire protection abilities, its plastic form and its relative cheapness (in purely financial terms), it is virtually unbeatable. Evaluation of concrete or any other material must then include the possibility of using alternatives. So for concrete, in some instances, there may be many alternatives but in others there may be very few.

The methods for evaluation and the language used is now also very diverse with many conflicting meanings. The term environmental design, for instance, can be used to describe the design of systems providing a building with its environmental services or alternatively it could be describing the design of a building and its interaction with the external environment.

In order to provide an attempt at a systematic process for environmental evaluation, a simple term 'ecology' will provide the starting point. A simple term it may be but the scope for its use and understanding is all encompassing.

Ecology as a science is concerned primarily with the relationship between organisms and their surroundings: the study of ecosystems in one respect or more specifically in this case and the study of man's relationship with the earth. The initial aspect of environmental evaluation, the ecology of a building material seeks to pull together as much information as possible to ascertain the material's relationship with man and the earth.

Initial assessment will include the relationships and degree to which each material involves:

- **work** – the methods involved in production
- **raw materials** – how much of it is there and how easy is it to access
- **energy** – energy used in its processing and transport (Berge, 2000).

These processes go on to pose a number of further questions with each of the sections above split into further divisions.

Work, for instance, can compare high-tech methods with low-tech alternatives with both providing positive and negative possibilities depending on the circumstances.

For example, the more efficient extraction of copper from the original copper ore or that left over from earlier less efficient extraction methods may be viewed as ecological improvements but at the same time viewed as the continuance of unsustainable exploitation of limited resources.

Raw materials can be classified as renewable if they are in some way regenerated in a relatively short period. Annual growth of plant material such as straw fits very well and so does the longer term growth of trees in the production of timber. Waiting for timber to rot down and eventually turn into oil does not count, however.

The availability of materials is also a major component of this form of assessment. For example, it is generally accepted that an abundant source such as clay may be acceptable ecologically even though it involves much disruption and work to retrieve it whereas the exploitation of renewable but environmentally sensitive tropical timber is not. The use of recycled or reuseable materials will also have major impact on this initial assessment, but they can fit into a standard method without requiring any special rules to accommodate them. The ability to reuse materials after a project has completed

Straw: Highly renewable but is monoculture acceptable?

Timber: Renewable but what about tropical hardwoods?

Oil: Orginates from rotten timber?

10.2

its lifespan is another issue, however, and will be dealt with later in this chapter.

Energy use is another complex area of assessment that can on the surface appear deceptively simple. Energy use is currently linked inextricably to carbon dioxide production, the consequent greenhouse affect and global warming. This has not always been the case although the over-reliance on fossil fuels has been a long-standing concern.

The issue of energy use is only important because of the limited supplies of fossil fuels and global warming. Consider a world where we were totally self-sufficient in energy terms, getting all we require from solar and related renewable sources. Would the high energy required to extract aluminium from bauxite supplied by renewable hydro-electric schemes still be a problem? Excepting the ecology of hydro-electric production, the high-energy cost would not be an issue.

The lesson here is that the rules for ecological assessment of materials are constantly changing. Of current significant importance, however, is the issue of total energy and consequent global warming represented by specific materials – the embodied energy.

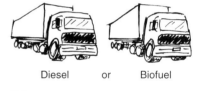

Diesel   or   Biofuel

10.3

Embodied energy is intended to be a sum of all the energy involved in bringing that material or product into its final position in a building. This therefore includes all the energy used to find and extract the raw materials, that used in the manufacturing and building process plus the transportation involved in all the previous aspects as well. Figures available will not generally be site specific but buildings are and so specific materials may have very different values depending on the location of the site.

For example, the good old brick again can have very different values dependent on manufacturers, sourcing of raw materials, transportation systems and the distance to the site.

There are also other significant concerns when working with published figures, however, such as whether or not the energy used in maintaining the transport infrastructure is included, the manufacture and location of the machinery involved at all stages or the involvement of people in these processes.

It becomes a very complex process to fully calculate accurate figures but the major energy inputs can provide useful if not totally accurate information. The actual contribution of the energy used to transport people to the brick factory is important but a relatively small proportion of the total involved.

Embodied energy therefore becomes a tool for comparison rather than empirical fact. The assessor must then add a degree of interpretation and assessment of the likely conditions to obtain definitive information.

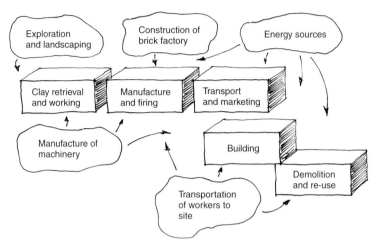

10.4

Using the brick again, the assessor can compare between supply companies, evaluating their respective processes, raw material sources, energy systems, etc., before making an equally important assessment on the transportation systems available, the distances involved and vitally the alternatives available.

In summary, embodied energy is a much used gauge to evaluate the environmental performance of materials, it is commonly used in this book, but it should be used with caution as there may be many alternative calculations available. A brick produced in India may be very different to one produced in the UK for instance.

Another important form of environmental evaluation of a material is knowledge of its **lifespan**. This form of assessment relates to many aspects of a material including issues such as durability and maintenance but also to its eventual degradation or demolition. Stainless steel, for example, could be viewed as performing very well in this assessment as it requires little maintenance, it is very durable and can be recycled at the end of its useful lifespan. How does it compare then to the hand-applied clay render on an earth wall that requires constant maintenance but can simply be scraped up of the ground and reapplied as required. Clearly, very different concepts and ones that cannot be viewed in isolation because stainless steel requires much energy in its production, manufacture, installation and recycling whereas clay plaster requires virtually none, simply the food to feed the plasterer.

As with embodied energy there are problems associated with assessing materials in this way because it is difficult to set clear parameters for the assessment. Should it include the period before its location in a building or is it simpler to avoid this issue altogether as it can be very complicated.

Cellulose insulation is derived from recycled newspapers; do we need to go right back to the felling of trees to make the original newsprint or can the discarded newspaper be viewed as the source? Similarly, once the stainless steel referred to above is recycled into new steel, do we stop the assessment process? This works for steel but may not for concrete where it may remain as low-grade building rubble for the foreseeable future.

As with the other forms of assessment, there seem to be more questions than answers but this is precisely the lesson to be learnt – there are no definitive answers and the responsibility of designers is to recognise this and the transient nature of information, style and fashion regardless of how important they may seem.

Recyclability is not a word recognised by most dictionaries but one that serves a useful purpose here. It refers specifically to the ability of materials to be successfully recycled at the end of a building project's lifespan. It is therefore distinctly separate from the use of recycled or reused materials in the design and construction of a building. The reason for this distinction is that it is relatively easy to source recycled materials or products containing recycled materials. Planning for the future recycling of all the materials in a building design is a far more onerous task.

The automobile industry through mass production can claim to produce cars that are almost totally recyclable. For example, European legislation will require 95% recycling of all new cars by 2015. Unlike the automobile industry, most new buildings are one-off designs, so this is more difficult to achieve but by no means impossible.

This last in the standard forms of environmental evaluation places a burden on designers not commonly encountered up until very recently. It is not very different from the health and safety requirements of CDM regulations, however, in that they demand that designers design safe buildings, including the eventual demolition. It is not a major step to include the selection of recyclable materials in this longer term view of buildings. The responsibility for this requirement can be directly attributed to the designer.

95%
Recyclable

10.5

General evaluation

The criteria governing the selection of materials fall within a highly complex series of events in the process of design so that examination of the individual elements can appear somewhat unrealistic. However, it is in this abstracted examination that a more conscious approach and therefore more sustainable and responsible method can be learnt.

So far in this chapter, we have discussed the two distinct restraints on the selection of materials, namely professional liability and environmental responsibility. In more general terms, however, the selection criteria for materials falls into three distinct categories:

- project-specific demands
- performance requirements and allied to this
- functional properties.

These three areas of choice could do with further clarification.

Project-specific

Project-specific choices are those where decisions already seem to be made from the moment the clients first conceive of the venture. The visual or **aesthetic quality** of the project will be defined by the client in the early stages by the mental pictures they develop – will it be an ultra-modern house extension or a traditional cottage style or will it be a simple, low-cost, framed industrial shed or a highly visual and stylised car showroom? These decisions impact greatly on the choice of materials in that their final appearance is critical in how the vision of the project is interpreted.

The aesthetic aims of the project will also influence the financial constraints and subsequent choice of materials. This is not to state that there is a direct and proportional relationship between aesthetics and cost, as even high-quality buildings can be constructed simply and cheaply but a suggestion that **cost constraints** may well exert some control over the aesthetic aspirations.

Also directly linked to the aesthetic and cost implications of a project is the **availability** of materials. As a general rule, the less available a material is, the more expensive it will be to get hold of. Even materials for very cheap building systems such as the earth for a rammed earth wall become much more difficult to acquire and transport if it is not available on site. So as cost will exert some control on aesthetic aims, so will the availability of materials.

The three aspects above lie to some degree within the control of the designer and the response to the client's brief but to a lesser degree is the influence of **health and safety** concerns. Legislation will play a vital role in the choice of materials when responding to the health and safety demands of a specific project, from the onus on the designer to design safe buildings to the regulations governing the use of particular materials.

Project-specific evaluation therefore provides selection criteria that are exclusive to each individual project, but so are all the other selection criteria in that each building project is a one-off building, however,

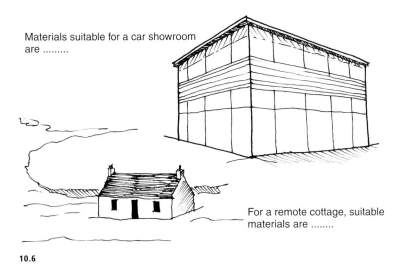

Materials suitable for a car showroom are ....

For a remote cottage, suitable materials are ....

10.6

similar to the one next door. The project-specific criteria therefore lead on to more defined criteria within the same scheme.

Performance requirements

Performance requirements clearly come about in response to project-specific requirements but for convenience can also be viewed as a separate consideration. The example of the car showroom above could be designed around a structural system based on steel framing, cast in situ or precast concrete framing. If all of the project-specific selection criteria provide no clear preferences, the individual performance criteria might. For instance, the improved fire protection of the concrete might prove preferable or the high strength to weight ratio of steel may provide a better solution.

In Chapter 8, we examined some of the basic requirements of performance criteria such as:

- structural stability
- durability
- health and safety
- fire.

These first four criteria are of fundamental importance but may not always be applicable. The process of evaluation and possible subsequent selection depends on identifying the appropriate performance criteria. For example, the underwater structural supports for a seaside pier may not require high degrees of fire protection but those above the water level may do so. Also the insulation material used in a domestic

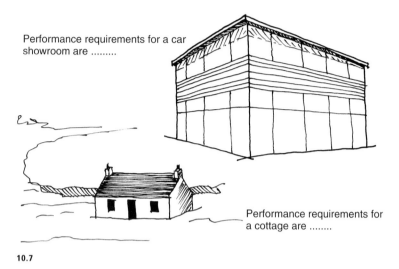

Performance requirements for a car showroom are ....

Performance requirements for a cottage are ....

10.7

loft space may not require significant structural strength but when used to provide fire protection in a cavity wall, it may do.

The fundamental performance criteria above are likely to be considered in response to legislation and the requirement to produce safe buildings and so are not normally in the 'negotiable' range.

The second level of performance criteria include:

- appearance
- weathering performance
- serviceability.

These criteria do have a significant impact on the evaluation and selection process in that they respond directly to the project-specific requirements although they are often also a consequence of the more fundamental performance criteria. The finish of a particular material will have a significant impact on the final appearance but also potentially, the weathering performance and the maintenance required.

For example, stainless steel cladding may be chosen for its shiny, reflective appearance, its corrosion resistance and low-maintenance requirements. Sadly, however, experience has shown that the jointing methods and compounds can cause severe staining, negating a good deal of the planned for benefits. Equally, copper cladding may be chosen for its ability to 'corrode' in a manageable way where the products of initial corrosion form a protective barrier and a green surface veneer that is desired although very different from the shiny copper original. These different performance characteristics are based on the distinctive properties of each material, and these can lead on to another form of evaluation, that which allows certain functions to be performed – its functional property.

Functional properties

Functional properties are those that make any particular material useful in dealing with specific requirements. This will derive from inherent physical properties such as stiffness, plasticity, strength, etc. but then be related to its functional use.

Structural stability is one of the inherent properties of all materials and is explained with the appropriate amount of detail by Taylor in his book *Materials in Construction* (2000). It is summed up as encompassing:

- **strength** – may be defined as the ability to resist failure or excessive plastic deformation under stress
- **stiffness** – is the ability of a material to resist elastic deformation under load
- **toughness** – is the ability of a material to absorb energy by impact or sudden blow
- **hardness** – is resistance to indentation under stress
- **creep** – is the effect of long-term stress, leading to additional distortion or failure
- **fatigue** – is the effect of load reversals such as vibrations that lead to failure at relatively low stress.

These are very useful definitions in adding to the general level of understanding but of little value to the technical designer without context. A crushing strength of 7.0 kN/mm^2 is meaningless unless it is considered in relation to the **shape** of the object. In addition to the shape is the overall size. The common 100-mm thick concrete block wall may have a similar crushing strength to a 450-mm thick rammed earth wall, whereas compared in isolation, rammed earth is much weaker than concrete.

Functional properties therefore rely to a large degree on the shapes available, which is also directly related to the specific properties of the material. Steel, for example, can be formed into an 'H' shape in cross section, making it very useful as a stanchion (steel column) in framed construction. It can have its load-bearing properties improved by changing the shape of the same amount of steel to hollow round section but making joints becomes more difficult. Concrete (or even rammed earth) may be able to provide similar load-bearing capacity but reliant on different shapes – solid with steel reinforcement to resist buckling for the concrete and massive structure for the rammed earth.

The introduction of steel into the concrete column above illustrates how the functional property of one material can be altered by the addition of another. Another example is that of plasterboard, now a very common building material in developed parts of the world. Essentially, plasterboard is a board of plaster about 12 mm thick but with properties that plaster on its own does not have. Plaster, unless applied in a wet state to a suitable substrate (normally walls or ceilings), is a brittle substance, liable to break under its own load.

By the addition of paper sides to the panel and some reinforcement, a relatively strong board is created that can be nailed or screwed into place but still is essentially plaster.

What the plasterboard and steel examples also serve to illustrate is that when materials are formed under factory conditions, there is also the potential to provide standard sizes.

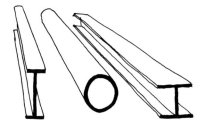

10.8 Steel shapes

Standard sizes allow the introduction of modular design where all the materials in a particular detail can be specified in sizes that will match up during construction. This **modular capability** is another functional property that makes certain materials more or less useful. Even gravel could be considered in this way where grading provides size ranges suitable for addition to concrete allowing varying properties and placement potential.

The modular capability of gravel is a relatively insignificant property when compared to the main advantage of the concrete in which it is commonly found and that is its plasticity. **Plasticity** in this case being used in the architectural sense to illustrate the ability to take on any 3D form so long as the mould can be constructed and kept in place until the concrete has cured.

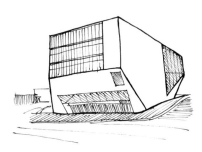

10.9 Plasticity of concrete – Casa da Musica in Porto by Rem Koolhaas

This very special property is not limited to concrete because steel could be said to have similar properties, but what makes concrete different is that the raw materials are relatively cheap and that mostly, all of the chemistry takes place at room temperature.

The now almost universal reliance on concrete in building is due to this functional property. It can be used to pour foundations taking on the shape of the hole in the ground, it can be formed on site into rigid-framed structures or formed into any amazing shape. It can be supplied as precast elements for assembly on site or it can be moulded into finished forms as building products such as roof tiles or cladding systems. There is no end to the uses that can be found for concrete because of this plasticity.

Another property of concrete that is related to its density is its ability to store heat and to be used to contribute thermal mass to a structure. There are other functional properties that also contribute to the thermal management of buildings and this is thermal insulation.

10.10 Plasticity of concrete – a roof tile

Insulation properties are not confined to thermal behaviour as sound insulation is also highly relevant. The behaviour of various materials in the relation to how they 'insulate' is very much dependant on the physics of heat transfer and its various forms. Double-glazed windows will resist heat loss through convection and conduction but not much

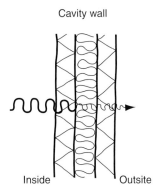

Cavity wall

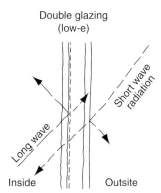

Double glazing
(low-e)

10.11

radiation (unless treated with a low-e coating). In this example the material glass, contributes little other than providing a transparent separation. This is true of most thermal insulation in that the resistance to heat flow is normally provided by air pockets trapped inside. The low-e coating is different, however, and works like the shiny surface found in vacuum flasks or some modern insulation products where the shiny surface has a property called low emissivity, which means it does not radiate heat very well. The exact opposite of matt black, that does radiate very well. In this case, the heat loss by radiation is much reduced.

There are many other ways to classify materials by their functional properties but those discussed above represent the most common. Many of these properties are known about through common experience such as those associated with stone, timber, etc., but others can confound such as the way cast iron performs more like concrete than it does like steel.

Chapter review

- The risks associated with technical design are numerous, and there is therefore a relationship between degrees of risk, creativity and also security.
- Evaluating a material for its environmental credentials goes beyond the material itself, however, and has to also include assessment of the alternatives.
- The initial aspect of environmental evaluation, the ecology of a building material seeks to pull together as much information as possible to ascertain the material's relationship with man and the earth:
  - embodied energy
  - lifespan
  - recyclability.

- Project-specific choices are those where decisions already seem to be made from the moment the clients first conceives of the venture:
  - aesthetic
  - cost considerations
  - availability
  - health and safety.
- The process of evaluation and possible subsequent selection depends on identifying the appropriate performance criteria:
  - structural stability
  - durability
  - health and safety
  - fire.
- Functional properties are those that make any particular material useful in dealing with specific requirements. This will derive from inherent physical properties such as stiffness, plasticity, strength, etc. but then be related to its functional use:
  - shape
  - modularity
  - plasticity
  - others such as insulation, etc.

Chapter 11

Choosing materials

When finally getting down to making decisions on the choice of materials, there are two ways in which these decisions can be made. Firstly, there is identification of the function that the material will have to provide and secondly there is the property that the material requires to fulfil this function. Both choices are valid and appropriate for different situations.

By fully understanding the functions that materials are required to perform in specific situations as a result of the construction systems that they are part of, we can then by also understanding the properties of particular materials make the appropriate decisions on which are more or less likely to provide the performance characteristics we desire.

By function

Definition of the function goes a long way towards making decisions in that the choices narrow down to those commonly in use and those that may potentially also work. There are other pertinent parameters as discussed previously, but the initial process is simple and logical. The first question of any technical design is what is holding the structure together, in other words, what structural system is employed?

This could then be load-bearing walls with spread loads, structural framing with point loads or a mixed system with tensile membranes where the point loads can be either compressive or tensile.

Structural systems

Taking the example of **load-bearing** walls, many materials are available but only a few are truly suitable and probably even fewer are available.

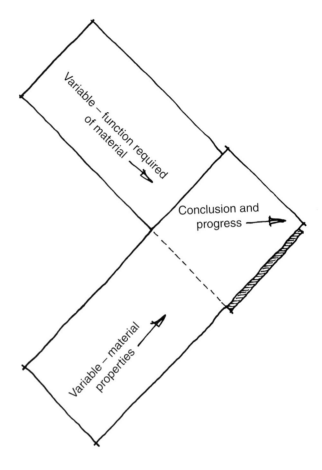

Variable – function required of material

Conclusion and progress

Variable – material properties

11.1

The basic function, however, is that the load transmitted to the walls is spread evenly across the entire wall structure.

Suitable materials are therefore those that can take compression well, can be built into a monolithic structure and have sufficient self-strength to avoid buckling under load. The term monolithic here describes both truly monolithic cast material such as in cast in situ concrete and the semi-monolithic structures where the wall is built up in sections but eventually acts in concert such as bonded brickwork.

Standard materials include:

- concrete as cast in situ or blocks
- stone and brick masonry
- earth in its many forms ranging from rammed earth to adobe or compressed blocks
- timber in the form of the load-bearing panels of the panel frame system.

Other suitable but less common materials could include:

- straw bales
- straw clay and its derivatives
- rubble-filled gabions
- earth-filled car tyres.

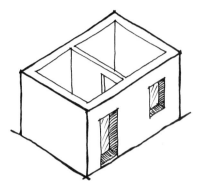

11.2 Load-bearing walls

The choices for a load-bearing wall are therefore very limited particularly if the building is to achieve any significant height. The more specific selection criteria discussed in Chapter 10 will then come into play to make the final decision.

A structural system based on **framework** has fewer materials to choose from than load-bearing methods but a significant number still remains. As framework consists of beams and columns, it is usual for the material chosen to provide adequate performance in both of these forms. The action of a beam under load shows areas of compression and tension as do columns where the compression is obvious but the tension, in the tendency to buckle, less so.

As the function here is to provide a framework than can withstand both compressive and tensile forces, the materials available to choose from are limited to those with the required inherent properties or those where these can be added. Standard materials include:

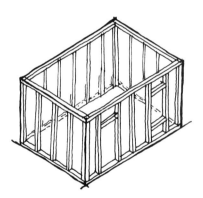

11.3 Framed structure

- steel and other metals
- timber
- reinforced concrete (really a composite material).

As standard materials, these three come in a wide variety of forms, however. Steel, for instance, is available in many different profiles, providing significantly different structural performance but can also have its own properties altered to produce high-tensile steel or maybe even in the form of cast iron.

Timber in the form of laminated beams (Glulam) has performance characteristics beyond standard timber in both the lengths available and the predictability of the performance. Timber can also be used as simple tree trunks or highly engineered into structural products with accurately predictable performance characteristics.

Concrete has even more potential for variety in that the concrete itself can be varied, the reinforcement characteristics are also variable and so is the choice of placement method, i.e. precast or cast in situ.

Steel can be welded, cut and bolted, making it relatively easy to alter once in position. Timber can also be cut and altered on site, but unlike steel, it cannot so easily be joined structurally as in welding. Concrete on the other hand is very difficult to alter structurally once in position, so the placement aspects become vitally important.

Load-bearing systems as discussed previously provide a monolithic structure, which also provides a continuous shell between the internal and external environment. It is therefore a dual purpose system that explains its popularity in simple domestic building.

Framed structures, although more sophisticated structurally, require a separate system for providing separation of the internal and external environments. For the sake of convenience, this system could be described as the infilling of the gaps between the framework although this could also be misleading as in reality the framework could be clad externally, totally covering the frame system or indeed, even have a shell system, suspended on the inside.

The 'shell' system could therefore be used to describe whatever process is used to provide the required separation although the term cladding may be more appropriate in most modern systems as it describes what is actually being done.

Interface systems

The materials suitable for providing the shell at the interface between internal and external environments are extremely wide and varied as are the forms these materials can take. At one end of the scale, natural materials could include thatch, timber in its many forms such as shingles, panelling, etc. or slate and tiles, etc. At the other end of the scale high-tech stainless steel cladding systems, glass or composite plastics may also be appropriate.

The design of interface systems has to be site specific in that the degree of separation required and the profile of that separation will vary considerably from site to site and from climate zone to climate zone. The requirements can be separated out and summarised, however, as normally having to control or provide:

- thermal insulation (in both directions)
- light penetration (windows and glazing)
- weatherproofing (water and airtightness)
- controllable ventilation.

There are numerous materials suitable for each of these applications, with the same material on occasion providing more than one of the

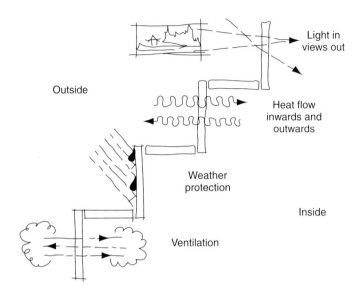

Light in
views out

Outside

Heat flow
inwards and
outwards

Weather
protection

Inside

Ventilation

11.4 Interface requirements

requirements. The glass in windows, for instance, can provide for almost all although it does not perform particularly well as an insulation material.

Materials in this instance can be chosen as part of a complete system, and understanding of the construction and scientific performance of the interface is required to make the correct choices. For instance, the choice of a specific insulation material could involve its ability to withstand possible moisture ingress or its ability to provide some degree of structural stiffness where it is required to be self-supporting. This will be in addition to providing its primary function of insulating against the flow of heat outwards (or inwards as well).

Common to all of these functions, however, is the need to provide adequate and controllable separation of the two environments. This means providing a sealed or sealable system at some point in the construction of the shell and could include a sealed external face as in most glazing systems or the weathering system such as rainscreen cladding where the seal is placed within the shell system. The practice relies heavily on jointing mechanisms and/or sealants. Vapour barriers, for instance, must be continuous and sealed at the joints, sealants must be flexible to withstand expansion and contraction but also able to withstand exposure to weathering and ultraviolet light if in contact with the external environment.

Full understanding of the function that a particular element of the interface system is required to perform is therefore vital in choosing the correct materials. The role of a slate in a traditional pitched roof is reliant on its structural strength and ability to shed water. It is not required to

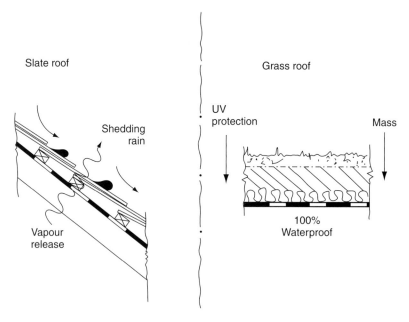

Slate roof

Shedding rain

Vapour release

Grass roof

UV protection

Mass

100% Waterproof

11.5

provide a continuous waterproof membrane (indeed it is sometimes required to allow the free passage of water vapour in an outward direction) but is required to withstand severe exposure to the external environment.

The role of the waterproof membrane in a green (grass) roof system will be to guarantee 'waterproofing' particularly at the joints because subsequent access for repair will be very difficult but other standard roofing requirements become less onerous. Ultraviolet protection and resistance to wind uplift is provided by the soil cover as is a degree of structural protection from penetration, etc. The slate roofing system is therefore more suited to pitched roofs and the green roof to lower or flat roofing systems.

By property

Definition of the function required of a material helps to narrow down the choices available but this is based on the inherent properties of particular materials. The previous discussion on the functions required of materials provided solutions but based on assumed properties. Insulation materials were assumed to insulate and steel was assumed to be strong and rigid. The process involved the definition of a required function and then provided a choice of ready-made solutions in the form materials with known properties.

Another route to choosing materials suggests that by defining the required property, an alternative list of potential materials can be accessed. Clearly, function and property are closely aligned when choosing materials, in that function dictates requisite properties but the suggestion here is that by separating out these two elements, the identification of the required property without prejudice may produce innovative solutions.

There are many ways to classify the properties of materials, but for the sake of convenience, we will limit this discussion to three:

- the inherent properties
- those that manifest themselves in performance
- the visual features.

Inherent properties

These are the 'obvious' properties of materials such as density, strength, etc. and as such form the foundation of our relationship with materials.

Density can be scientifically described as mass per unit of volume (Kg/m^3), and although this is critical in the scientific prediction of performance, it can also be used in a more conceptual but equally important route to understanding materials.

Dense materials are heavy, which limits their uses if they are not equally strong as in the case of steel or strengthened as in reinforced concrete. Dense materials usually would also be able to absorb large amount of heat so providing useable thermal stores as thermal mass. Low-density materials tend to have large amounts of gas entrained within them and so perform well as thermal insulators or as resilient materials (those that can absorb movement).

Materials can therefore be evaluated on their density with a very wide range from very dense to very low density. Some can be adjusted to provide different levels of density and therefore different performance characteristics. An example of this would be concrete where the very dense can provide radiation protection and the less dense, thermal insulation properties.

Density is directly related to weight but strength is also another variable. Concrete is dense but weak in tension, whereas steel is also dense but strong in tension.

Strength is the ability of a material to resist forces applied to it. As these forces can be applied in many different ways and directions, the material will have inherent properties that respond to these forces. The example of concrete above is weak in tension but is strong in compression. Steel, however, is strong in both directions. Forces can be applied as pushing (compression) and pulling (tension) forces but also as chopping/cutting (shear) and twisting (torsion) forces.

The strength of a material must therefore be characterised in relation to the forces acting on it.

This applies to all materials in use in building, so even apparently weak materials such as vapour barriers or insulation materials have to be sufficiently strong to resist the forces acting on them.

These last two examples serve to illustrate further properties than can be utilised, water resistance and insulation properties.

Water resistance is an interesting variable property that can be used in many ways. At one end of the spectrum, vapour barriers are virtually totally impermeable to both water and water vapour. Breather membranes, however, can provide water resistance but still permit vapour transfer by incorporating holes small enough to allow vapour to pass through but too small for water droplets.

Insulation can also be classified as thermal insulation or acoustic insulation where the physics associated with these particular properties will be fundamentally different. The same material could provide both forms of insulation although perhaps not to the full capacity of either.

The last of the inherent properties that can be considered to be fundamental in building design is the **combustibility** of individual materials. Buildings must be safe places to live and work in, and last in this particular sequence, there is also a requirement to protect property in buildings. This area of materials choice is highly regulated in the UK with limitations on the use of certain materials in specified situations.

Generally, however, materials can contribute to the overall combustibility of a building by being highly combustible or resistant to combustion in themselves or to the spread of fire by surface combustion or the transfer of heat to other combustible materials by virtue of their high-conduction rates. Very diverse materials such as concrete and certain forms of insulation such as rockwool can have very favourable combustion properties, whereas steel, although not truly combustible, performs poorly in fire.

There are other inherent properties that could be discussed here, such as hardness, but these are best considered as performance properties, i.e. those that affect the way the material behaves in use.

Performance properties

The inherent properties discussed above are clearly of considerable importance in the way these materials perform in use but some performance properties are better viewed in isolation. These performance properties may be better described as resistant properties such as the 'resistance to combustion' or 'resistance to water penetration' discussed previously as an inherent property. Durability is also a term that encompasses most of these properties but without being sufficiently specific.

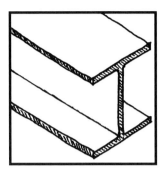

Steel
1. heavy (dense)
2. strong
3. high conductivity
4. water resistant (corrodes)
5. poor in fire.

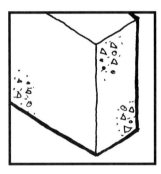

Concrete
1. heavy (dense)
2. strong (compression)
3. thermally massive
4. water resistant
5. good fire resistance.

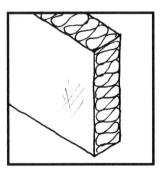

Insulation
1. light weight
2. weak (needs support)
3. thermally insulating
4. water resistance – variable
5. fire resistance – variable.

11.6 Inherent properties

For instance, a material may be termed durable but without being resistant to staining.

The first and most important of these properties is the **resistance to deterioration**. That is the ability to last for a specified time without loosing the ability to perform the function it was chosen for. The classic example illustrating this aspect is the debate surrounding the choice of window frames in the UK. Window frames are subjected to a large range of imposed agents for deterioration, being exposed to ultraviolet light, water run-off from the glazing and having to move in order to open and shut.

Traditionally, softwood frames lasted for between 10 and 100 years depending on the maintenance regimes and crucially the weatherproofing paint system. Steel was tried but found to conduct heat too effectively, hardwoods were more successful but reliant on imported and environmentally suspect supplies and lately aluminium and particularly PVC have gained popularity. Purely in terms of resistance to deterioration, softwood is the worst possible choice, but it can also be claimed that it is derived from the most sustainable source and therefore worth pursuing. In this example, the resistance to deterioration of aluminium and PVC could still be utilised by providing thin layer protection to the outer surface of softwood frames.

The next in this list of 'resistances' is the **resistance to abrasion**, in other words the ability to stand up to the wear and tear expected of it. This wear and tear can take many forms, from the movement in the hinge on a window system to the steps in front of a building. Most of us are surprised when we first see the worn stone steps in an ancient cathedral or even the weathered stones forming the exposed turrets of the same building but even the hardest of materials will be worn down with time.

Clearly, some will wear down quicker than others and it is the resistance to the abrasion that comes from all sorts of exposure, be it the feet of millions of visitors or the effect of wind over time that we are discussing here. Just as with the resistance to deterioration mentioned above, increased resistance to abrasion can be added by the application of resistant coverings. These can take the form of paints or tiles protecting walls and timber work, various floor coverings or the application of sacrificial coatings where they serve to protect the materials beneath.

Generally, however, it is the material itself that is chosen to provide the requisite resistance and there is a close relationship between this resistance and another, the **resistance to staining**. This refers to an ability of a material to maintain its original appearance or to achieve a predictable appearance and then maintain that. The 'greening' of copper is a prime example of the latter and the requirement that stainless steel remains shiny, an example of the former. Both of these materials are expected to provide a predictable appearance for a significant period of time in addition to their other requirements.

Traditional building materials such as stone, clay tiles, etc. are expected to discolour with age, adding to their visual appeal. Timber on the other hand can age gracefully in some limited circumstances but generally, if left exposed, will stain through the effects of fungi and water leaching.

To understand staining is to understand how materials interact with the external atmosphere. Possibly the hardest and most difficult to stain in common use is glass, and although glass will collect dirt and dust over time, it is easily cleaned. This is because the surface of glass is not greatly affected by airborne gases or water.

Metals oxidise however, and even the most resistant to staining achieve this by forming a thin, stable layer of oxidised material on the surface. This is not seen in stainless steel, it is the desired green layer on copper or the undesirable rust in ordinary steel (rust is not stable, however, and continues to produce more increasing the staining). These oxidised surfaces may appear smooth to the eye but are in fact quite rough at microscopic level, which means dirt and dust can adhere to the surface which in turn can feed fungal or algal spores leading to further staining.

Other materials such as stone and fired clay products absorb moisture into their surfaces, allowing a much quicker staining action than that for metals although because of their rough surfaces, it may not be noticeable until well advanced. Timber and other organic materials can absorb moisture into their surfaces as well but then allow fungal action to take place within the material structure itself, leading to significant staining that is almost impossible to remove. The effects of fungal staining on timber can be more than cosmetic, but the most immediate change will be to the visual appearance.

Visual properties

The last of these material properties that influence our choice is their visual appearance. The visual interaction with buildings is based on much more than the finished form; it includes colour and particularly texture. Colour and texture come from the materials chosen to provide the finish. Texture gives us some of the optical interaction with surfaces, but it also includes degrees of transparency and reflection.

The **appearance** of materials, i.e. what they look like, is on one hand a superficial characteristic but on the other, it is based on a deeper psychological interaction with the viewer. Consider the current vogue for timber flooring; the general requirement is not just for floors made of timber but for floors that have a certain 'look'. This must be neatly laid without gaps (normally associated with timber flooring) and usually in

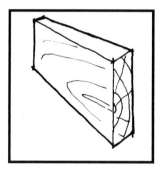

Timber
1. wears with time
2. easily stained
3. deteriorates easily.

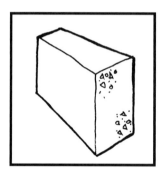

Concrete
1. wear resistant
2. easily stains
3. resistant to deterioration.

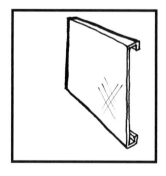

Metal
1. wear resistant
2. mostly stain resistant
3. resistant to deterioration.

11.7 Performance properties

lighter tones, resembling expensive and well-constructed hardwood flooring. The reality, however, is that for most a form based on photo realistic surface treatment on reconstituted timber is acceptable because of its lower price. In addition, timber effect plastic flooring systems may be preferable for bathrooms or other wet areas.

This requirement for a 'look' is the first priority, but most people confronted with this choice would still rather take the 'real' wood if it was possible within budget. In other words, the appearance is of prime importance, but there is a level of interaction that goes beyond the purely superficial.

The interaction with the appearance of materials is a deep and complicated one, with issues of perceived quality high on the list but beyond that there are many more layers. The 'real' timber floor is considered by many to be of higher quality, but it may require far more onerous maintenance than a 'plastic' equivalent. The 'real' floor may last a lot longer if properly cared for, but this might actually go beyond its current vogue. Many surface finishes get covered over or replaced for this reason.

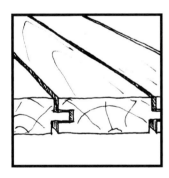

Real wood

Advantages
1. quality
2. long lasting.

Disadvantages
1. maintenance
2. expensive.

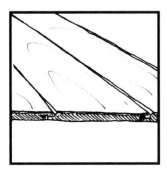

Fake wood

Advantages
1. low maintenance
2. easily changed.

Disadvantages
1. low quality
2. damage is apparent.

11.8

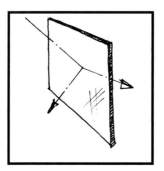

Glass
1. can be reflective
2. can be transparent
3. can be colourful
4. can be diffusive.

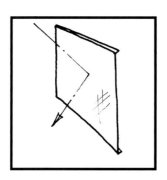

Metal
1. can be reflective
2. can be diffusive
3. can be highly coloured.

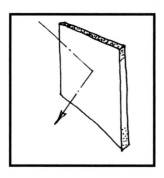

Plasterboard
1. can be highly coloured
2. can be diffusive.

11.9 Optical properties

This discussion touches on a much deeper philosophical argument that is well beyond the scope of this book; the point, however, is to suggest that the appearance of a material is much more than what it looks like. It cannot be divorced from the interaction with the viewer, providing additional interpretations such as good, bad and indifference or the whether the material is actually what it looks like.

The **optical qualities** of the material involve how it interacts with light. Colour is perceived by the reflection of certain electromagnetic wavelengths and the absorption of others. This interaction is further complicated by surface conditions, with reflection and scattering of light in many different directions and shadows providing texture. Highly polished and therefore reflective surfaces give a smooth mirror-like quality by reflecting light in an ordered and predictable way.

Transparency is a quality based on how much light can travel through a material. Standard glass is highly transparent, but this can be adjusted by the addition of colour pigments or simple surface treatment. The pigments involved will reflect or absorb certain wavelengths giving the effect of colour.

Consider frosted glass however: normal glass with a roughened surface that disperses and scatters the light falling on it or travelling through the glass. Materials that appear transparent also rely on surface treatments to provide the quality required. Glass was known about as a material for thousands of years before a production system was invented that provided the smooth surfaces required to effectively see though it.

Clearly, glass is not the only transparent material but what it does allow is an examination of a common interaction that can then be translated to other similar materials. For example, why can polished stone be almost as reflective as glass or why can some plastics be almost as transparent as glass?

Chapter review

- Materials can be chosen by the function that the material will have to provide and secondly there is the property that the material requires to fulfil this function.
- **By function**
- Structural systems:
  - load-bearing walls
    concrete as cast in situ or blocks
    stone and brick masonry
    earth in its many forms ranging from rammed earth to adobe or compressed blocks
    timber in the form of the load-bearing panels of the panel frame system.

- o   framework
    steel and other metals
    timber
    reinforced concrete (really a composite material).
- Interface systems:
    - o   thermal insulation (in both directions)
    - o   light penetration (windows and glazing)
    - o   weatherproofing (water and airtightness)
    - o   controllable ventilation.
- **By property**
- Inherent properties:
    - o   density
    - o   strength
    - o   water resistance
    - o   insulation
    - o   combustibility.
- Performance properties:
    - o   resistance to deterioration
    - o   resistance to abrasion
    - o   resistance to staining.
- Visual properties:
    - o   appearance
    - o   optical qualities.

Chapter **12**

Materials: case studies

This chapter is based on three hypothetical case studies, each aiming to illustrate a different approach to the selection of materials. Although these studies will highlight the process for choosing materials, the process cannot be viewed in isolation, it is indeed an integral part of technical design, and the same studies will be examined again in Part 4, where the 'detail design process' is observed.

Case study 1: starting from first principles

The idea of this case study is to examine the process as a hypothetical example where little or no experience is available although precedents may exist to copy from. In Chapter 2, we discussed the example of the roof to an environmentally responsible dwelling, which can now form the basis of this particular case study. The scenario is this:

> A client would like to build a sun lounge on to the south-facing elevation of an existing single storey rear wing of the dwelling in North East Scotland. This rear wing is traditionally constructed in random stone rubble with a natural stone slate covered roof in diminishing courses. The client has requested that the design involves minimal alteration to the existing roof structure meaning that the roof will be essentially flat. In addition, the client is aware that 'normal' flat roofing materials do not perform well in this part of the world and also that the low winter and summer sun paths suggest that an insulated solid (non-glazed) roof would be preferable.

The decision has been made on environmental grounds to opt for a green roof on a timber-framed structure. The task is therefore to find

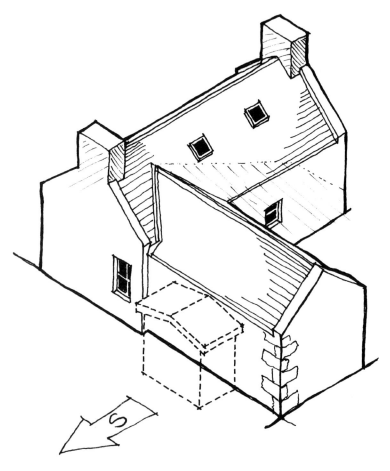

12.1

and select appropriate materials for this roof construction. The technology chosen is that for an 'unventilated, warm flat roof construction' based on a portal frame with 175 x 63 mm timber rafters at 800-mm centres with a nominal pitch of 10° providing a slope for rain run-off.

Research into unventilated warm roof technology for flat roofs and green roofs will suggest that we need to find the following materials:

- grass/planting system
- soil or equivalent substrate
- drainage/water retention system
- water-proof membrane with root protection
- structural insulation
- vapour control layer
- structural decking system

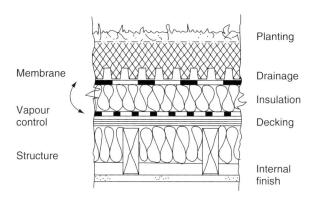

12.2 Typical green roof make-up

- more insulation?
- internal finishing.

Decision 1: the roof covering

- Question: do we opt for a proprietary green roofing system or try our own site-based version?
- Answer: research proprietary systems to fully understand the requirements and limitations of the technology and materials, then decide. In this case, we opt for our own version of a brown roof – using the existing subsoil and relying on natural colonisation by local flora.
- Question: do we still need a drainage/water retention layer?
- Answer: no, because we are opting for a very simple system with little requirement to support particular plant species, but we do need to protect the water-proof membrane from possible root damage.
- Question: what materials will be suitable?
- Answer: tough (to survive inexperienced handling), single ply membrane (to avoid complicated application procedures and provide 'loose-fit' for movement) with guaranteed jointing methodology and integral root deterrent.
- Question: where do we find this material?
- Answer: research to concentrate on case studies, technical data files, Internet and local suppliers of similar materials.
- Result:
- Architectural technologists data file suggests some products but none are suitable.
- Try the Internet for a 'rubberised roofing membrane' based on something locked away in a brain memory file, very many to choose from but one with fully illustrated fitting details and British Board of

Agrément certificate is a likely candidate – proceed with this assumption for now but check for local availability.

Site sourced substrate on EPDM rubber flat roofing membrane.

Decision 2: the insulation requirements

- Question: what are the specific requirements of this project?
- Answer: to maximise the insulation thickness, to provide support for the membrane system and to provide insulation to the upper side of the roof structure (to prevent condensation on the cold side).
- Question: what materials will be suitable?
- Answer: stiff for upper layer but any for the lower portions.
- Question: where do we find these materials?
- Answer: research to concentrate on case studies, technical data files, Internet and local suppliers of similar materials.
- Result:
- Architectural precedents and publications suggest 100-mm thick extruded polystyrene (waterproof) or cork as a natural alternative, laid on 'standard vapour barrier', supported by roof decking.
- Stick to 'safe' known product; extruded polystyrene as it comes complete with fully illustrated fitting details and British Board of Agrément certificate – proceed with this assumption for now but check for alternatives.

Locally sourced 100-mm thick 'extruded polystyrene' insulation with tongued and grooved joints.

Polythene vapour barrier with taped joints (to manufacturer's specification).

Decision 3: the roof structure

- Question: what support does the insulation, membrane and roof covering require?
- Answer: continuous and sufficient to span between rafters at 800-mm centres.
- Question: what materials will be suitable?
- Answer: tough and workable, so (from experience or precedents) either plywood-type board material or timber planks with tongued and grooved joints to provide required performance.
- Result:
- Choose locally sourced, plywood-type material for its multi-directional strength at 25 mm thick due to wider span (note: check this with structural engineer or calculate loads later).

Locally sourced 25-mm thick 'sterling board' fixed directly to rafters.

Decision 4: the internal finishing

- Question: what internal finishings (including more insulation) are required?
- Answer: timber to provide warm feel, extra insulation to prevent heat loss due to high surface area to volume ratio of a small extension. Decision made to locate wiring for lighting elsewhere.
- Question: what materials will be suitable?
- Answer: any insulation material, provided it can be supported by ceiling finish. Ceiling could be any ceiling material – decision to stick to 'safe' solutions so either plasterboard or timber panelling.
- Question: how will these be fixed?
- Answer: underside of rafter to be exposed so plasterboard or timber panelling to be nailed to 50 × 25 mm timber battens nailed to side of rafters. Battens will hold cellulose insulation (in batts) in place before final panelling (check with client) is fixed. (note: check cellulose insulation is available like this to ensure a tight fit, otherwise fibre glass or polystyrene may be fallback position).

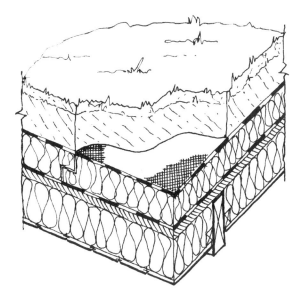

12.3

150-mm thick cellulose insulation (or equivalent) between rafters with 12.5-mm thick softwood-tongued and softwood-grooved ceiling panelling on 50 x 25-mm battens fixed to either side of rafters.

Note: check details with colleagues.

This hypothetical case study has illustrated that even apparently new systems still rely to a large degree on existing knowledge and design processes. The information sources can be varied and wide but the choice of materials is usually very narrow as only a few will fit the exact requirements of the project. In Decision 3, for example, the decision to stick to polystyrene may seem unadventurous but this is because experience suggests that this particular aspect of the roof system is most likely to provide problems. In response to this, it seems wise to stick to proven technologies even though the overall concept may be fairly innovative.

Case study 2: modifying a comparable model

In this case study, the aim is to 'copy' an existing example but making adaptations to fit a new situation. The precedent has well-documented and published details of the technology involved, and as it was designed in conjunction with the manufacturer, a great deal of expertise is available to support the detail design process.

The requirement is for a new hostel building including relatively high environmental performance credentials but with a very short lead in time, in other words it needs to be completed in a very short space of time. The occupants are likely to be in residence for a good part of the day but for relatively short spells of time. It was decided that lightweight, quick heating and quick heat loss was not suitable, so a system that provided some access to thermal mass was required.

An interesting precedent was a new apartment construction that used precast concrete wall panels. These load-bearing precast concrete-insulated sandwich panels were constructed off-site and included the external finishing and integral insulation. The reason for opting for this particular precedent was because the sponsor of the new building is a prominent ceramic tile manufacturer and they were very keen that the building should reflect this.

In brief, the system is based on load-bearing walls constructed as complete units, incorporating a 150 mm thick concrete inner leaf panel with the insulation (75 mm) and vapour barrier enveloped between it and the 75 mm thick concrete outer panel. The outer panel has the finishing material embedded in it as part of the casting process. The inner leaf

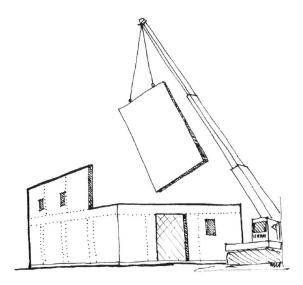

12.4

takes all the loads with the outer leaf and insulation suspended of it with stainless steel wind/shear tie connectors.

Phase 1: initial research

- Background research into precedent study to establish whether or not it is a suitable method. All indications suggest that it will provide a suitable method:
  - available thermal mass, very fast construction method and very good internal acoustic insulation. See Chapter 18 for further discussion.
- Background research into ceramic tiles to ascertain whether there are any particular concerns regarding their use as an external finish. Initial research (*Materials for Architects and Builders* by Arthur Lyons) suggests that ceramics are suitable, provided they are manufactured correctly – client to provide suitable tiles. Ceramics can be rendered unsuitable by impact damage, and this system will make replacement of individual tiles very difficult – consider a different, maybe contrasting finish at lower levels.

Phase 2: external finish

- **External finish** – tile manufacturers to provide suitable tiles manufactured with extra key to rear surface and 'specials' for exposed corners and sills. Placement to include 2-mm joints for subsequent grouting and polishing.

Proprietary load-bearing precast concrete-insulated sandwich wall panels incorporating client's tiling system laid out to pattern provided by conceptual designer.

Phase 3: internal finish

- Question: what internal finishings (including further insulation) are required?
- Answer: good surface for decoration, extra insulation to prevent heat loss due to lower initial external wall insulation (75 mm). Decision made to locate electrical wiring elsewhere.
- Question: what materials will be suitable?
- Answer: any insulation material, provided it can be accommodated by wall covering. Covering could be any material – decision to stick to 'safe' solutions so plasterboard chosen for its speed of fitting and insignificant drying out time. Foil-backed plasterboard to provide the extra insulation due to its lower emissivity.
- Question: how will these be fixed?
- Answer: plasterboard can be fixed directly to external wall panel with plaster dabs – skill-dependent operation that can be problematic if rushed and no space for insulation behind. Batten system provides space and accurate alignment.
- Decision: investigate full range of proprietary support systems by typing 'plasterboard support systems' into Internet search engine.

Proprietary metal furring fixing system (cold rolled steel section bedded in plaster base to provide aligned surface) and 12.5-mm thick foil-backed plasterboard.

Note: check details with colleagues, and check the overall availability of thermal mass.

This hypothetical case study was based on a real system provided by Techcrete and served to illustrate that the adoption of existing technology with minimal adaptation can provide appropriate solutions whilst still satisfying the client's demands. As with the example above, the information sources can be varied and wide, but the choice of materials is usually very narrow as only a few will fit the exact requirements of the project.

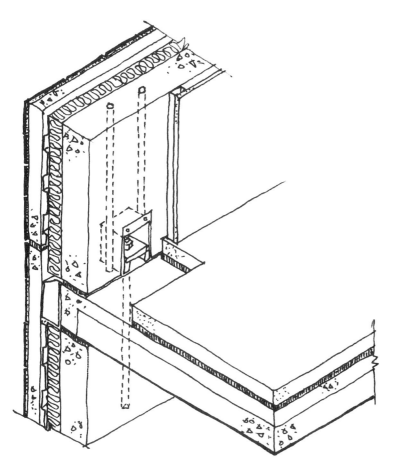

12.5 Adapted from detail by Susan Dawson (Techrete)

The main intentions of the scheme, however, to provide the design for a hostel that could be constructed in a short period of time and with a distinctive external appearance were accomplished without unnecessary risk to either client or designer.

Case study 3: compilation of a standard solution

In the first two of these case studies, a roofing detail and a wall detail were portrayed; in this third study, a floor detail will form the basis for the case study. In this instance, however, the requirement is for a standard detail that could be applicable to many situations.

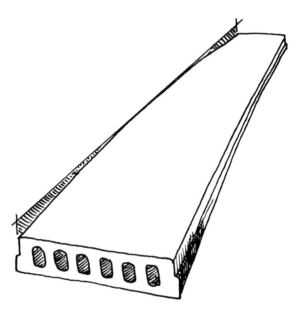

12.6

The study is intended to address the issue of the varying thicknesses that come with various floor finishes, particularly when used in conjunction with prestressed concrete structural systems. These prestressed systems normally include an in-built camber which means that the floor structure is not level – it rises towards the middle. A system is therefore required that will negotiate this bump and provide a predictable final level, suitable for most floor finishes, insulation (thermal and acoustic) and underfloor heating possibilities. The requirement for the predictable final level is so that in multi-storey buildings and staircases systems can be designed accurately and that different flooring systems could also be accommodated without changes in level.

Phase 1: background knowledge and process

Selecting materials to complete a task is clearly very difficult without considering the technology at the same time. This particular study is a good example of this as the properties of the materials involved form an integral aspect of the technology. For example, the floor structure requires levelling and any unevenness sorted out, so a material that can easily be adjusted to suit minor differences but also provide structural stability is required. In this case, cement mortar forms the fallback material; previous knowledge suggests that it will work, but if a better material is available it could be used.

Mortar can accommodate a high degree of unevenness on the underside but will still require levelling on the upper side, so an accurate and easily reproduced method is required. As well as achieving a level finish, a predictable height is also required. Again a standard method is to bed timber battens into the mortar, tapping down to achieve the required height and level (in addition to an even spreading of loads). The timber battens can then form the basis of the subsequent flooring system with timber flooring fixed to the battens or a concrete screed poured between the battens.

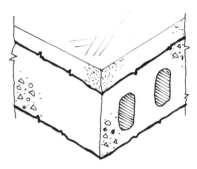

12.7

Phase 2: project-specific requirements

In this instance, a system is required that will form a standard solution for an entire scheme but still allow a selection of different flooring systems and heating arrangements throughout. The flooring systems can be selected from standard timber floorboards, chipboard floating floor with carpet overlay or ceramic floor tiles. The heating system will include underfloor heating only in the areas with ceramic tiles, either encased in a concrete screed or within a proprietary insulation support system. Acoustic considerations are limited to structure-borne sound and a resilient layer must be incorporated at some point.

The system described above, incorporating timber battens bedded in mortar will work well for the timber flooring systems as a resilient layer (5-mm thick rubber-based padding material) can easily be attached to the top of the battens. This system does not work for the ceramic tiles, however, as they require a firm base to avoid movement and subsequent cracking.

Phase 3: project-specific solutions

Decision 1

The knowledge described in *phase 1* is pertinent and forms the basis for arriving at a possible solution, i.e. use the properties of mortar but using a structural concrete screed instead to level the entire floor system. Thickness required – refer to Detail Design phase in Part 4.

Disadvantages:

- More expensive in that it uses more concrete.
- More difficult to provide a consistent final level.

Advantages:

- provides a seal to floor system eliminating airborne sound travel
- provides an even and monolithic structural base.

Precautions:

- system required to guarantee finished height and level
- propose fixed level points prior to structural screeding.

Suggest 25-mm thick (minimum) concrete levelling screed.

Decision 2

The resilient layer can be added at this point, covering the entire floor. Thickness required – refer to Detail Design phase.

Disadvantages:

- more expensive in that it uses more insulation.

Advantages:

- provides a thermal insulation to floor system as well.

Precautions:

- suitable product required – research needed.

Suggest 25-mm thick rigid insulation such as expanded polystyrene or equivalent.

Decision 3

The finishing screed required to take final floor covering. Thickness required – refer to Detail Design phase.

Disadvantages:

- more expensive in that it uses more concrete
- more difficult to provide a consistent final level.

Advantages:

- provides an even and monolithic structural base
- provides good base for 'floating floor' systems.

Precautions:

- system required to guarantee finished height and level
- propose fixed level points prior to screeding.

Suggest 75-mm thick concrete floor screed incorporating underfloor heating pipes as required.

Note: check details with colleagues.

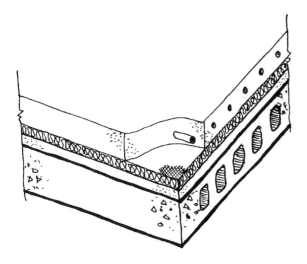

12.8

This hypothetical case study has served to illustrate that the provision of standard solutions can be difficult if it attempts to cover too many possible variations. As with all the examples above, the choice of materials is integrated with the technical design process and a full understanding of all possibilities is required before a realistic 'standard solution' is possible.

The prime requirement of standard solutions is to be reproducible, which means it must be robust (suitable to many circumstances) and simple (to avoid mistakes). This justifies the extra research required at an early stage and also provides a sound rationale for compromise solutions.

Chapter review

- Even apparently new systems still rely to a large degree on existing knowledge and design processes.
- The information sources can be varied and wide, but the choice of materials is usually very narrow as only a few will fit the exact requirements of the project.

- The adoption of existing technology with minimal adaptation can provide appropriate solutions whilst still satisfying the client's specific demands.
- The prime requirement of standard solutions is to be reproducible, which means it must be robust (suitable to many circumstances) and simple (to avoid mistakes).

Part **3**

Bibliography

Berge, B. (2000) *Ecology of Building Materials*. Oxford: Architectural Press.

Construction (Design and Management) Regulations (1994) London: Stationery Office.

Emmitt, S. (2002). *Architectural Technology*. Oxford: Blackwell Science.

Loosemore, M., Raftery, J., Reilly, C. and Higgon, H. (2006) *Risk Management in Projects*. 6th edn. Oxon: Taylor & Francis.

Lyons, A. (2004) *Materials for Architects & Builders*. 2nd edn. Oxford: Elsevier Butterworth Heinemann.

Oakland, J. and Marosszeky, M. (2006) *Total Quality in the Construction Supply Chain*. Oxford: Elsevier Butterworth Heinemann.

Taylor, G.D. (2000) *Materials in Construction: An Introduction*. 3rd edn. Harlow: Pearson Education Limited.

Wienand, N. and Watson, P. (2006) *Integrating and Managing a Sustainable Approach for Construction Projects*. International Conference on Construction and Real Estate Management (ICCREM 2006) Collaboration and Development in Construction and Real Estate.

Webliography

British Standards Institute, www.bsi-global.com

British Board of Agrément, www.bbacerts.co.uk

Chartered Institute of Architectural Technologists, www.ciat.org.uk

Construction (Design and Management) Regulations 1994, www.opsi.gov.uk/SI/si1994/Uksi_19943140_en_1.htm

European Directive on recycling new cars, http://europa.eu.int/eur-lex/pri/en/oj/dat/2000/l_269/l_26920001021en00340042.pdf

European Standards, www.cenorm.be/cenorm/aboutus/index.asp

International Standards, www.iso.org

Techrete website, www.techrete.co.uk/techrete.htm

Vinyl loop process, www.vinyloop.com/vinyloopprocess/0,,2036-2-0,00.htm

Part 4
Detail design

Part **4**

Introduction

The aim of this book has been clearly set out to explore the practice of technical design in architecture and to many, that process manifests itself in the design of technical details – detailing. The fact that we have needed 12 chapters to get this far is testament to the misconception that it might be a simple process. This section will now examine the approach to the design of technical details in depth, but it must be stated again that this dissection of the various aspects of design is to a large degree a false picture as the design process is a very complicated one with many aspects occurring simultaneously.

The first chapter in this section will summarise the main requirements before the following chapters break these down into the more identifiable aspects of the detailing process.

Chapter **13**

Summary of requirements: detailing

The importance of detail design in the production of buildings cannot be over-estimated as this is the point at which conceptual designs are converted into buildable schemes. This conversion of a conceptual idea into a set of plans is not simple, and it is an essential development in making it possible. It is therefore a point where the success or otherwise of a scheme can be determined.

> In practice the detail design phase is a complex process involving the co-ordination of diffuse information, the management of disparate consultants and the making of thousands of decisions which will affect both the appearance and design life of the building, not to mention its cost in use and its durability.
>
> (Emmitt, 2002)

The output from this stage may be a set of detail design drawings that are required to inform the next stages of the process with precise costing or production information, but as Emmitt (2002) suggests, there is a great deal of preliminary work that goes into creating that information.

Essential link: transformation of concept design into production information

This essential link in the transformation of concept design into production information is one that has been undervalued historically and traditionally in the UK, assigned to architectural assistants or technicians. Fortunately, the Oxford conference of 1958, in creating a formal two-tier system of architects and architectural technicians permitted the eventual development in 2005 (28 July 2005) of the chartered architectural technologist. It could be argued that if the process had been instigated by technicians themselves, it could have happened sooner, but a reconsideration of history will add little to this particular discussion.

The development of the role of the technologists has been in response to significant changes in building generally, with the traditional roles and relationships now subject to constant evolution.

The traditional role of the architect as team leader is moving to one of conceptual designer with architectural technologists increasingly taking on full responsibility for the technical design process in a framework of multi-disciplinary teams. In addition, chartered architectural technologists can also practice independently, providing a full range of design services, including taking projects from 'inception to completion', and are required by their professional body to carry full PI insurance.

The role of the architect has not been curtailed in this development, more the role of the architectural technologist has matured into a fully developed professional discipline that now sits alongside architecture without any difficulty. In recognition of this new status, the two UK professional bodies (RIBA and CIAT) signed a Memorandum of Agreement in 2004 (29 January 2004) recognising their complementary roles.

CIAT describes chartered architectural technologists as follows:

> Chartered Architectural Technologists (MCIAT) provide architectural design services and solutions. They are specialists in the science of architecture, building design and construction and form the link between concept and construction. They negotiate the construction project and manage the process from conception through to completion. Chartered Architectural Technologists can manage a project from inception through to completion.
>
> The Chartered Architectural Technologist is a vital component within the construction process and is complementary to the architect and other professionals within the construction industry.

Incidentally, CIAT has maintained a technician category of membership which they describe as follows:

> Architectural Technicians (TCIAT) are specialists in the application of technology to architecture, building design and construction. Technician members of CIAT (TCIAT) are an integral part of an architectural design service, working alongside fellow Architectural Technicians in support of Chartered Architectural Technologists, architects, engineers, surveyors and other professionals within the

Chartered Institute of Architectural Technologists

13.1 Courtesy of CIAT

construction industry. Whilst Technician members of CIAT (TCIAT) cannot practise on their own account, they are an integral part of the architectural design process.

These definitions are included in recognition of the particular roles performed by this professional discipline. Both technicians and technologists are specifically charged with the creation of technical details required to form the link between concept and construction. Architects and other building professionals are not excluded from this practice although they are responsible for other aspects of the process as well.

Whoever is responsible for this stage of the design process, however, be they architects, technologists or engineers, the basic process remains the same and that is the production of the detailed information required to take the conceptual design forward into a completed scheme. This task comes with certain responsibilities.

Responsibility

In previous chapters, we have already discussed the various responsibilities that fall on technical designers, but it is worth revisiting these as we look specifically at the detail design phase. It is at this point that many decisions are made that may go unnoticed in the overall scheme but can have a major impact on the future of the building. Many of these responsibilities are covered by legislation and will be discussed further, but this cannot be allowed to remove a general responsibility to design a building that is both healthy and safe for the occupants and also healthy and safe for the builders, maintenance staff and the subsequent demolition team.

This does not mean that technical designers should have to agonise over every decision being made to guarantee no adverse effects will possibly occur, but it does mean that no decisions should knowingly be made where there is a known and unacceptable degree of risk. In other words, there is a requirement beyond the legal to exercise a reasonable degree of care in this process.

This responsibility goes beyond the production of safe designs for buildings and includes concepts of sustainable design practices. This involves aiming for environmental design principles, avoiding waste and choosing materials that fit within this overall concept. Generally, the authors of this book have attempted to avoid making categorical statements, preferring to provide the arguments in favour but leaving the ultimate decisions to the reader. In the area of environmental responsibility, however, it is more difficult to avoid being fairly dogmatic.

History may prove that the current obsession with sustainable design was misplaced, but there is such a phenomenal amount of evidence now confirming global warming and the role that humans and our buildings in particular play in it that we simply cannot afford to ignore it. The argument is therefore very clear, as designers, we have a fundamental responsibility to design in sustainability wherever possible regardless of how difficult or resistant the situation may appear.

Contractual responsibility may require the technical design of a building that reflects the initial conceptual design, but this should still be possible alongside those environmental responsibilities outlined above. If this is not possible, serious consideration should be given to the merit of the project.

Form and function

So far, we have examined the requirements of the detail design process in purely abstract terms. In other words, just as the 'link' between concept and construction. This link is more than just a connection, however, it is a relationship that involves a great deal of philosophical as well as physical communication.

The concept of quality was discussed previously and again serves to illustrate the demands of this philosophical communication. A conceptual design, aiming for a particular level of quality, needs that same level of quality reflected in the technical details. For example, a modern celebrated restaurant design cannot rely on the detailing suitable for a roadside café and a bank will have very different requirements to a supermarket.

Detail design therefore has to achieve the appearance, quality and durability dictated by the conceptual design by following the forms and functions conceived. In addition, however, there are other aspects that arrive in conjunction with these requirements such as buildability and serviceability. The detail design process takes the conceptual form and converts it into a buildable scheme so the degree to which the design is buildable is an important aspect. This may seem to be a very obvious statement, but it can be illustrated by comparing the process involved in two very different schemes.

A highly prestigious public building such as the Scottish Parliament building (2004) that aimed for a very strong image in terms of form and quality could just about get away with 'difficult' buildability because there would always be funds available and because it was a one-off design.

13.2 The Scottish Parliament building by Enric Miralles

In contrast, however, the large shed design for a popular DIY chain would not be acceptable if it was anything other than highly buildable and relatively inexpensive.

The term buildable has been used here to describe the ease of building but equally important is the ease of demolition or indeed, disassembly. The section above, discussed the responsibility for sustainable design practices, suggesting that the inclusion of and future planning for the eventual deconstruction of the building is now of equal importance.

13.3

Coincidentally, as discussed in Chapter 10, European legislation now requires that all new cars are at least 95% recyclable. Buildings can go one better at least in ensuring that they are reuseable as a whole or at least as parts. This concept does add greatly to the load on individual designers but cannot be avoided in the long term; it may be that this level of responsibility cannot be carried by individuals but must be spread over larger multi-disciplinary design teams.

Chapter review

- The output from this stage is a set of detail design drawings that inform the next stages of the process with precise costing or production information, and there is a great deal of preliminary work that goes into creating that information.
- Architectural technologists are specifically charged with the creation of technical details required to form the link between concept and construction.
- Responsibility goes beyond the production of safe designs for buildings and includes concepts of sustainable design practices. This involves aiming for environmental design principles, avoiding waste and choosing materials that fit within this overall concept.

- The 'link' between concept and construction is more than just a connection; however, it is a relationship that involves a great deal of philosophical as well as physical communication.
- Buildability describes the ease of building but equally important is the ease of demolition or disassembly. The planning for the eventual deconstruction of the building is of equal importance.

Chapter **14**

Technical information sources

The process of technical design was discussed in some detail in Chapters 2 and 3 although this was in mainly abstract terms. In this chapter, the aim is to examine in greater depth, the real sources of information that form the foundation for developing detail design solutions. The assumption is therefore made that this refers to completely new information or that which alters the way in which existing knowledge is used. In doing this, four distinct sources have been identified and these are:

1 **building science**, where empirical scientific information can be used to inform the design
2 **manufacturer's information**, where the results of research and development conducted on behalf of manufacturers can be used to develop or modify the design process
3 **standard details**, where previous successful work can remove some of the more onerous design development
4 **technical literature**, available from various sources such as the Building Research Establishment or trade associations such as the Concrete Association can also be highly influential in design development.

It is important, however, that these sources of information are used in a systematic approach to research generally so that a complete picture is available. The idea that a particular method was chosen because a company representative left a leaflet in the office reception is not what is being suggested here but that the method was chosen after evaluating a defined list of alternatives. The amount of relevant research required is an impossible concept to quantify, however, as it will reflect the gaps in current knowledge, the degree of development required and the level of risk involved, i.e. the prestige and stature of the particular project.

Building science

In one respect, the concept of incorporating new ideas gleaned from the work of scientists into a new design is potentially the most exciting form of technical design. The reality, however, is that although this work is extremely valuable, it is also probably not cost related or intended to be readily incorporated into the building process.

The first step, however, is answering the question – what areas of building design are covered by this term 'building science'? Attempting to list all the possible areas is well beyond the scope of this book and will almost certainly leave out some vital area.

Generally, however, the important areas that can produce valuable new information can be grouped under a number of significant headings such as:

14.1

- **construction and structural design** – covering all aspects of construction technology and structural innovation, so curtain walling, green roofs, timber engineering, etc. will fall into this category
- **materials and performance** – covering all aspects of new and existing material combinations and uses, so concrete, plastics, glass, timber products, etc. will fall into this category
- **environmental design** – covering the consideration of environments created by buildings, so thermal, acoustic, solar interaction etc. will fall into this category
- **building services** – covering all aspects of the servicing of buildings, both standard forms and new alternatives, this area is of course closely linked to environmental design but will include water and waste management, energy management and internal transportation.

There are other significant areas such as **green building design and construction** and **design for disassembly** although they could also be encompassed by the categories listed above. **Building performance evaluation** and **conservation** are other areas that may not necessarily fit easily into specific categories but can and do provide significant and valuable contributions to building design knowledge.

The second question requiring an answer is – where can this information be found? An important qualification to this question, however, is the observation that it is ideas that designers require not necessarily facts alone. So where a search for the most up-to-date information could preclude information published in books as already 2–3 years out of date, ideas can come from any source. Books therefore represent one of the most consistent and accessible forms of scientific information available to inform the technical design process. Volume 2 in this series, **Environment, Technology and Sustainability**, is an excellent example of this type of information and clearly there are libraries full of many more.

Another valuable source of new information is available through structured learning. This is available in many forms, from in-house office-based seminars to degree courses in Higher Education Institutions (HEI's). Continued professional development (CPD) events are organised by all sorts of interested parties, such as manufacturers, professional bodies, legislative authorities, etc., all of whom have an interest in the design teams working with more current or specific information.

Whilst signing up for a degree course may be beyond many working in practice, it does still represent one of the most consistent ways of acquiring large amounts of new and relevant information. Post-graduate courses may have more to offer with shorter time scales involved and more specific subject content. Subject areas such as environmental design, sustainable architecture and now more recently technical architecture are available from many UK HE institutions. Professional bodies are the best source of this information as they have a vested interest in keeping their members up to date.

14.2

There is another reason for maintaining a working relationship with HEIs and that is because much relevant research takes place in universities but more significantly, those involved in teaching are more aware of what research is being conducted and where this information is available, be it through conference papers, journal publications or recently published books.

The Chartered Institute of Architectural Technologists (CIAT) has two committees aimed at providing members with relevant and forthcoming new information. The Innovation and Research Committee aims to develop and support a culture of innovation and research by working with manufacturers and other bodies to enhance 'cross fertilisation and knowledge/technology transfer'.

The Technical Committee aims to keep members abreast of new developments in legislation but also to build on established links with other professional bodies and research establishments.

The Royal Institute of British Architects (RIBA) has a Research and Development Department whose aims are to bring together those requiring information, those able to provide the research facilities and those able to fund that research. In addition they aim 'to publish, encourage publication and otherwise disseminate and implement the outcomes of research for both applied and academic purposes'. This work is supported by a Research Committee who aim to **inspire and steer** the work of the department.

The Association of Building Engineers (ABE) who represent 'those specialising in the technology of building', also publish very relevant information, maintaining a significant database of CPD events and other relevant courses. In addition, they aim to 'publish, encourage publication and otherwise disseminate and implement the outcomes of research for both applied and academic purposes'.

Manufacturer's information: including trade associations

Although it has been suggested that this type of information should be viewed with caution, this must not in any way undermine this extremely valuable source of knowledge. The caution required is simply to ensure that one is not being seduced into one way of thinking by very well-produced technical details.

Manufacturers can provide very detailed information suitable for incorporating directly into production details, more and more often this information is delivered in CAD packages that slip right into the common drawing systems in use.

In the past, the information would be delivered in the form of robust details, with or without certification such as British Board of Agrément (BBA), usually in leaflet form or sometimes in larger technical volumes such as the White Book from British Gypsum. This meant that the information had to be read to be understood and transferred onto another drawing, again requiring some interaction and therefore knowledgeable interpretation. Nowadays, with information provided electronically through web-based sources and in a drawn form that allows direct importation into existing drawing systems, there is no longer the same degree of interpretation required.

This process must be controlled to avoid the systematic use of inappropriate products and methods that are not understood, simply because they are easy to 'lift' from the Internet. The task of the technical designer has always been to stay abreast of current developments, and this process for the transfer of knowledge is just another one of those responsibilities.

Before we attempt to evaluate this type of information, it is worth to take another look at the motives behind their production. Manufacturers need to sell their products in order to survive: they need to develop their products to keep ahead of any opposition, and any information they provide is linked directly to these two objectives. In other words, the excellent technical information provided by some is intended to make that product more irresistible to technical designers and any research conducted is also aimed at making their product more saleable.

In contrast to this, however, is the fact that, wary of negative feedback and even possible litigation, manufacturer's information is usually extremely well researched. This research costs money, and so to recuperate this outlay, they need to sell significant amounts but at realistic

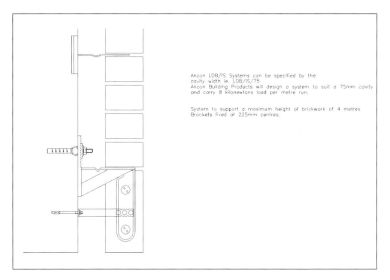

14.3 Manufacturer's CAD detail (Ancon Building Products)

prices – hence, the high-quality service that often accompanies this type of information. Often it will include complementary associated design services – all intended to help in 'making the sale'.

Advantages:

- well researched (usually)
- certified (usually)
- readily useable (CAD details, robust details, etc.)
- current (up to date with regulations)
- can offer back up design services (such as calculations, etc.)
- can work with manufacturers to develop products.

Disadvantages:

- can limit further relevant research
- can make unsubstantiated claims (all products now claim 'green' credentials)
- can pressurise sales by providing back up design services
- sales techniques can be subliminal, so beware.

There is little doubt, however, that this source of information is also the mainstay of most technical design and detailing that currently occurs in UK architectural practice. The main reason for this is to allow technical innovation to progress without being weighed down by the **thousands of decisions** referred to in the introduction to Chapter 13. The repetition of standard solutions is a reduced risk design process that may not necessarily even qualify as design. By using and relying on manufacturer's details for new areas of design, it allows designers to concentrate on the more

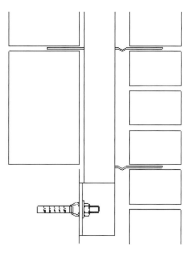

14.4 Manufacturer's CAD detail (Ancon Building Products)

problematic areas whilst feeling confident that those reliant on the manufacturer's information should under most circumstances work as predicted.

The much used specification clause 'installed as per manufacturer's instructions' is testament to the reliance placed on these details, and it is only to avoid a possible over-reliance that some doubt has been shed on the custom. In practice, however, it is a process that frees up technical designers to work on the problematic areas suggested above but also allows a consistent overview of the information that would not be possible when having to deal with the thousands of minor decisions required to construct an integrated series of detail design solutions.

Standard details

In looking at manufacturer's details above, we concluded that by the process of relying on others to cover some of the more mundane design details, the designer can concentrate on more important aspects. Standard details provide the same assurance but are not generally produced by manufacturers, instead they can be based on a set of details developed in-house to cover details for problems commonly encountered or can be produced by legislative bodies for similar reasons. Sometimes termed **robust details** in the past, they are intended to produce the required outcomes in many circumstances but without necessarily being innovative or ground breaking. Their role is primarily to ensure conformity with particular requirements rather than anything more ambitious.

The term **robust details** has now been overtaken by the formation in 2004 of the company Robust Details Limited, a non-profit distributing company who work in accordance with a memorandum of understanding with the Office of the Deputy Prime Minister (now, Communities and Local Government). Their role is to:

- approve new robust details as a method of satisfying Building Regulations
- manage the use of robust details in the house-building industry by enabling builders or their representatives to use them in new homes
- monitor the performance of robust details and withdraw any that consistently fail to meet the required standards
- promote the use of robust details and publish information to help the industry improve the sound insulation performance of separating walls and floors in new homes.

In-house standard details refer to a set of drawings primarily, that are kept in most architectural practices, known to satisfy certain building regulations or common (but mundane) details such as door jambs or floor systems. Their role is to provide support to applications for building approval or to provide contractors with construction information.

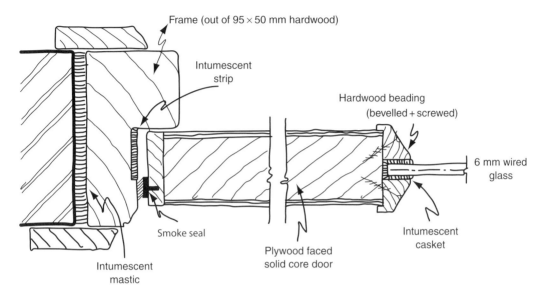

Frame (out of 95 × 50 mm hardwood)

Intumescent strip

Hardwood beading (bevelled + screwed)

6 mm wired glass

Smoke seal

Intumescent casket

Plywood faced solid core door

Intumescent mastic

14.5 A standard detail

The more responsible practices will ensure that these details are updated periodically to ensure compliance but also to keep abreast of developments in sustainable design practices.

Often these in-house versions derive from manufacturer's details, those available from other authorities or establishments such as the National House Building Council (NHBC) and those mentioned above.

Equally, they can represent the result of significant in-house research in order to provide a stock solution but one that reflects the ethos and character of the practice. Examples here could include a detail illustrating a system for incorporating cellulose insulation into timber-framed walls or a detail for a green roof system.

As with manufacturer's details, it is necessary to avoid a possible over-reliance on these details, but in practice, however, it is a process that frees up technical designers to work on the problematic areas. As suggested above, it also allows a consistent overview of the information required to construct an integrated series of detail design solutions.

Technical literature

The last in these information sources, technical literature probably forms the most dependable form in that it tends to be independent (and so responsible), reliable (fully tested) and applicable (suitable for the task of building). However, even with these sources, designers must be prepared to balance the motives of sponsors of the information against what they already know or are prepared to research further. A very good example of this is the excellent information produced by the Concrete Centre. Their website contains very helpful design information and a considerable amount of information on the sustainability of concrete. Their role is to promote the use of concrete, and the emphasis on sustainability is not surprising although in stark contrast to the commonly perceived view that cement-based products are highly unsustainable. This is due to the high levels of energy used in the production and subsequent CO_2 release.

The message of this book is very clear in this respect, however; do not trust any information at first hand – also that which states that cement is responsible for global warming. Look into both sides of the argument before making an informed decision and then be prepared to modify this

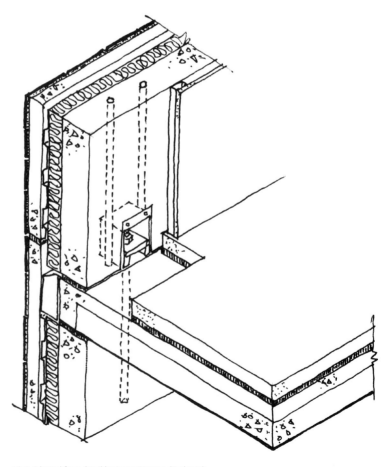

14.6 Adapted from detail by Susan Dawson (Techrete)

view as more information becomes available. This statement is in no way a support for concrete but nor is it a support for the contrary view; it is a demand that designers think for themselves and are also prepared to think the unthinkable.

At one end of the scale, technical literature can be little more than standard details but at the other end, they can offer a complete package of information on particular building themes. Publications from establishments such as the Building Research Establishment (BRE) will include all the information needed from background scientific theory to standard details. The information provided by the BRE is not free, however, and it is an independent organisation and therefore not beholden to any major sponsor. This puts a certain value on the information, both the obvious economic one and it also adds to the authority of the information provided.

The specific value to designers of the product-specific certification scheme, the BBA, was discussed in Chapter 9, where new products or techniques not covered by the other standards are tested, usually in context and come with approved installation methodologies. To repeat, these are product-specific tests, so the manufacturers will arrange for the testing process to be carried out, but the BBA conducts the assessment and produces the independent information. It includes laboratory testing, on-site assessment and production controls.

The BBAs suggest that 'every Agrément Certificate contains important data on durability, installation and compliance with Building Regulations, not just in England and Wales, but in Scotland and Northern Ireland, too'.

Their certificate search section covers a whole host of technologies by subject which then links to the individual certificate numbers and in turn to the contact details for each manufacturer. This can form a very useful search engine for new systems and products and is inextricably linked to the quality assurance of the BBA certificate.

The BBA also links into the European dimension by providing European Technical Approvals and information on other standards such as the British Standards, European Standards and the International Standards (ISO).

Common to all of these information sources, however, is the requirement for designers to fully understand the technology involved but also to be aware of the implications on other aspects of the detail design solutions. Acquiring the knowledge required is a time-consuming process and has to be organised just as the production of design details requires management, but great care should be taken to ensure that the knowledge gained is authentic and, above all, unbiased.

Chapter review

- It is important that sources of information are used in a systematic approach to research generally so that a complete picture is available.
- Building science information is found under the following headings:
  - Construction and structural design
  - Materials and performance
  - Environmental design
  - Building services.

  plus:
  - Green building design and construction
  - Design for disassembly
  - Building performance evaluation
  - Conservation.
- The CIAT, the RIBA and the ABE all have a vested interest in aiding the dissemination of technical knowledge.
- By using and relying on manufacturer's details for new areas of design, designers can concentrate on the more problematic areas whilst feeling confident that those reliant on the manufacturer's information should work as predicted.
- Standard details can be based on a set of details developed in-house to cover details commonly confronted or can be produced by legislative bodies for similar reasons. Their role is primarily to ensure conformity with particular requirements rather than anything more ambitious.
- At one end of the scale, technical literature can be little more than standard details, but at the other end, they can offer a complete package of information on particular building themes.
- Acquiring technical knowledge has to be organised, and great care should be taken to ensure that the knowledge gained is authentic and above all unbiased.

Chapter **15**

Process and choices

The previous chapters in this section on detailing have been setting the scene for the main event that is the actual process of detail design. This particular aspect of detailing is in fact relatively simple to describe as a great deal of the decisions are made prior to this process and others such as those discussed in the following chapters are complementary rather than fundamental.

Autocad and other computer drafting software allows the viewer to take a sketch scheme at the equivalent of 1/100 scale and to zoom into an equivalent scale of 1/5 or similar. Most CAD systems work at full size but with the viewer at differing distances from the object to create the effect of scale; the scale equivalents are used here to give some idea of the size of the drawn objects. This zooming in to an area of greater detail is possible but only worthwhile if the detailed information is in place, otherwise all that will be seen is one or two lines and wide open spaces.

This same approach can be adopted mentally, so the primary task of detailing is to provide the information required to fully understand a view of any particular part of the building at full size, should you wish to zoom in that far. In other words, detailing attempts to represent the **construction process** of a building, in all its parts at full size although scaled drawings may be used to represent this. The task is therefore to convert conceptual ideas and drawings into detailed construction information. There are particular stages involved in this process, but as in many aspects of technical design they may occur simultaneously or even be by-passed in many circumstances.

The main stages are:

- **concept to detail** – the zooming in for greater clarity
- **decision-making** – what goes into the detail
- **control of creativity** – what systems control this process.

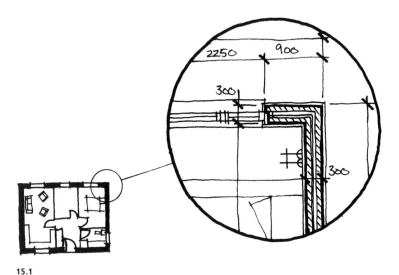

15.1

There are follow-up procedures to assess the details and others that simplify the process but essentially, the three steps above, provide a profile of the process.

Concept to detail

This important aspect of the detail design process was discussed above as **zooming in for greater clarity**, which it clearly is but it is also about an interpretation of the conceptual aims of the original scheme design. It is about understanding the aims of the original concept and converting these to construction details but while still honouring those aims and aspirations.

In simple schemes where the concept designer prepares the details, this process is almost automatic with the details possibly already in the mind of the designer during the conceptual stages. On larger schemes or where the process of concept design is separated from the detailing phase, this transfer of conceptual aims has to take place.

The most important aspect of this phase is who controls the transfer of conceptual ideals. There are many possible permutations to this relationship, but the following list identifies three key routes:

1   **Conceptual designer dictates transfer** – detailer has to understand and follow the concept designer's aims and instructions.
2   **Scheme design dictates transfer** – detailer has to understand and interpret the conceptual aims of the scheme.
3   **Client dictates transfer** – detailer has to understand and interpret the client's requirements.

In reality, most detailing happens in an atmosphere where all three dictate the process but with varying degrees of influence. This range of influence will vary from project to project but also between different aspects of the same project.

For example, in a new office block, the conceptual designer may retain a high level of control over the external finishes required to provide the requisite 'look'; the detailer may have to control the make up of the walls to ensure they perform as a building of this type must and the client's requirements may dictate the internal finishes to ensure the building provides the internal environment aimed for.

This phase may appear to be somewhat superficial but in reality is one of fundamental significance. Mies van de Rohe (1886–1969), one the best 'technical' architects and designers of the twentieth century, claimed that 'God is in the detail'. This statement is very important as it recognises that the essential 'feel' of a building is provided by the quality of the detailing. This is not to suggest that all buildings should aim for perfection regard-less of cost and consequence but that, for example, a timber garden shed should be detailed as a garden shed and that a modern high-tech office building should be detailed as a high-tech building.

The designer of technical details therefore has to respond to these influences, taking a lead from the dictates of the particular scheme, but essentially they have to get into the correct frame of mind. This act is mostly intuitive and often only becomes apparent when the process fails and breakdowns occur. The next phase involves making decisions regarding the content of construction details, and this 'frame of mind' will have a direct bearing on these decisions.

Decision-making: fear of failure or innovation

The next phase in the process of detailing is making specific decisions on what actually goes into the detail. Sometimes this can be a simple arrangement of information that has already been decided, such as the detail of a timber-framed wall where the finishes, technology and dimensions follow a prescribed route. On other occasions, however, it can involve completely new scenarios that require solving from first principles such as the lintel detail over a circular window in the same timber-framed wall. In this instance, standard solutions could be sought, the structural engineer (if employed) could be asked to provide solutions or the designer could decide to come up with their own solution, maybe trying something new.

The decision-making process in this case will depend on the individual designer and their knowledge levels, experience and desire to experiment.

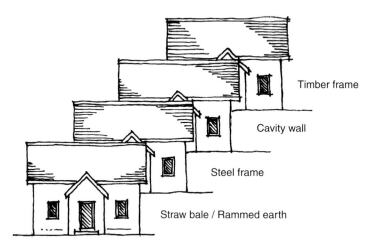

Timber frame

Cavity wall

Steel frame

Straw bale / Rammed earth

15.2

Added to this is the culture of risk-taking and the atmosphere that this process is taking place within.

This can vary from playing absolutely safe, working on the assumption that in the case of the timber-framed walls again, the potential for problems in what is essentially an organic material is too large to risk, to the contrasting concept that timber frame is a highly sustainable material, representing the future for small-scale building and therefore requires an innovative approach to its design.

The individual relationship with risk was discussed in depth in Chapter 10 but here is where that relationship can be responsible for some fundamental decisions. A principal aim of detailing is to provide a buildable scheme, and as such it makes complete sense to stick to existing 'standard' solutions. However, designers are also working in an environment where creativity and innovation are required so they need to address the relationship between degrees of risk and creativity but also security.

The risk to reward ratio is not favourable in technical design (Wienand and Watson, 2006a) because most creative or innovative technical details are hidden deep within building structures, which in turn may serve to discourage innovation. However, the creativity of individual designers and the aspirations of innovative design teams are in contrast to this incentive. So, even though technical design may appear to be a risk-averse process, at the level of detail design, a full range of relationships with risk is still possible.

> The variation in this relationship is based not only on the personality of the design organisation but also the variety in the form of the potential rewards. The rewards are unlikely to

be financial, so they fall into categories such as personal satisfaction and peer recognition.

(Wienand and Watson, 2006a)

There is therefore a wide range of personal experiences possibly
involved in detailing. Some designers may be too conservative to the
point where the full potential of the scheme is not being met, whereas
some designers may be too ambitious where the full potential is being
jeopardised because of inappropriate risk-taking. With the former example, little is possible other than encouragement, particularly as the building should still perform well, but with the latter, the potential for failure is
high so there are controls in the form of regulations that serve to protect
the client's, user's and public's interest.

Control of creativity: regulations

It may appear on occasion that regulations, and specifically Building
Regulations (Building Codes), have been invented explicitly to subvert
the innovative aspirations of designers. This is clearly not the case, and
in some cases, it can be argued that regulations have actually been
responsible for significant innovation.

In the UK, thermally efficient buildings existed before the regulations
required higher levels of performance, but it was undoubtedly the introduction of specific requirements that now ensures that all relevant buildings achieve at least minimum standards. A contrary argument suggests
that regulations lead to too many schemes providing just the lowest
acceptable levels.

There is little doubt that creativity has to be channelled and controlled to
an extent, and regulations do provide this controlling factor. They do
provide more than control to the detailing process, however, in that they
dictate the design parameters, thereby guiding the process to ensure
that all the important issues are addressed. Designing without constraints can be very difficult particularly when confronted with the
many decisions required in technical design. Narrowing down these
choices by working on individual aspects of a conceptual scheme in
ways discussed above helps to concentrate the design process, and
the imposition of regulatory requirements can add to the simplification
of technical design so that the number of options available becomes
more manageable.

Although UK Building Regulations (Communities and Local
Government) have simple aims – to set standards that ensure buildings
are healthy and safe for people in and around them, with energy conservation and access also important – the further clarification of these
aims results in detailed regulations under the following headings:

15.3

- Part A – Structure
- Part B – Fire safety
- Part C – Site preparation and resistance to moisture
- Part D – Toxic substances
- Part E – Resistance to the passage of sound
- Part F – Ventilation
- Part G – Hygiene
- Part H – Drainage and waste disposal
- Part J – Combustion appliances and fuel storage systems
- Part K – Protection from falling, collision and impact
- Part L – Conservation of fuel and power
- Part M – Access to and use of buildings
- Part N – Glazing, safety in relation to impact, opening and cleaning
- Part P – Electrical safety.

The Regulations set out the broad objectives or functions that the individual aspects of the design detail should achieve. Meeting these 'functional requirements' is an integral part of detail design and a working knowledge of the relevant Parts is very useful. However, the Regulations are constantly being updated suggesting that a knowledge of how to respond to them and how to use the system is a more important skill as it allows technical designers to work in any of the areas without having to retain large amounts of technical information.

The other major form of UK regulation that affects detail designers directly is the CDM regulations in that they place a direct legal responsibility on designers to design safe buildings. It may not be possible to discuss these regulations in depth in this book, but the important aspect of this regulation is that building designs should not only be safe for the users but also for the builders and the eventual dismantlers.

In addition to responsibilities involving the client, these regulations expect the designers to:

- ensure that any design he prepares and which he is aware will be used for the purposes of construction work includes among the design considerations adequate regard to the need:
  - to avoid foreseeable risks to the health and safety of any person at work carrying out construction work or cleaning work in or on the structure at any time, or of any person who may be affected by the work of such a person at work
  - to combat at source risks to the health and safety of any person at work carrying out construction work or cleaning work in or on the structure at any time, or of any person who may be affected by the work of such a person at work and
  - to give priority to measures which will protect all persons at work who may carry out construction work or cleaning work at any time and all persons who may be affected by the work of such persons at work over measures which only protect each person carrying out such work.
- ensure that the design includes adequate information about any aspect of the project or structure or materials (including articles or substances) which might affect the health or safety of any person at work carrying out construction work or cleaning work in or on the structure at any time or of any person who may be affected by the work of such a person at work and
- co-operate with the planning supervisor and with any other designer who is preparing any design in connection

with the same project or structure so far as is necessary to
enable each of them to comply with the requirements and
prohibitions placed on him in relation to the project by or
under the relevant statutory provisions.

[Construction (Design and Management)
Regulations, 1994]

As with the Building Regulations, knowledge of how to respond to these
requirements and how to use the system is a more important skill than
total knowledge of the complete CDM regulations.

Working with and within the scope of regulations is therefore a reality in
technical design. This controlling mechanism can be embraced as a
guidance tool or it can be wrestled with at every opportunity, but the
option for either approach is usually available.

Pragmatism is another valuable capacity that successful technical
designers should aim to develop. The regulations are normally phrased
in such a way as to allow some degree of flexibility in their interpretation, but this understanding of the regulations has to be shared by those
responsible for its enforcement. Experience of working with the
Regulations, knowledge of the local 'understanding' and the pragmatism to know when and where to push the limits can achieve much
apparent yielding of the regulations.

This is in no way to suggest that regulations should be broken, indeed
their role is not being questioned in any way, but it does suggest that
constructive interpretation of the flexibility can actually benefit everyone
concerned. Technical design solutions therefore need to be understood
and assessed in order to progress and high-quality detailing forms an
integral part of this process.

Assessment of technical information

There has been a great deal of discussion in this book regarding the
various aspects of technical design and how it relates to designers and
the construction of buildings. The discussions have involved the ideas of
quality and responsibility but so far have not confronted one particular
simple question – how can we be sure that the correct decisions are
made? In other words, where does some form of assessment of the
technical solutions fit into the design process?

This question covers many aspects of the detail design development
including:

- interpretation of the brief
- choice of materials
- choice of technology

- choice of precedents
- choice of risk strategy
- choice of solutions.

For design teams, this may be well structured with defined areas of responsibility, whereas for individual designers, this includes those working within defined parameters of teams, it is about their personal relationship with risk as discussed previously but also their desire to control and/or share information and responsibility.

Take the example of a design team working on the details for an environmental flagship project. A team member has been designated to find the most appropriate green roofing system and has come up with a solution. How can the team leader or any other member of the team feel confident that the most appropriate solution has been found and indeed should they even be considering this issue? Clearly, it comes down to trust but particularly team management and organisation.

Risk is not just about the solutions adopted but also involves the degree of reliance based on individual decision makers. Experience is probably the most successful way of dealing with this issue, where experienced team leaders will be familiar with the characters in their team, knowing where to check and where to trust.

There is a formal solution, however, and it comes in the form of structured team learning. The simple concept of a **spiral of intelligence**

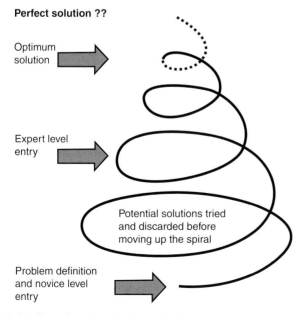

Perfect solution ??

Optimum solution

Expert level entry

Potential solutions tried and discarded before moving up the spiral

Problem definition and novice level entry

15.4 Spiral of intelligence from Wienand and Watson (2006)

describes the learning process for individual designers going through a design exercise (Wienand and Watson, 2006a). This presupposes that the observation that many designers feel as though they are going around in circles is in fact a positive movement towards a successful conclusion and not the negative regurgitating of the same ideas that it may sometimes feel like. In other words, each time the same apparent point is reached, it is in fact only after having gone through a further process of elimination, development and therefore refinement from the previous stage. Even if nothing actually comes out of the process, the designer can at least feel assured that they have checked their arguments one more time.

The concept of **triple loop learning** can be applied to this **spiral of intelligence** and used to provide a useful working model for design team management that can address this issue of assessment and responsibility. It is more about instilling a formal culture of learning than about directing responsibility for checking and evaluation. In order to fully understand **triple loop learning**, one must first appreciate **single** and **double loop learning**. Single loop learning is when a team or individual responds to a deviation from a set plan by detecting and correcting errors in order to maintain the central features of the strategy. Double loop learning involves 'thinking' about the deviations from the plan and what actions should be taken and learning from the experience.

> In Triple Loop Learning a reflection phase is incorporated to support or improve the thinking phase and hence to improve the decision making process, leading to more efficient and effective actions being taken.
>
> (Wienand and Watson, 2006a)

A formal design team management structure that incorporates **triple loop learning** is illustrated in Figure 15.5. The most important aspects, however, as far as assessment is concerned are the 'thinking' and 'reflection' phases but also the requirement that information is managed up as well as down. In other words, that all team members are encouraged to participate in all aspects of the design process in order to avoid working in 'silos', where individual team members or subteams work in apparent isolation or, even worse, competition.

The adoption of some form of design management strategy goes beyond the structure and working of the team; however, it can and should also inform the approach of individual designers. The simple aim being to ensure that the most appropriate solutions are found and that every reasonable step has been taken to do so. This requires knowledge of standard procedures for accessing and exploiting the resources available.

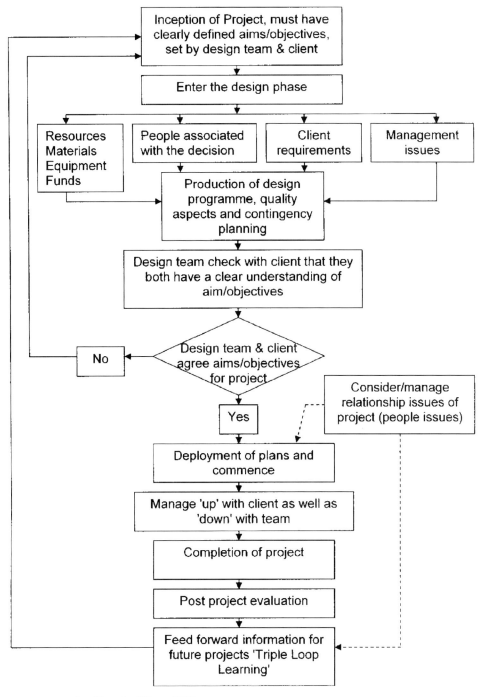

15.5 Design team management from Wienand and Watson (2002)

Procedural resources: precedent, typical standards and manufacturer's details

There are three standard procedures for finding out new information from existing sources – precedent studies, typical standards and manufacturers details. This process is not just about finding examples to **copy** but can be vindicated on many other levels as well. Some designers may not feel comfortable copying a detail from elsewhere whilst others wholly embrace the concept. In very simple terms, copying a detail from elsewhere is generally only a problem if the original design was totally unique and it is then reproduced in its entirety.

There are very strict copyright laws in the UK and internationally, so care should be taken and advice sought if there is any suggestion of copyright infringement (UK Patent Office). However, the standard view in architectural technology is that technology evolves from one successful solution to another so that very few examples could be classified as unique or totally original. Continuation of this process of evolving designs is normally considered to be standard practice.

The **study of precedents** is standard practice in architectural teaching generally and can be particularly rewarding at the level of finer technical details. Reading drawings and developing an understanding, firstly of the problem and then of the solution, leads to a depth of learning that generally is only possible by direct experience. It also helps to gain further understanding of the project being undertaken.

In the example of the green roof used previously, the study of how other design teams tackled their particular problems may suggest an alternative way of approaching the current one but may also identify areas of concern that were not immediately obvious.

The study of precedents is not just about reading published work, but it also includes the inquisitive observations of building sites to build up knowledge and also the 'reading' of existing buildings. Students of architectural technology may not have this awareness built into their characters at the beginning of their studies but soon develop it. Every interesting building (or even the dull ones) becomes a technical construction manual that demands 'reading'. Holidays abroad or even films on television become sources of technical design information simply by observing, 'reading' and attempting to understand.

This discussion on the value of precedents has only concerned the almost accidental interpretation of exemplars; what is actually required of a procedural system is the deliberate acquisition of useable information by the systematic study of precedents. This step simply needs to be acknowledged and included in the design schedule.

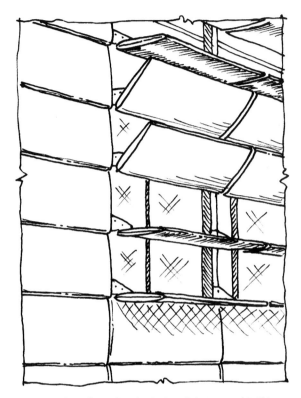

15.6 An interesting precedent – the Nordic Embassies in Berlin by Berger and Parkkinen

Typical **standard details** were discussed in Chapter 14 as sources of technical information. The issue here is to place the study or use of standard details into a structured procedure for developing design solutions. The value here is very similar to the study of precedents with less of the serendipitous learning associated with 'reading' buildings but with the real benefit of the knowledge that these are generally tried and tested methods. So just as for a systematic study of precedents, a systematic study of standard solutions should be acknowledged and included in the design schedule.

Manufacturer's details fall into a similar category to the precedents and standard details above but with the proviso that a certain degree of

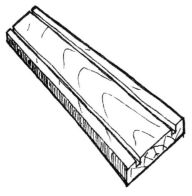

15.7 A larch tile/shingle

interpretation is required. The reason is that during this stage, it is not necessarily aiming to adopt a particular method or system but to understand and learn from them. Also as discussed in Chapter 14, manufacturer's details tend to be aimed at maximising sales of their products and any added learning is either accidental or a costed trade-off. Having said all this, these details can still be a very useful addition to the procedural process of gaining and building the technical knowledge required to make fully informed decisions. The study of these details therefore also fits neatly into a structured design schedule.

Feedback loops: builder/designer

The main criteria that distinguished triple loop learning as discussed and illustrated in Figure 15.5 is the thinking and reflection stages that should inform future learning. Probe any successful technical designer and you will find an experienced learner, someone who has the ability to recall similar situations where thoughts were developed and enhanced. For technical designers, this process has to include two critical elements – the design phase and the construction phase.

The design phase is one that has been subjected to a great deal of scrutiny in this book but the construction phase, less so. The particular emphasis here is on learning from the construction phase but also including this into a structured approach to good design. Designers should always be aware of the need to have their designs constructed and the potential for both negative and positive effects that this can have on the design process.

It is not usually feasible to involve the builder or site operatives in the early design phase but on occasion it is possible. Knowledge that the joiner, for instance, fully understands your intentions but not only that was also able to offer suggestions as to how your design might be made more buildable will make the design process far more rewarding but also add to the security of knowing that the design solution is probably a sound one.

This level of input at the front end of a project is rare but should it always be so? The answer is difficult to predict as it generally reflects the way in which building projects are procured although design and build schemes maintain their popularity despite the unease of the architectural professions.

There are still very positive ways of ensuring this practical or similar knowledge is gained, however, and that is through a genuine and meaningful approach to gaining feedback. There is a view that designers avoid feedback as it is generally unconstructive because it is usually only the negative aspects that necessitate noting. However, a structured

15.8

approach to gaining feedback by actively searching it out can fit very well into a triple loop learning environment.

The opportunities for feedback and consequent design enhancement do not only present themselves at the beginning or end of projects. There are many stages in the procurement of buildings that would allow a meaningful dialogue with both builders and site operatives. This information could be used to forward into the next similar scheme, but it could also be sought after throughout the life of a project and used to inform a continuing design evolution during a project.

In some of the successful technical designers referred to above this inclusion of feedback learning into their portfolio of design skills may be accidental, but for others, it is a genuine reflection of their management of the learning process and simply just good design practice. There is a distinct requirement in the technical design of buildings generally for this system of learning to be formalised into structured aspects of design team management.

The desire for greater control of the design process is not simply for the sake of control but is in recognition of the ever increasing technical complexity of modern buildings. This is apparent even before the requirement for more sustainable solutions is put into the equation. The technical design of buildings incorporating sustainable technologies is now such an intricate and convoluted process that to be certain that all reasonable attempts were made to examine all alternatives, a fully structured approach to the design process is required. This includes a need for the management of the process in the form of design team management.

Chapter review

- Detailing attempts to represent the **construction process** of a building in all its parts at full size although scaled drawings may be used to represent it.
- **Concept to detail – the zooming in for greater clarity**
  - The most important aspect of this phase is who controls the transfer of conceptual ideals? There are three basic routes:
    - **Conceptual designer dictates transfer** – detailer has to understand and follow the concept designer's aims and instructions.
    - **Scheme design dictates transfer** – detailer has to understand and interpret the conceptual aims of the scheme.
    - **Client dictates transfer** – detailer has to understand and interpret the client's requirements.
- **Decision-making – what goes into the detail**
  - Some designers may be too conservative to the point where the full potential of the scheme is not being met.

- ○ Some designers may be too ambitious where the full potential is being jeopardised because of inappropriate risk-taking.
- **Control of creativity – what systems control this process**
  - ○ The regulations provide a controlling factor. They dictate the design parameters, thereby guiding the process to ensure that all the important issues are addressed.
- A formal design team management structure that incorporates **triple loop learning** will include 'thinking' and 'reflection' phases but also the requirement that information is managed up as well as down.
- A structured procedural system is the deliberate acquisition of useable information by the systematic study and critical evaluation of precedents, standard details and manufacturer's details.
- A structured approach to gaining feedback by actively searching it out at all stages of a design project can fit very well into a triple loop learning environment.
- The technical design of buildings incorporating sustainable technologies is now such an intricate and convoluted process that to be certain that all reasonable attempts were made to examine all alternatives, a fully structured approach to the design process is required.

Chapter **16**

Tolerances and joints

During the life of a building, it will go through many changes but many of these will be unseen; they will be settling, flexing and swelling and shrinking from the very first day that work begins. The act of building is very much about the assembly of materials in a particular pattern in order to produce a structure that will be useful. This act relies on materials being able to stick together, whether through joints and connections or through the inherent properties of the materials and the jointing materials.

Firstly, there is the need to gain some understanding of the hidden movement of buildings. Anyone familiar with life in a tent will know almost intuitively that a fabric construction accommodates wind loads by flapping movements and thereby absorbing some of the energy; the guy ropes perform a similar function. When a wet towel is draped over the tent, it also sags to accommodate the load but when dry, the tent regains its original shape.

These are the obvious load adjustments, but there are others, sometimes the tent will change in shape from slack to taught as the fabric absorbs moisture and then dries out. Sometimes these changes in moisture can be seen as a direct consequence of condensation, the inner surface on cooler mornings can be dripping with condensation before drying out through evaporation and ventilation. The direct effects of rain and wind are clearly seen and expected, the loads imposed by snow and the subsequent temperature variations related to the wind conditions also become known.

All buildings are subjected to these same loads although the movements and condensation effects may not be so obvious. Buildings need to accommodate movement caused by loads being imposed and then removed, whether its weather-related loads or those resulting from

16.1

changing use patterns. The same is true for the effects of moisture whether generated internally or precipitation from the outside.

A building therefore needs to accommodate these movements in its own structure and the air in and around it. Designing for this involves understanding how different materials and structural elements come together and are held together. An example of this knowledge is in understanding the exact role of mortar in a brick or stone joint and the nails in a simple timber joint.

Much is spoken about the mortar in a brick joint not being a glue but a mechanism for spreading loads evenly. What it actually does is quite simple: being soft and pliable, the mortar can shape itself to the exact shape of both the bricks above and below; in other words it provides a precise fit.

This then allows the even transmission of loads but also seals the gaps between the bricks.

Traditionally, lime mortar was used or a weak cement mortar that also allowed a certain degree of gradual settlement to be absorbed without breaking these joints. Larger panels of brickwork need special expansion joints or strengthening to avoid cracking due to thermal expansion and contraction. Bricks are already a material that has been 'assembled' by using the properties of clay to stick together and then be favourably altered by firing. The mortar is a mixture of sand and cement that sticks together because of the inherent chemistry of hydration and the manufacture of cement.

A nailed timber joint takes the properties of timber, the ability to stick together through its natural growth plus the inherent structural

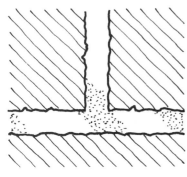

16.2

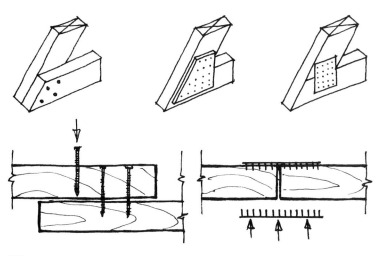

16.3

flexibility of wood, and adds the strength of steel to hold them together. This joint is very different to a brick mortar joint in that it relies on a steel nail being forced through one piece of timber with a hammer and then gripping the second piece of timber simply by virtue of it being forced into it. Timber must therefore be soft enough to push the nail through but also strong enough to grip the nail. It is the flexibility of timber that allows this although nails can be ribbed to provide a better grip.

When joining one piece of timber to another in this fashion, one has to overlap the other so that the nails can penetrate both pieces. This limits the range of joints possible and the subsequent shapes available (gang nail systems do allow butt jointing), but a full understanding only comes from knowledge that the strength of nailed joints relies on the shear strength of steel so it is perpendicular to the direction of the nail and also utilises the friction between the two pieces of timber being tightly forced together.

The joints between different materials relies very much on the nature of the materials involved, the structural performance required and the nature of the task involved. Essentially, however, joints:

- hold the building together
- make it possible to assemble
- ensure the performance required (Bryan, 2005).

This chapter seeks to explore these issues in more depth but taking the view that understanding the principles involved is more important than providing definitive answers.

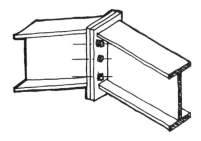

16.4

Structural and technical design factors: buildability, intersections and interfaces

The assembly of a building as we have seen involves the bringing together of different materials to provide various functions. The joints between these materials will have different requirements depending on the roles they are intended to perform.

The role of timber in a traditionally designed rafter, nailed together as described above will be very different to the timber slats in a rainscreen cladding system or that involved in a plywood sheathing panel. The requirements of joints between materials will therefore be dictated by the structural or technical requirements of that jointing system. In addition, however, the limitations of the material will also be an overriding factor.

The first of these design factors is the **buildability** of the design solution and the limitations of the material. The limitations of materials are based on the inherent properties discussed in Chapter 11 plus the shapes and sizes available. The great advantage of concrete is its plasticity, in other words, it can be provided in almost any shape imaginable.

Bricks are different in that they are limited in overall size because of the drying out of clay and firing systems, but by using small sizes, larger shapes can be formed but not nearly as versatile as concrete. Timber on the other hand, comes in a greater variety of forms than bricks, in that it is available in forms such as wooden beams, plywood panels or engineered beam systems.

These properties of materials are recognised and exploited in the successful design of buildable schemes. There is the added requirement,

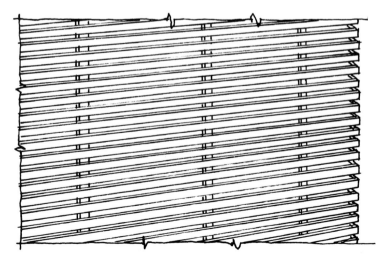

16.5 Timber rainscreen cladding

however, that there is a logical and achievable sequence to the assembly that fits into the norms of construction practice. This point takes account of the problems associated with the reality of building systems.

A flooring system that provides the finished surface as part of the structural assembly will then necessitate many precaution systems to protect it during the remaining stages of construction. The value of the system will then have to be balanced against the probability of damage. Although building has always involved a degree of off-site manufacture, this somewhat old fashioned view is still applicable but is being over-taken by building systems that rely increasingly on prefabrication.

Buildability therefore takes into account the limitations of the material in its particular form and also includes acknowledgment of the proposed construction methodology. The buildability of a proposed technical design solution will be governed by the:

- material properties
- material shapes and sizes available
- jointing requirements
- jointing systems available
- sequence of assembly.

The precise nature of the joints will depend largely on what is required of that particular **intersection**. The terminology involved can be confus-ing with a suggestion that 'joints', 'connections' and 'fixings' all have specific meanings and there is a sound argument in favour of this position. However, there are also situations where the boundaries get confused, so it is more important to understand what exactly is required and the nature of the task the joint is required to perform. Defining the requirements of the intersection therefore goes a long way towards deciding on the type of joint involved. These can be basic requirements such as:

- simple joining of materials to increase size
- connections between different elements
- structural load transmission.

These basic functions of joints can have further detailed requirements such as having to accommodate and control:

- weathering
- physical movement
- heat transmission
- fire protection
- sound attenuation.

Each of these basic functions and added control requirements will dictate further mechanisms for providing joints. Although very much

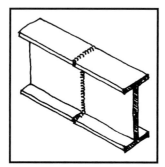

End to end weld
to increase length.

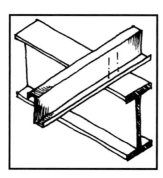

Connection of elements
to hold in place.

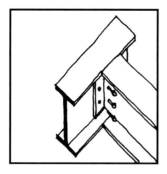

Connection of elements
to transfer load.

16.6

material related, these mechanisms are surprisingly small in number and include variations on the following simple concepts:

- **glues, adhesives, etc.** – materials that stick one material to another and these can include inherent 'glues' such as welding
- **mastic** – similar to glue but it also fills joints with a flexible filler to accommodate some movement
- **bolts** – joins two materials together with length of metal that goes right through and is threaded to allow tightening up
- **penetration (nails)** – steel or similar is punched trough one material and is held in the second by friction and can also include 'push-fit' connectors and wedges of various types
- **screws** – similar to nails but allow the tightening up similar to bolts due to the threaded section 'screwing' into the second material
- **gravity** – materials simply sit in place due to heavy weights involved and well-constructed joints such as bricks and mortar or tiles with lips that locate over battens.

Jointing systems can be just one of these or a combination of many in varying degrees. The choice of system will depend largely on the material but also to a degree on the particular nature of the intersection. These intersections often form the **interface** between elements of the building and its interaction with different environments. Where intersections are concerned with joints connecting materials together, interfaces are the establishment of surface boundaries between different significant areas.

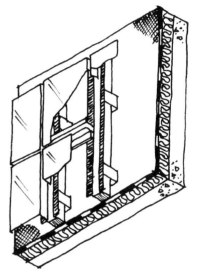

16.7 Rainscreen detail

Interfaces may therefore be concerned with moisture movement through the establishment of vapour barriers or more sophisticated pressure-equalised rainscreen cladding systems.

Thermal insulation could also be a requirement of a particular interface, maybe including the whole of the construction element or just particular parts. Issues such as cold bridging and its control are fundamentally important to the successful detailing of the joints at these interfaces.

Other interfaces may need better control of sound transmission or movement, etc. One of the main aids to controlling the performance of these interfaces is providing materials in a form that fit together effectively and integrate well with the joints.

Integration and coordination: tolerances, dimensions and modular matrices

In the past, the assembly of buildings owed much to the fact that materials could be formed into shape and altered on site. Until fairly recently, pre-fabricated parts were limited to elements such as doors and windows. Although bricks, timber and steel come in standards sizes, these materials are still easily and commonly adjusted on site to fit particular project needs.

Modern building techniques where high levels of economic efficiency are required regard this site work as a severe waste of time. Environmental efficiency would also see the waste of materials and energy caused by unnecessary alteration on site as non-sustainable.

There is therefore a pragmatic incentive to provide detail design solutions that are based on the efficient integration of materials, and this includes consideration of the assembly processes. The integration of materials and coordination of the assembly process requires recognition of the human element including all aspects of the initial placement but also the maintenance and repair of the various parts. This coordinated integration can no longer rely on adjustment on site and so needs to have this facility built-in.

The concept of the correct fit is a compromise between the need for easy handling and the need for a tight fit. Most systems therefore incorporate the idea of **tolerances**, where the space required to fit an object is acknowledged as needing to be greater than the object itself but is adjusted to take account of the particular materials and trades involved.

Materials vary in their manufacture, some being quite inconsistent in size such as hand-made bricks. Other similar materials such as concrete blocks may be reasonably predictable in size but due to the method of placement, still provide a variable end product. The tolerance generally used for structural openings in masonry walls may be 10 mm to accommodate these variations whereas when working only with manufactured items, this can be reduced. The greater the tolerance, the easier the fit

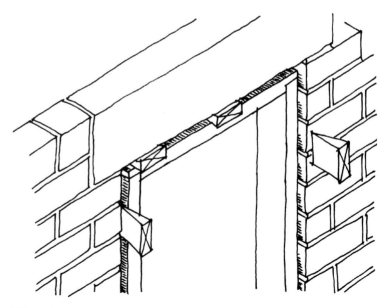

16.8

but the more difficult to cover, and the smaller the tolerance the neater the fit but the more difficult to install.

The responsibility of the designer to specify tolerances is outlined by Stephen Emmitt in his book *Architectural Technology* (2002), where he suggests that there are three interrelated forms of tolerance to be considered. These are:

- **manufacturing tolerances** – those that are fundamental to the manufactured product
- **positional tolerances** – those that result from on-site activities and setting out
- **joint tolerances** – those that can be either functional and/or aesthetic in their origin.

This last point is worth further consideration as it requires an aesthetic consideration of what is normally seen as a purely technical aspect of design. It also recognises that what may be correct may also appear to be incorrect or simply 'look' wrong.

Functional tolerances are set and need to be fully understood by the detail designer; issues like the moisture movement in timber or the thermal expansion of sheet metals need to be accommodated in detail design proposals. Lead flashing being a prime example with the requirement to allow controlled movement in order to avoid stress fractures caused by repeated expansion and contraction.

Aesthetic tolerances could include examples of the sheet metals where structural integrity may not be affected by movements but buckling of the surface would 'look' very bad.

Other simple examples such as the minor differences in the level of floor slates may look very obvious if the slates were placed very tightly together, whereas a wider gap of 5 mm or more would make this difference much more difficult to spot. Another similar aesthetic tool is the creation of shadow gaps where provision of a deliberately sized spacing provides a noticeable delineation of certain components.

Successful coordination, including the provision of suitable tolerances, involves designing to and providing the correct **dimensional information**. One of the prime tasks of detail design is coordination of dimensions.

Manufactured components come in standard sizes or can be requested in sizes that allow coordination. Others have to be realistic and suitable for the task. So where steel components may be expected at very tight tolerances, other site-based activities have to be more realistic.

There is a suggestion that to expect site sizes to any more accurate than building to the nearest 25 mm is being unrealistic. This may have been a pragmatic assumption in traditional lower quality building but must be less acceptable in modern high-quality design details. The acceptance of

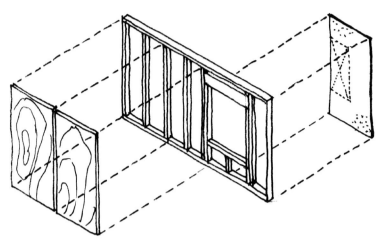

16.9 Modular wall matrix

such a large dimensional tolerance as 25 mm may have been due to the nature of building where so much was constructed on site and derived from variable materials.

The move to a greater coordination of materials and dimensions relies very much on the production of building components in standards sizes. However, a further requirement is that these sizes fall within a **modular matrix**. This means that larger dimensional requirements can be made up of smaller elements.

A modular matrix means that standard dimensions can be used to build up larger structures by simply adding on more 'standard' dimensions. Dimensional coordination is nominally based on a 100-mm grid (Emmitt, 2002), and a good example of this process is the standard size of plasterboard being 2400 mm × 1200 mm. This allows it to fit standard timber stud or ceiling ties spacing at 400 mm or 600 mm or non-standard spacings of 300 mm, 800 mm or 1200 mm.

A build up of this matrix would see the floor to floor dimensions assuming an internal ceiling height of 2400 mm (with tolerances).

Modular matrices can involve most building materials and if used successfully, can avoid much on-site waste although there may be conflict with aesthetic design: should aesthetic considerations dictate a window position, for instance, or should it be the daylight access or should it coordinate dimensionally?

Prefabrication and assembly

As we have seen, even the most traditional of building systems involved some prefabrication in the form of windows or even more simply, the manufacture of bricks or the cutting of timber. Until very recently, this proportion has remained fairly small. There is now, however, a very strong tendency to move towards ever increasing levels of prefabrication and a brief discussion on the merits or otherwise is valid. The concept of prefabrication is based on the manufacture of major elements of the required building under factory conditions where quality can be strictly controlled, waste reduced to a minimum and weather dependency virtually eliminated.

The benefits in terms of quality and economic efficiency are the main arguments in favour and will be discussed in greater depth later in this section. The counter-arguments are almost all based on the sustainability theme and therefore of value but again worth considering in more depth.

The suggestion that the most sustainable form of building is based on earth construction where the soil is dug directly from the site using the lowest energy source possible – the future occupants, digging the soil and forming the walls – is a difficult one to beat.

Closer examination, however, will come up with a counter argument that although this method is suitable for warm dry climates, what happens in cooler wetter climates where some degree of heating and therefore insulation is required as well, or to make maximum use of solar gain, south-facing (prefabricated) windows would probably be needed.

Sustainable solutions will almost always involve some degree of compromise and it is in the understanding of the compromise that sustainability can be maximised. Prefabrication is of potential value in achieving this compromise. The main drawback is the reduction in low skill, on-site work and therefore labour costs – a very strong economic argument for the system but weak in human terms.

If the reduction in human efficiency is accepted, the benefits of prefabrication can be fully appreciated, as the reduction in on-site activities excludes incumbent weather from the construction process.

The successful introduction of timber-framed construction into the UK was delayed because of poor construction techniques that allowed timber to be soaked during rain showers and subsequently rot when encased in the finished building envelope.

In the UK, unfavourable weather is common and affects the use of concrete through temperature variations, timber through water ingress and also in a general acceptance of mud and dirt as being part and parcel of new building. Prefabrication can reduce all of this, and the main incentive should be in the comparison with the motor industry. However, the concerns of internationalisation where uneconomic factories can be shut down overnight, moving production to cheaper countries, create a real and pertinent fear.

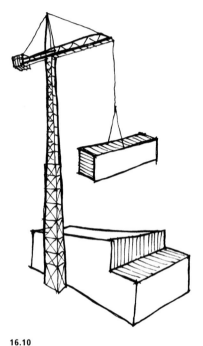

16.10

The thought that your brand-new car was made in a field with the workers walking in and out in muddy boots and constructed in conditions that were just about okay would soon have you looking elsewhere, so why is it acceptable for new buildings? This argument is clearly less applicable to larger commercial projects where the percentage of time spent working on the ground is less and the subsequent structure itself, to an extent, becomes a controllable factory environment.

Prefabrication still relies on a good deal of the actual assembly taking place on site; however, the process needs careful consideration during the detail design phase. A project considered as traditional in most respects may struggle to incorporate a highly prefabricated element in isolation, mainly because the ethos is not fully inculcated into the process. So to make maximum use of the benefits of prefabrication, it should form part of an overall approach to providing a quality-assured building process, starting with the design phase and leading into the on-site assembly.

Potentially, this means involving the manufacturers at a much earlier stage than would normally be the case to allow their expertise to inform the detail design and also to allow the detail design to be fully cognisant of the assembly requirements. The detail design phase becomes much more of a team-based exercise, where the manufacturers and erectors play an equally important role as the technical designers and design engineers do in traditional design practices. This does change the relationship between clients, designers and contractors, and although there are contractual models available to cope with these circumstances, they have not yet found a place in the common vocabulary of construction practice.

Chapter review

- During the life of a building, it will go through many changes but many of these will be unseen; they will be settling, flexing and swelling and shrinking from the very first day that work begins.
- The joints between different materials rely very much on the nature of the materials involved, the structural performance required and the nature of the task involved. Essentially, joints:
  - hold the building together
  - make it possible to assemble
  - ensure the performance required.
- The buildability of a proposed technical design solution will be governed by the:
  - material properties
  - material shapes and sizes available
  - jointing requirements
  - jointing systems available
  - sequence of assembly.

- The precise nature of the joints will depend largely on what is required of that particular intersection. These can be basic requirements such as
  - simple joining of materials to increase size
  - connections between different elements
  - structural load transmission.

  Or detailed requirements such as having to accommodate and control:
  - weathering
  - physical movement
  - heat transmission
  - fire protection
  - sound attenuation.
- The concept of the correct fit is a compromise between the need for easy handling and the need for a tight fit, so most systems incorporate the concept of tolerances.
- A modular matrix means that standard dimensions can be used to build up larger structures by simply adding on more 'standard' dimensions.
- Prefabrication still relies on a good deal of the actual assembly taking place on site; however, the process needs careful consideration during the detail design phase.

Chapter **17**

Presentation of solutions

During the detail design phase, many sketches will be produced, manufacturer's detail collected plus other forms of technical information assimilated. The actual technical design solutions may not actually be available as discreet documents but may still be a concept lodged in some designer's mind as a 'good idea'. There is now a distinct need to translate that information into a form that is useful in both transmission of the idea to others and also as a record before events overtake the process and the idea is forgotten. These are the **developmental drawings** referred to in Chapter 4.

The main requirement at this stage, however, is the accurate transmission of information to a specifically targeted audience. These are the **production drawings** referred to in Chapter 4. In Chapter 5, we examined the standard drawing conventions in more detail, asking questions such as:

- Who needs to know?
- Why do they need to know?
- What do they need to know?

This is the point, however, where the theoretical discussion of communication methods turns into the specific task of 'getting the message across'. It is worth taking some time out to consider these basic questions, as it may affect or alter the standard conventions in place, for the better.

Criteria

The word criteria, the plural form of criterion, means **the standard that something is judged on**, and in the case of design details it can only be the success or otherwise of the translation of the technical concept into

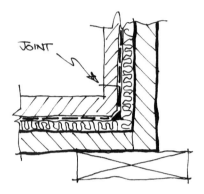

17.1 Tanking sketch idea

the built form. For this to happen, the concept has to be communicated successfully to all parties involved and this includes:

- **visual representation** – to allow the readers to form a 3D mental image
- **precise technical information** – to allow manufacture.

Firstly, the visual representation has to take account of all the potential readers, so will include initial assessors, i.e. fellow designers who may be required to comment and to add extra information. An example would be a structural engineer updating dimensions and other details in response to further calculations. There may be a need for regulatory authorities to understand the information but they should fit into this initial category of reader who all share a common technical design language.

The next group of potential readers are the manufacturers, whether they be factory or site based, they differ from the initial set in that there is less likelihood of a common language. The visual representation therefore needs to take this into account. It could be that some in this group are very familiar with certain forms of representation involving highly advanced technical language but not others. The form of visual presentation used, therefore, has to accommodate all of the prospective readers. This may vary from project to project, but common forms are possible to cover all possibilities.

Secondly, there is the need to include accurate technical information in a form that is readily understood by all who need to but equally does not swamp the information with unnecessary detail. This particular

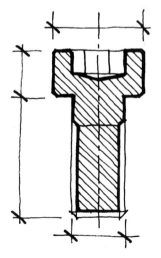

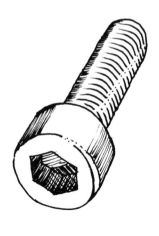

17.2

aspect of technical detailing is often handled poorly as it can be a disparate process involving two separate functions – drawing and specification. Clearly, these two functions are not separated in the design process but all too often they end up being produced on their own, independently.

The issue here is whether to include all the specification information alongside the visual imagery or to write it up separately. There is no clear standard solution as simple details will be best understood with all the specification information alongside the drawing, whereas the more complicated details will be swamped with too much information and the likelihood is that it would be ignored.

The standard format would see mainly dimensions added to fully describe the detail and then a minimum of additional notes to make the drawing legible. However, standard formats can be restrictive and design teams should look to break free of convention whenever possible, primarily to move forward and to increase the level of knowledge transfer.

Another interpretation of the task of technical details takes the two criteria mentioned above, the visual and the precision and gives them different weightings. This takes account of the primary purpose of the detail and asks:

- Is it to provide a requisite visual appearance? or
- Is it to provide a requisite technical performance?

In other words, is it a structural detail or an architectural detail? The requirements of the technical information provided may be very similar but they could also be very different.

Structural details

This area of technical design is aimed very much at providing a predictable performance. In doing so, it has to provide all of the information needed to produce that performance, including information on its manufacture or construction but also information on its required performance.

There is an overlap here with the concept of formal specification methods, where the choices involve the specification of expected performance (performance specification) or the description of a detail that provides that performance (prescriptive specification).

These systems will be discussed in much more depth in the following section of this book, Part 5 which is based specifically on specification writing but should not serve to confuse the specific requirements of a technical detail. Here, the primary task is to convey the technical information required to understand the structural requirements of the

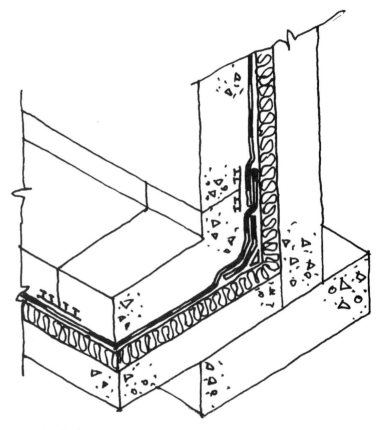

17.3 Tanking detail

proposed detail. Both methods are possible but without removing the requirement to provide very detailed information on what is being asked for in the design.

An example that illustrates this requirement is the detailing of a water-proof tanking system for a concrete basement. The successful detail design will indicate the dimensions involved, i.e. sizes and thickness of concrete, protective screeds, insulation, etc., it will also be very specific about the location of the waterproof membrane and, in particular, the sequence of placement in order to make sure it is possible but also to ensure that minimum damage occurs in its placement.

In addition, the detail will cover jointing methods and specific protection elements such as corner details.

Whether the precise system is specified or a performance requirement is specified is secondary to the main requirements of the detail – that it is technically robust, buildable and accurate.

In other words, the specification method cannot be allowed to compromise the structural performance requirements of the basement, whether it be part of the building's foundation design or some other aspect of the structural integrity. The requirement of a structural detail is to ensure structural performance above all else.

There are particular parts of buildings that are crucial to its effective performance, and traditionally, structural details have concentrated on these areas. Stephen Emmitt, in his influential book, *Architectural Technology* (2002), suggests the following critical intersections:

- **wall to ground** – whether a sloping or flat site or whether the building appears to float above the ground, this detail is crucial in avoiding problems
- **wall to floor** – primarily it is the juxtaposition of vertical and horizontal planes that need resolution structurally
- **wall to roof** – starts with the structural integration of the vertical and angular planes but can also include the horizontal in addition, plus the weathering aspects, ventilation and transfer of forces, making this a complicated junction

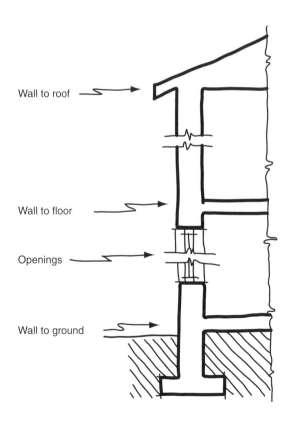

Wall to roof

Wall to floor

Openings

Wall to ground

17.4

- **openings** – all openings to the external environment have the potential to create a weak point in the envelope, so details need to address weathering and structural considerations as well as need to provide moving parts.

Structural details are therefore crucial to the effective operating performance of a building, influencing the perception of success or failure on the level of individual interaction. In other words, how the actual users of the building feel about it in addition to the more fundamental concerns such as its ability to stand up.

Architectural details

Unlike structural details, architectural details are concerned primarily with appearance. These are the details that are seen and go a long way towards forming the character of a building; however, they cannot be achieved without also providing an adequate level of structural support.

For example, the external staircase and ramped access to the front of a prestigious building is a major architectural feature requiring careful consideration and detailing. Its appearance is fundamental to its success but so is its structural performance.

The true value of architectural detailing cannot be overestimated as it defines the character of a building and is therefore fundamental in achieving the true transfer of concept into built form.

To again refer to Stephen Emmitt (2002), in particular his suggestion that the need for 'harmonious' detailing, where the requirement that all the architectural details follow the character theme of the conceptual design, is part of the 'creative art' of detailing. This states the need for a consistent theme that could be a project-based or an office-based development and could also be manifested in standard details. The internationally famous architectural practice, Foster and Partners, has a reputation for highly technical detailing where the technology is celebrated visually. This practise is a fusion of the art of structural detailing with that of architectural detailing where the technology takes centre stage. It does, however, generally rely on expensive materials and production methods to fully reveal the aesthetic qualities of the technology on display. Glass, stainless steel and high-quality finishes are normally required but not exclusively so.

Generally, the cheaper the material, the more difficult to detail well architecturally, but this is balanced by the more onerous requirement that expensive materials should be well detailed.

Normal details such as the architrave around a door opening are intended to cover the gap around the frame caused by the tolerance

17.5 The Louvre Pyramid by Ieoh Ming Pei

between the structural opening and the door frame. This highly visual form of architectural detailing can be designed in many ways, some adapting the covering principle but others expose the gap and celebrate its features. This latter approach needs careful design consideration, however, as one of the reasons for the covering plate is to hide the common variations in structural sizes. In other words, it is a way of compensating for 'standard' quality workmanship, and by trying a new version, is the quality of workmanship expected possible under normal circumstances?

Choosing drawing styles: sketches, hand-drafted, CAD or 3D

The style of drawing chosen to illustrate technical details is fundamental to the flavour of the understanding transmitted with it. Essential information can be portrayed by any system even without the aid of drawn material. Words, both verbal and written with a rough model or photograph of a similar example could replace a drawn detail but with major consequences to the level of understanding imparted.

The various styles of drawing were discussed in Chapter 4 with the conventions covered in Chapter 5, so a swift re-read may be of some use here. The first decision to make in choosing a drawing style is to be sure of the intended audience. The degree to which the subliminal messages contained in the various styles available must not be underestimated.

For instance, the relationship between designer and on-site operatives can unfortunately be very sensitive at times and problems can be easily exacerbated by the production of inappropriate details. Details perceived as too sketchy can be assumed to be poorly thought through, details with too much detail can be assumed to be too complicated or details produced in 3D with full rendering could be interpreted as a waste of the client's money. Yet, all of these styles are appropriate under different circumstances – the timing of decision is vital as is the flavour of the message mentioned above.

The flavour of the information is similar to the tone in a voice, and so on occasions, it may be required to demonstrate authority whilst on others, inclusiveness may be more suitable.

These are extreme examples as most details will be designed in advance without any 'personalities' involved, yet they can be aimed at the likely readers and thereby given the requisite flavour. Details produced purely for structural engineers may benefit from being sketchy to encourage a dialogue whereas those required as instruction for a plumber on the position of lead flashing may be very different, having to convey the authority of the design and thereby discouraging any dialogue.

17.6 Sketch idea

The first level of detail design representation will be the **sketch** proposal, often on a scrap of paper, 'the back of an envelope' equivalent. Often thought of as 'designing on the hoof', some see this as the indications of a highly creative designer, others as an incompetent professional having to make things up on site.

The reality is probably neither, but it is biased against a favourable impression. These sketches are suitable for working up concepts, for discussion with colleagues and rarely suitable for anything else. It is important not to confuse these rough drawings with details that have deliberately been made to look sketchy, where a deliberate decision has been made to encourage dialogue.

The ability to produce competent sketches is one worth developing; however, as there will certainly be occasions when it will be called upon. Detail designs inevitably go wrong, even with the most thorough preparation, and on these occasions, it can very useful to demonstrate technical knowledge with skilful rendering of remedial ideas. The point is that they should be kept in reserve and used to retrieve tricky situations rather than possibly being the initial cause.

The idea of **hand-drafted** details is a very useful tool and may be better described as hand-crafted in respect of the amount of information contained within them. As discussed previously, the idea is to convey an open mind on the further development of the concept but simultaneously making sure that the design is well thought through and tested as far as possible.

The dialogue with engineers was cited as an example above, but this particular flavour may be pertinent to many other professional relationships as well.

Consider the dialogue with a system builder where the designer hopes to enlist the manufacturing expertise of the manufacturer or even the example of the plumber where, in this case, their local knowledge may just produce a better or at least more relevant solution.

This last example also reflects on the fact that contractors may produce better quality results if they are producing work based on their experience and existing knowledge rather than attempting something new for the first time. Also and equally as relevant, however, plumbers in this example are in the main experts at plumbing and their professional knowledge must not be underestimated. The art is in recognising the good ones.

Final details and standard details are invariably produced as firm-lined drawings, suggesting well thought through design concepts that have stood the test of time or at least have been through many design stages. More often now available as **CAD** files, these details can be reproduced very quickly or slipped into other drawing files.

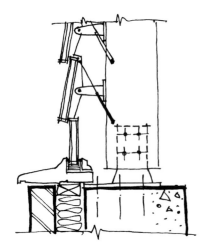

17.7 Hand drafted sketch

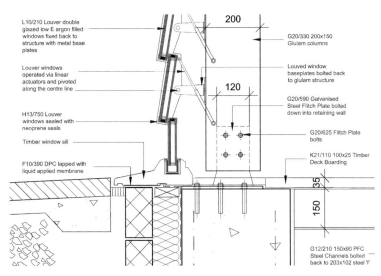

L10/210 Louver double
glazed low E argon filled
windows fixed back to
structure with metal base
plates

Louver windows
operated via linear
actuators and pivoted
along the centre line

H13/750 Louver
windows sealed with
neoprene seals

Timber window sill

F10/390 DPC lapped with
liquid applied membrane

200

120

G20/330 200x150
Glulam columns

Louved window
baseplates bolted back
to glulam structure

G20/590 Galvanised
Steel Flitch Plate bolted
down into retaining wall

G20/625 Flitch Plate
bolts

K21/110 100x25 Timber
Deck Boarding

35

150

G12/210 150x90 PFC
Steel Channels bolted
back to 203x102 steel 'I'

17.8 2D CAD detail (Jonathan Arksey)

The flavour or message contained in these details must be authoritative, but care must be taken to ensure their relevance and that they are as up to date as possible. This is simply in recognition of the fact that their authority will be lost if they are found to be lacking.

For many technical designers, these technical drawings are the culmination of the technical design process, and very fine examples of the art of detailing can be produced. It is vital to maintain the link with production, however, so a technical designer or illustrator who never gets to see the work produced will be working at a great disadvantage. The task is to convey the technical information required to build, so this element of the process should be under constant review.

A major factor in the understanding of drawn material is the ability to imagine the object in three dimensions. The process of **3D imagery** was discussed in some depth in Chapter 4, and it has a vital role to play in the comprehension of detail designs. The task of the drawn detail is to convey, among other things, the information required to allow the reader to form a 3D image in their mind. How much easier would this be if the original detail was also constructed in 3D.

Generally, sketching in 3D is difficult and depends on the individual skill of draftsperson. This skill can be developed, however, as it is a very useful way of forcing the designer to think in three dimensions as well.

Before the advent of CAD, 3D drawing systems took longer to produce than two dimensions and so were only used for important aspects. CAD, however, with the proper training can permit 3D images to be built up fairly easily.

17.9 3D CAD detail (Jonathan Arksey)

These images can be extremely valuable to technical designers as they allow manipulation of the image to provide not only the best view but also multiple and potentially interactive views.

This is clearly the future for technical detailing, and although the architectural professions and allied building professions can be conservative and slow to change, the building industry is currently in the grips of an IT explosion with many new possibilities opening up.

Control

The choice of drawing style and the technical content of design details are mostly decided by the design team generally or specifically by the individual designer. The process is geared, as it should be and as discussed at some length, towards an efficient transfer of conceptual ideas into the technical information required to build. The aim is for an efficient transfer of information, and this process requires some control. There are many areas that require some form of control and those at the initial technical design stage include:

- concept to technology transfer
- maintaining client's best interests
- maintaining the aesthetic design concept
- avoiding unnecessary work
- avoiding unnecessary risk.

As we have seen, the technical design phase is followed by the transfer of that information to various 'readers' and that process also requires some form of control, including:

- the style of drawing
- the information content
- the degree of instruction.

This leaves the final stage where manufacturing, production or construction happens, and this process is normally outside of the immediate control of the designer, apart from occasional site visits. Very occasionally, designers are site based, but this is not the norm.

So this leaves another phase requiring some form of control. Because this last phase is so difficult to control, as many safeguards should be put in place before the project begins as is possible. This includes being aware throughout the detail design phase that the information produced will have to work without the aid of the designer's explanation. In other words, it has to stand alone as design instructions. This means that anyone who has to read the information and interpret the instructions should be able to do so without difficulty. The presentation of technical details as offered in this chapter is all about providing the knowledge and understanding to exercise the required control.

Chapter review

- The translation of the technical concept into the built form has to be communicated successfully and includes:
    - **visual representation** – allows readers to form a 3D mental image
    - **precise technical information** – to allow manufacture.
- Structural detailing is aimed at providing a predictable performance. It has to provide all of the information needed to produce that performance, including information on its manufacture or construction but also information on its required performance.
- Architectural detailing defines the character of a building and is therefore fundamental in achieving the true transfer of concept into built form.
- The style of drawing chosen to illustrate technical details is fundamental to the flavour of the understanding transmitted with it.
- Sketches are suitable for working up concepts, for discussion with colleagues and rarely suitable for anything else. It is important not to confuse these rough drawings with details that have deliberately been made to look sketchy, where a deliberate decision has been made to encourage dialogue.
- Hand-drafted details aim to convey an open mind on the further development of the concept but simultaneously making sure that the design is well thought through and tested as far as possible.
- Final details and standard details are invariably produced as firm-lined drawings, suggesting well thought through design concepts

that have stood the test of time or at least have been through many design stages. More often now available as CAD files.

- The task of the drawn detail is to convey, among other things, the information required to allow the reader to form a 3D image in their mind.
- The transfer of conceptual ideas into the technical design required to build should involve an efficient transfer of information, and this process requires effective control.

Chapter **18**

Detailing: case studies

In the previous section on the **selection of materials**, the final chapter was based on the study of three separate hypothetical case studies, each aiming to illustrate a different approach to the selection of materials. Although these studies highlighted the process for choosing materials, the point was made: that it is an integral part of technical design and cannot be viewed in isolation. These same studies will be examined again in this chapter where the 'detail design process' will be examined.

Case study 1: starting from first principles

To repeat, the idea of this case study is to examine the process as a hypothetical example where little or no experience is available although precedents may exist to copy from. The basis of this particular case study is the roof to an environmentally responsible dwelling and the scenario is this:

A client would like to build a sun lounge on to the south-facing elevation of an existing single storey rear wing of a dwelling in North East Scotland. This rear wing is traditionally constructed in random stone rubble with a natural stone slate covered roof in diminishing courses. The client has requested that the design involves minimal alteration to the existing roof structure meaning that the roof will be essentially flat. In addition, the client is aware that 'normal' flat roofing materials do not perform well in this part of the world and also that the low winter and summer sun paths suggest that an insulated solid (non-glazed) roof would be preferable.

The decision was made on environmental grounds to opt for a green roof on a timber-framed structure. The technology chosen is that for an

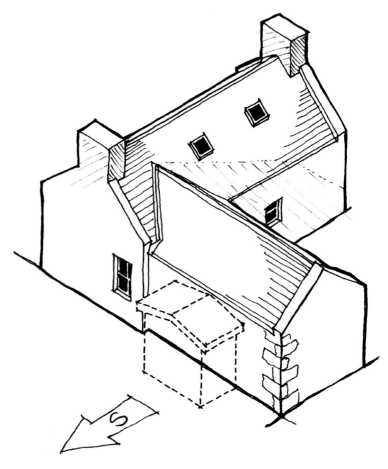

18.1

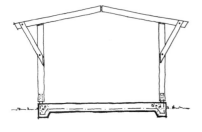

18.2

'unventilated warm flat roof construction' based on a portal frame with 175 × 63 mm timber rafters at 800-mm centres with a nominal pitch of 10° providing a slope for rain run-off. The task here is to see why these decisions were made and to look at some of the details.

Phase 1: the initial decisions

- Low Scottish sun path in summer and winter allows a solid roof to retain heat and also minimise overheating through excessive solar gain – some loss of maximum light penetration.
- Flat roof allows minimal disturbance of existing roof structure but requires sensitive aesthetic design – architectural detailing must dictate.

- Traditional flat roof materials suffer from extreme exposure – both frost damage and wind uplift.
- Green roof methods provide sensible protection of roof covering – brown roof chosen to avoid excessive growth because the roof will be low down and very visible – local species suitable for exposed habitats.
- Timber construction was chosen to give a 'warm' feel, to allow modular-framed structure to maximise light penetration and to offer an environmentally friendly building material.

Phase 2: the consequential decisions

- Portal frame technology was chosen to provide an open internal structure.
- Large section timbers at wide span were chosen to expose the structure internally to emphasise the construction and environmental material choice – also to reduce the number of portal frames required.
- Wider span (800 mm) provides an 'architectural' structural opening for the window dimensions and fits a standard modular construction – e.g. 3 × 2400 mm.
- 175 × 63 mm timber rafters at 800 mm centres with a nominal pitch of 10° providing a slope for rain run-off – from experience; note: engineer to check or calculate loads.
- Roof pitched from centre line providing symmetrical and lesser impact on existing roof than a mono-pitched, lean-to roof.
- Unventilated warm flat roof was chosen to avoid the need for ventilation – extremes of temperature make the ventilation requirements of cold roofs difficult to achieve and externally placed insulation (inverted warm roof) was considered inappropriate for the small and exposed roof.

Phase 3: technical research

Research into unventilated warm roof technology for flat roofs and green roofs will suggest that the following make up is required:

- grass/planting system
- soil or equivalent substrate
- drainage/water retention system
- waterproof membrane with root protection
- structural insulation
- vapour control layer
- structural decking system
- more insulation?
- internal finishing.

Phase 4: materials research (see Chapter 12)

- Site-sourced substrate on EPDM rubber flat roofing membrane on
- 100-mm thick 'extruded polystyrene' insulation with tongued and grooved joints on
- polythene vapour barrier with taped joints (to manufacturer's specification) on
- 25-mm thick 'sterling board' fixed directly to rafters with
- 150-mm thick cellulose insulation (or equivalent) between rafters with
- 12.5-mm thick softwood tongued and grooved ceiling panelling on
- 50 × 25 mm battens fixed to either side of rafters.

Phase 5: design details required

- Decision process
  - critical areas:
    - standard section through roof structure
    - roof/existing roof junction to include flashing detail capable of handling brown roof/slate interface
    - glazed timber wall/roof junction to include rainwater collection and disposal
    - architectural detail required for dominant front elevation.
- Style
  - key readers of details – in order of importance:
    - builder
    - engineer
    - building control officer
    - client
    - planning officer – maybe.
  - style choices:
    - sketch – too informal
    - CAD detail – too technical looking for domestic dialogue
    - hand-drafted – perfect, invites dialogue with all interested parties.

Phase 6: design details (to be provided as hand-drafted)

1. Roof/wall junction illustrating top of glazed detail, eaves construction (including holding back of soil substrate) and rainwater collection
2. roof/wall junction to front elevation to accommodate roof slope and internal ceiling finishes
3. roof/existing roof junction to include flashing detail capable of handling brown roof/slate interface
4. structural detail illustrating portal frame construction.

Note: check details with colleagues.

This hypothetical case study that must be read in conjunction with the equivalent materials study in Chapter 12 has also illustrated that even

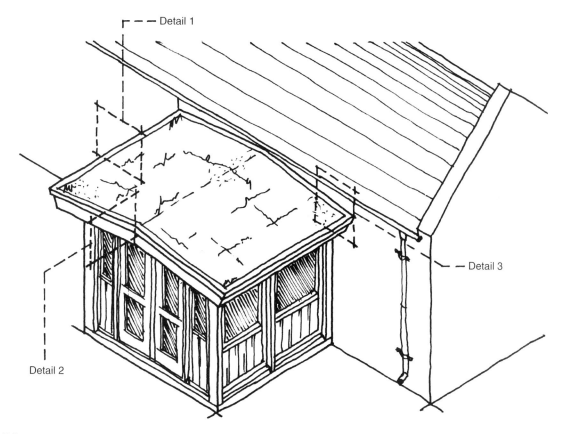

Detail 1

Detail 3

Detail 2

18.3

apparently new systems still rely to a large degree on existing knowledge and design processes. The choices may seem to be endless initially, but as soon as one or two initial decisions are made, these choices
rapidly decline in number.

Two other observations are the decision to stick to proved technologies,
even though the overall concept may be fairly novel in the locale, and the
high number of technical details proposed. Both of these decisions
reflect the fact that this is an unusual solution for this area of the UK,
so the details have to provide extensive information and that information should be based on standard technologies, if possible.

Case study 2: modifying a comparable model

To repeat, in this hypothetical case study, as in Chapter 12, the aim is to
'copy' an existing example but making adaptations to fit a new situation.

The precedent has well-documented and published details of the technology involved, and it was designed in conjunction with the manufacturer.

The requirement is for a new hostel building including relatively high environmental performance credentials but with a very short lead in time, in other words it needs to be completed in a very short space of time. The occupants are likely to be in residence for a good part of the day but for relatively short spells of time. It was decided that lightweight, quick heating and quick heat loss was not suitable, so a system that provided access to thermal mass was required. An interesting precedent was a new apartment construction that used precast concrete wall panels. These load-bearing precast concrete-insulated sandwich panels were constructed off-site and included the external finishing and integral insulation. The reason for opting for this particular precedent was because the sponsor of the new building is a prominent ceramic tile manufacturer and they were very keen that the building should reflect this.

In brief, the system is based on load-bearing walls constructed as complete units, incorporating a 150 mm thick concrete inner leaf panel with the insulation (75 mm) and vapour barrier enveloped between it and the

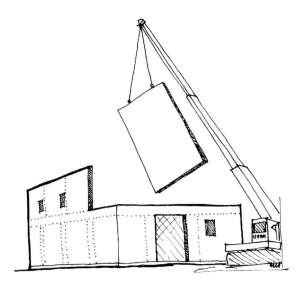

18.4

75 mm thick concrete outer panel. The outer panel has the finishing material embedded in it as part of the casting process. The inner leaf takes all the loads with the outer leaf and insulation suspended of it with stainless steel wind/shear tie connectors.

Phase 1: initial research

1. Background research into precedent study to establish whether or not it is a suitable method.
   - fast construction method with manufacturer sharing responsibility for delivery and construction
   - thermal mass available, suitable for continuous occupancy
   - very good internal acoustic insulation.

Phase 2: external finish

1. Background research into ceramic tiles suggests that they are suitable, provided they are manufactured correctly; however, ceramics can be rendered unsuitable by impact damage, and this system will make replacement of individual tiles very difficult – consider a different, maybe contrasting finish at lower levels.
2. External finish – tile manufacturers to provide suitable tiles manufactured with extra key to rear surface and 'specials' for exposed corners and sills.

Phase 3: internal finish

1. Good surface required for decoration
2. extra insulation to prevent heat loss due to lower initial external wall insulation (75 mm)
3. foil-backed plasterboard to provide the extra insulation due to its lower emissivity
4. plasterboard to be fixed directly to external wall panel to provide accurate alignment.

Phase 4: technical system chosen (see Chapter 12)

- Proprietary load-bearing precast concrete-insulated sandwich wall panels based on
- 150-mm thick structural concrete inner leaf with
- 75-mm insulation incorporating vapour control layer
- 40-mm cavity former with
- 75-mm thick concrete outer leaf connected to inner leaf with
- stainless steel wind-shear tie connectors

- outer leaf to incorporate client's tiling system laid out to pattern provided by conceptual designer
- inner face to have proprietary metal furring fixing system (cold rolled steel section bedded in plaster base to provide aligned surface) and
- 12.5-mm thick foil-backed plasterboard.

Phase 5: design details required

- Decision process
  - critical areas:
    - wall structure
    - openings
    - external wall/floor junction
    - floor details
    - dominant front elevation.
- Style
  - key readers of details – in order of importance:
    - engineer
    - building control officer
    - client
    - planning officer – maybe.
  - style choices:
    - sketch – too informal
    - hand-drafted – invites unnecessary dialogue
    - CAD detail – perfect, can incorporate manufacturer's details and looks highly professional;

Phase 6: design details (to be provided as CAD drawings)

1. standard section through wall structure and openings indicating internal finishes
2. external wall/floor junction to include fixing and grouting mechanisms plus floor details
3. architectural detail required for dominant front elevation.

Note: check details with colleagues.

This hypothetical case study that must be read in conjunction with the equivalent study in Chapter 12 was based on a real system provided by Techcrete. It illustrates that the adoption of existing technology with minimal adaptation, particularly that provided by manufacturers, can provide appropriate solutions whilst still satisfying the client's demands.

The main intentions of the scheme, to provide the design for a hostel that could be constructed in a short period of time and with a distinctive

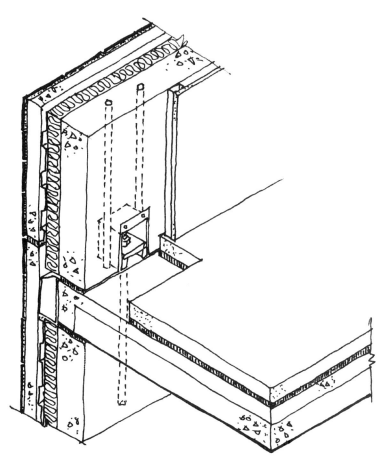

18.5 Adapted from detail by Susan Dawson (Techrete)

external appearance, are achieved. In addition, this is accomplished without unnecessary risk to either client or designer.

The main observation here is the relatively small number of details required; this is because the manufacturer's system is being employed and as such will rely on their standard details and the fact that it is a proved and certified 'system'.

Case study 3: compilation of a standard solution

As in Chapter 12, a floor detail will form the basis for the case study. In this instance, however, the requirement is for a detail that could be applicable to many similar situations and thus provide a standard detail.

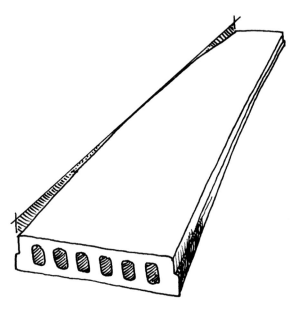

18.6

The study is intended to address the issue of the varying thicknesses that come with various floor finishes, particularly when used in conjunction with prestressed concrete structural systems. These systems normally include an in-built camber which means that the floor structure is not level – it rises towards the middle.

A system is therefore required that will negotiate this bump and provide a predictable final level, suitable for most floor finishes, insulation (thermal and acoustic) and underfloor heating possibilities. The requirement for the predictable final level is so that in multi-storey buildings, staircases systems can be designed accurately and that different flooring systems could also be accommodated without changes in level.

Phase 1: background knowledge and process

This particular study is a good example of the interrelationships that exist between materials and suitable technologies or indeed those that exist between technologies and suitable materials. In this case, the properties of the materials involved form an integral aspect of the technology.

For example, the floor structure requires levelling and any unevenness sorted out, so a material that can easily be adjusted to suit minor differences but also provide structural stability is required.

Previous knowledge suggests that the plasticity of cement-based products will even out the differences in level and also permit the formation of a level finish. The idea of timber battens embedded in the concrete was considered in Chapter 12, because it could aid the levelling process and provide a fixing point for certain flooring systems but was discounted because of the project-specific need to incorporate a sound deadening, resilient layer for all floor types.

Phase 2: project-specific requirements

As discussed in Chapter 12, a system is required that will form a standard solution for an entire scheme but still allow a selection of different flooring systems and heating arrangements throughout. The flooring systems can be selected from standard timber floorboards, chipboard floating floor with carpet overlay or ceramic floor tiles. The heating system will include underfloor heating only in the areas with ceramic tiles, either encased in a concrete screed or within a proprietary insulation support system. Acoustic considerations are limited to structure borne sound and a resilient layer must be incorporated at some point.

The system of battens was also excluded because of the need to incorporate the possibility of ceramic tiles as a floor finish as they require a firm base to avoid movement and subsequent cracking.

Phase 3: project-specific solutions

Decision 1

A structural concrete screed was chosen to level the entire floor system in order to:

- provide a seal to the structural floor system eliminating air-borne sound travel
- provide an even and monolithic structural base.

But subject to:

- system to guarantee finished height and level.

Suggest 25-mm thick (minimum) concrete levelling screed because it will accommodate any inconsistencies in level and provide its own structural integrity.

Decision 2

The resilient layer to be added, covering the entire floor, providing:

- acoustic resilient layer to floor system
- thermal insulation to floor system.

Suggest 25-mm thick rigid insulation such as expanded polystyrene or equivalent as it is required to support flooring loads from above as well.

Decision 3

A finishing screed required to take all final floor covering systems as it:

- provides an even and monolithic structural base
- provides good base for 'floating floor' systems.

But subject to:

- system required to guarantee finished height and level.

Suggest 75-mm thick concrete floor screed incorporating anti-cracking steel mesh reinforcement and underfloor heating pipes as required.

Phase 4: technical system chosen (see Chapter 12)

- Final floor finish installed as per manufacturer's instructions on
- 75-mm thick concrete floor screed with power-float finish, incorporating anti-cracking steel mesh reinforcement as per engineer's details on
- 25-mm thick rigid expanded polystyrene insulation or equivalent on
- 25-mm thick (minimum) concrete levelling screed on
- proprietary structural floor system.

Note: underfloor heating pipes installed as per manufacturer's instructions and heating engineer's details over steel mesh prior to the pouring of the floor screed.

Phase 5: design details required

- Decision process
  - critical areas:
    - floor structure incorporating reinforcement and heating pipes.
- Style
  - key readers of details – in order of importance:
    - builder
    - engineers (various)
    - building control officer.

- ○ style choices:
  - ▪ sketch – too informal
  - ▪ hand-drafted – possible as it invites dialogue
  - ▪ CAD detail – possible, useful as a standard detail.

Phase 6: design detail (to be provided as CAD drawings)

1. standard section through floor structure indicating levelling screed, resilient layer and floor screed incorporating steel mesh reinforcement and heating pipes location.

Note: check details with colleagues.

This hypothetical case study has served to illustrate that the provision of standard solutions can involve compromise in order to cover many possible variations. The reasons for this compromise may not always be obvious to the on-site operatives as it relies on a full understanding of all possibilities, and great care should be taken to insist that these details are followed in all respects.

To echo the conclusions in the equivalent section in Chapter 12, the prime requirement of standard solutions is to be reproducible, which means it must be robust (suitable to many circumstances) and simple (to avoid mistakes). As the choice of materials is integrated with the technical design process, the extra research required at an early stage is

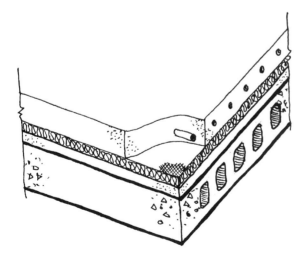

18.7

justified as it provides a sound rationale for compromise solutions before realistic 'standard solutions' become possible.

The final observation pertinent to this case study is the possible over-reliance on standard details; the advantages of having one system throughout a scheme and the quality control that this offers must be balanced against the losses in efficiency caused by the compromises needed to achieve standardisation.

Chapter review

- Apparently, new systems still rely to a large degree on existing knowledge and design processes.
- The choices may seem to be endless initially, but as soon as one or two initial decisions are made, these choices rapidly decline in number.
- Innovative solutions require a higher number of technical details reflecting the fact that they are unusual, so the details have to provide extensive information.
- The adoption of existing technology with minimal adaptation, particularly that provided by manufacturers, can provide appropriate solutions whilst still satisfying the client's demands. In addition, this is accomplished without unnecessary risk to either client or designer.
- When a manufacturer's system is being employed, the process will rely on their standard details that are based on proved and certified 'systems'.
- The provision of standard solutions can involve compromise in order to cover many possible variations.
- The reasons for this compromise may not always be obvious to the on-site operatives as it relies on a full understanding of all possibilities, and great care should be taken to insist that these details are followed in all respects.
- The prime requirement of standard solutions is to be reproducible, which means it must be robust (suitable to many circumstances) and simple (to avoid mistakes).
- The advantages of standard details is having one system throughout a scheme, but the quality control that this offers must be balanced against the losses in efficiency caused by the compromises needed to achieve standardisation.

Part **4**

Bibliography

Berge, B. (2000) *Ecology of Building Materials*. Oxford: Architectural Press.

Bryan, T. (2005) *Construction Technology Analysis & Choice*. Oxford: Blackwell Publishing.

Construction (Design and Management) Regulations (1994) London: Stationery Office.

Emmitt, S. (2002) *Architectural Technology*. Oxford: Blackwell Science.

Endacott, A. (2005) *Forty Years On, The Official History of the Chartered Institute of Architectural Technologists*. London: Chartered Institute of Chartered Architectural Technologists.

Wienand, N. and Watson, P. (2006a) *Obtaining Technical Innovation Within Integrated Project Teams*, Paper submitted to the Structural Engineering & Construction Conference (ISEC-4) 2007.

Webliography

British Board of Agrément, www.bbacerts.co.uk

British Gypsum Literature, www.british-gypsum.com/literature.aspx

Building Research Establishment, www.bre.co.uk

British Standards Institute, www.bsi-global.com

Chartered Institute of Architectural Technologists, www.ciat.org.uk

Communities and Local Government – previously Office of the Deputy Prime Minister, www.communities.gov.uk

The Concrete Centre, www.concretecentre.com

Construction (Design and Management) Regulations 1994, www.opsi. gov.uk/SI/si1994/Uksi_19943140_en_1.htm

European Directive on recycling new cars, http://europa.eu.int/eur-lex/pri/ en/oj/dat/2000/l_269/l_26920001021en00340042.pdf

European Standards, www.cenorm.be/cenorm/aboutus/index.asp

Foster & Partners, www.fosterandpartners.com/Projects/0102/Default. aspx

Holyrood – the Scottish Parliament building, www.scottish.parliament. uk/ vli/holyrood/index.htm

International Standards, www.iso.org

National House Building Council, www.nhbc.co.uk

Robust Details Ltd, www.robustdetails.com

Royal Institute of British Architects, www.riba.org/go/RIBA/Home.html

Techrete website, www.techrete.co.uk/techrete.htm

UK Patent Office, www.patent.gov.uk

Part 5
Specifications

Part **5**

Introduction

This part of the book deals with a process that has often been misunderstood. It has sometimes been treated as though it were a bolt-on optional extra, but it is one that is essential for every designer to command. Having identified and analysed the problem presented by the client, the team have reached the optimum solution. The specification lies at the heart of the processes by which this is succinctly conveyed not only to the contractor but between every participant in the design process.

The preparation of specifications is, it will be seen, an extremely responsible role. It is indeed an integral part of the design process from which it cannot be divorced. Although for practical reasons the two activities of detailing and specification have been separated in this book, they should never be considered as though separate.

Ideally, notes compiled during briefing will have been carried forward into planning and detailing, and specification notes concerning all salient points will accompany sketch details to form the basis of the writer's work.

For the document to be properly valuable, it needs to be based on a proper understanding of its purposes, which are addressed in Chapter 19. Chapter 20 examines the types of specification available and their uses, Chapter 21 considers the composition of the document and Chapter 22 presents a helpful case study for guidance (but not as a model to be copied).

Chapter **19**

Purposes of the specification

Objectives

You will recall from the introduction to specifications in Chapter 6 that these documents are of considerable significance. Those who prepare them carry a large part of the responsibility for ensuring that:

- The quality of the completed work fulfils the requirements of the client. This is a matter which will have been fully investigated at briefing stage (see Volume 1). For example, necessary standards of hygiene in a hospital operating suite or of durability on the walls of a safe deposit vault are part of the brief and must be carried forward throughout the project or they can become side tracked. Equally, if the client is looking for a short-term building, for exhibition purposes perhaps, this would be relevant.
- The level of specification is appropriate to the economic parameters of the project. A matter that will also have been examined in detail during briefing will be the cost profile, related to life cycle costs, of the building required. The decisions reached must be respected. One of the most seriously irresponsible things a design team can do is to allow a project to creep over budget without warning. They must therefore select materials and methods of construction which they believe can be employed within the cost limits.
- Those tendering have comprehensive information on which to prepare their bids. If those tendering are left to make assumptions, they will be liable either to make expensive ones, to the detriment of the client, or to cut corners in order to win the contract, which benefits no one.
- All firms tendering do so on an equal basis. They are entitled to know that their competitors have precisely the same comprehensive information that is before them.

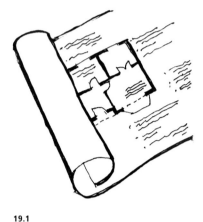

- Contractors fully understand what is expected of them. They need to know, among other things, to whom they will be responsible and what sanctions may be applied in case of failure to keep to time or otherwise.
- Those supervising work on site have clear criteria to apply.
- The law is respected. It is therefore imperative that any specific relevant provisions are alluded to.
- The interests of third parties are taken into account. This applies particularly to the insurance of passers-by and of adjoining property but may also refer to the rights of those who hold easements over the site, for example to gain access to other premises.

It used to be the practice that extensive (hand written) notes were appended to drawings as the sole description of materials and quality. This of course obviated most danger of conflict but was in the event only adequate where designer and builder were used to working closely together in a near symbiotic relationship. While specification notes provide helpful explanations on drawings, it is unlikely that, even in the simplest case, such notes alone would suffice to fulfil the objectives listed above.

To take a very simple example a householder wishes to have the front garden to his property repaved to provide hard standing for his cars. He might (though he would be very ill advised to do so) discuss the matter with someone quite unknown to him who happened to knock on his door 'because he was doing some work further down the street'. The householder just indicates that he wants the space paved. The tout hazards a guess that the work would take x number of days to complete and cost around £yyy. He asks for £zzz up front to buy the materials.

One should not be unduly surprised, six weeks later, to hear that the front garden has been ripped out but no more has been heard of the perambulating workers.

At the other extreme, our householder might have heard of cases like that and be very determined not to be caught. He therefore investigates the various available materials and instructs an architectural technologist to measure up the space and make a drawing of exactly what's wanted, as well as getting a surveyor to take off quantities to provide a schedule of work. He then enquires of the relevant trade organisations for the names of suitable contractors, obtains the names of satisfied clients from them, takes up these references, and invites five firms to tender for the work. He accepts the lowest price, the work goes smoothly and he finishes up with a nice forecourt.

In this case, one ought not to be astounded that the final price comes in at a good three times the cost of the perfectly acceptable driveway his neighbour has just had completed.

19.1

19.2

It is reasonable, therefore, to understand that there are interactions between responsibility, quality, time and cost, which need to be taken into account when determining the level of sophistication to which a specification needs to be prepared – but this understanding needs to fall within an overall acceptance that standards of quality, of both materials and workmanship, and the conditions under which the work is to be completed, must always be established by some means and accepted by all parties.

Users

Specifications are used by several different groups of readers, and the requirements of each need to be kept in mind during composition. These include:

19.3

- The design team, for interoffice communication during development of the proposals. It is essential that when decisions are taken the outcomes are recorded in a way that will inform everyone concerned. The evolving specification is the ideal vehicle for this.
- The quantity surveyor, when a BoQ is prepared and during the contract when variations have to be valued.
- The builder's estimator, preparing a tender, so that he knows his process is strictly comparable with those of his competitors.
- The site manager as a reference during construction, to ensure that the instructions of the designers are strictly followed.
- The clerk of works or other supervisor on site to provide criteria for assessment.

Content

There are three main elements in any specification:

- Preliminary clauses, which set out the legal and practical conditions under which the work will be done.
- Trade preambles, which home in on particular elements of construction, such as masonry or plumbing.
- Detail clauses, referring to individual items or stages.

Prime costs to cover the cost of components such as a heating system, still to be determined and often to be provided under subcontracts, are also frequently included. They need to be based on careful estimating, and to included not only for all attendance that the main contractor will have to provide but also for his profit. There will also, invariably, be an allowance for contingencies – which is money set aside to cover genuinely unexpected occurrences and not changes of mind by client (or designer!).

Subcontractors appointed in this way become nominated subcontractors, with whom the general contractor is directed to enter into a relationship and for whom he becomes responsible although he had no say in their appointment, and these additional sums take this into account. The general Contractor may also have subcontractors of his own, and what financial arrangements he makes with them is usually outside the conditions of the specification although his selection of them will be subject to certain conditions that will be described later.

Provisional sums may be included to cover items yet to be decided upon but which will not be the subject of subcontracts, and the most important of these is the contingency sum that should always be included to allow for totally unexpected circumstances that may rise during the course of the works. This is not money included for either the designer or the client to spend on a whim!

Classification

The hierarchy set out below is very simplified and must be understood to be a guide against which a decision on the appropriate level of sophistication can be made in a particular case.

Very small work

Very small work being undertaken for a single property owner by a single tradesman or a small firm.

In this case, it is desirable that the requirements should be set out in writing and include details of such things as:

- the times at which the site will be accessible
- responsibility for statutory approvals
- responsibility for the provision of mains services
- the materials to be used, where these are critical to safety, durability or appearance
- to whose satisfaction the work is to be done
- responsibility in the case of failure
- insurances for the property and persons and for third parties
- schedule of payments.

A small single building

In the case of, for example, a house for a private client, it will generally be appropriate for tenders to be obtained and the work to be done against a set of detailed drawings and a specification. One of the case studies in Chapter 22 deals with such an example.

19.4

The specification will usually be written from first principles, since the bulldozer approach of the national standards would be inappropriate, and the preliminary clauses will include the most essential details specific to the project.

Topics covered in the preliminary clauses will include such matters as:

- The form of contract to be adopted.
- The location of the site and access to it.
- The availability of main services and the responsibility of the contractor (usually) to arrange the provision of temporary services for the works.
- Conditions imposed under Building Regulation or Planning Approvals.
- Application of standard regulatory codes, such as British Standards.
- Inspection.

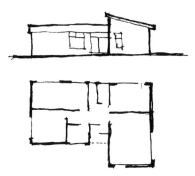

19.5

Additionally, each trade or constructional element will be covered by a separate section of the document, and clauses referring especially to acceptable practice in those activities will be included in trade preambles. For example, in the case of a specification for concrete works, such considerations as the weather conditions when work should not continue would be spelled out in the preambles.

The third major component of the document will consist of the detailed trade clauses for each element or trade, setting out (again taking the example of concreting) matters like the mix to be used in each element, such as foundations, oversite concrete, precast work and so on.

Major works

Major works will usually be contracted on the basis of BoQ, but this in no way minimises the importance of the specification, which must underlie the Bill and which must itself be prepared with comparable care to that which would be exercised in the previous instance. Decisions must be taken on all the same matters. In some ways, the precise wording may be thought to be even more critical, because those tendering will see no drawings to illustrate the intentions.

However, it is relatively common in this case for the specification to be prepared by extraction of appropriate clauses from a standard form, either in-house or national.

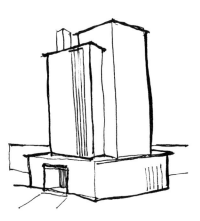

Responsibility

The responsibility for what is included within the specification is always that of the design team, just as much as the content of the drawings. This means that in cases where the actual task of writing the document is delegated, it must none the less be based on clearly understood decision

19.6

making and most carefully checked in detail, just as happens with design drawings. The practice of allowing a 'standard' set of clauses to develop over a period of years, and the unquestioned adoption of the resultant heterogeneous mix in all cases, is to be deprecated. To leave the detail of clauses within the BoQ to the quantity surveyor's experience can also prove to be an unfortunate short cut, unless that person has been fully involved in the development of the design from its initial stages – which is rarely the case.

Chapter **20**

Process and selection

There is one additional and very influential decision that must be taken before the preparation of the specification can be started. This is that between the prescriptive and the performance models. Making a selection between these depends on a number of factors:

- The vocabulary of up-to-date technology held by the design team.
- The existence of forward thinking research in a particular area of the industry.
- The likelihood of suitable construction firms being willing to assume the responsibility for what are in essence design decisions.

Prescriptive specifications

The conventional specification for many years has been one that encapsulates the considered decisions of the designers on the best ways of solving the accommodation problem set by the client.

Materials, including their source, quality and perhaps chemical make-up were described for the contractor to obtain where he wished, at the best price for which he could obtain them.

Standards of workmanship were stated or assumed to be those of properly trained tradespeople and specific standards to be met (such as the finish to which joinery timber was to be brought) described.

The conditions under which work was to be done, for example to ensure it was properly protected, were described.

In the case of manufactured items either:

- an actual product is named, sometimes with the option to offer an alternative if it is essentially the same but perhaps made by a different manufacturer

- a careful and detailed description of exactly what is required is set out, for the contractor to propose the materials or components offered on the basis of his knowledge of the industry, but leaving little scope for the contractor to offer alternative solutions or
- a PC sum was included in the specification and the contractor directed to order the particular object required adding on his required profit.

The examples given in the previous chapter were all of this type. In their preparation, the designer not only determines what has to be performed by the building but exactly how this outcome will be obtained. The responsibility for any failure to achieve the anticipated performance lies squarely with the designer.

Under this system, it is taken as read that knowing how to obtain a required result is part of the skills equipment of the members of the design team, so it is appropriate that the responsibility for doing so should remain with them.

This does not take account of the difficulty of keeping up to date with research and development across a wide variety of materials, components and systems. Contractors are sometimes assumed to be closer to these processes, but it is more realistic to say that this is true of the manufacturers and particularly the trade bodies that commission and disseminate the results of research.

The practice of performance specification has come into use as a way of tapping in to this store of up-to-date knowledge.

Performance specifications

Performance specifications describe what is required in behavioural terms: they state what is to be achieved but not how this is to be done.

There are various levels to which the process of specifying by expected performance can be pursued.

At a simple level, it is not unusual to require that concrete shall demonstrably reach a particular minimum level of compressive strength. Since the mixes necessary to reach specified levels are well known, this does not put an unacceptable level of design responsibility on to the contractor.

In addition, the practice of detailing the required performance of specialised components rather than making precise selections has come into use. This is done on at least two levels:

- There is a longstanding practice by which a selected item may be mentioned but an 'equivalence' clause be written around it.

For example, 'The lever handles are to be Messrs Brigand's catalogue no ... or other equal approved'.

In such cases, Messrs Brigand's product is almost always used, but the specifier hopes not to be accused of favouring an individual supplier:

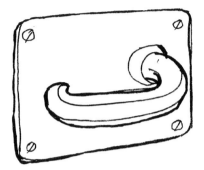

- In more sophisticated instances, the levels of heating and air change required from a heating and ventilating system might be stated, but the actual plant to be used is left to the choice of the (usually nominated) subcontractor, whose tender will have been based on his own assumptions.

20.2

Full performance specifications spell out in great detail the eventual result required while leaving decisions as to how that outcome will be obtained to the contractor. This means that instead of competing on efficiency, as is the case where a prescriptive specification is used, contractors are competing on the basis of their innovative ingenuity.

Against this, it has to be said that on the whole, contracting firms do not wish to assume the responsibility of design and have generally been reluctant to participate in such ways. The exception is in the case of design and build contracts, where contractors become developers and themselves commission designers. As an inevitable result, the weight of responsibility is shifted.

Performance specifications provide one way of utilising the undoubted skills and experience of the practical side of the industry, but it has sometimes been argued that a better means of achieving this aim would be to appoint a contractor on the basis of competitive tenders on a tentative BoQ and to invite his collaboration in developing detail.

Such specifications remain rare as applied to whole building projects but much more common where detailed and sophisticated components or elements are concerned. It is interesting that if you put 'performance specification' into a search engine, the first sites that come up deal with such elements as road markings. Safety and durability are paramount considerations in such a case, and a performance specification is the best way of ensuring that the most up-to-date research is accessed and applied.

Where innovation is essential in an extreme case such as the development of advanced sterile environments in operating theatres, the co-option of the knowledge and skills of the industry through the use of a full performance specification would be entirely appropriate. However, it would be reasonable to suppose that this is usually applied only to very large programmes (such as the theatres of a group of Health Authorities) in order to justify the time and costs of the necessary research.

It is important that the choice of this form of documentation and the variation in tendering practice implied is not made lightly. Performance

20.3

specifications are not always advantageous, are inappropriate for simple or conventional projects and have not always proved successful.

The advantages of performance specifications can be summarised as including the following:

- They open the door to innovative thinking and can stimulate research, provided the market justifies the outlay.
- They may encourage competition between firms anxious to establish reputations for advanced technological solutions.
- If criteria are set out skilfully, employing nationally agreed standards, it is possible to minimise the length of documents.

The disadvantages, however, have been thought to include the following:

- It can be difficult to enforce standards of quality unless very strict objective criteria are stated.
- A great deal of skill is needed to prepare effective lists of criteria.
- Sometimes longer documents are needed if criteria are set out in detail.

National Building Specification

The NBS is a subscription service that is kept constantly updated, produced by a consortium set up by a broad group of industry professions. It is part of RIBA Enterprises Ltd. and owned by the RIBA. The database includes a vast array of clauses that have proved their worth but among which careful choices have to be made. Many clauses need to have additional data inserted, so that this is not a fail-safe option. It is dangerous to include clauses that will not be invoked, as this practice weakens the authority of the whole document.

The sequence of clauses in the NBS follows the CAWS that is itself compatible with the Standard Method of Measurement (SMM7).

There are minor works, intermediate and standard versions. What is particularly helpful is that there are guidance notes included against many of the clauses to explain their use.

The NBS has the advantage of being widely adopted and therefore well understood, which should lead to a reduction in disputes as to interpretation.

Green specifications

There has more recently been a movement to encourage environmental awareness in the industry, associated with the use of the so-called green clauses. These are based on the perceived necessity to conserve natural resources by the use of 'sustainable' materials, products and methods.

'Sustainable' is defined by Chambers Dictionary of Science and Technology (1999) as 'Involving the long term use of resources that do not damage the environment'. The implication, therefore, is that renewable resources will be chosen wherever possible, emissions will be minimised and waste will be avoided.

A very large number of organisations have been set up to pursue this end. (Please also consult Volume 2 of this series on this topic.)

The National Green Specification website, www.greenspec.co.uk, which is generic and refers to the whole movement within the construction industry, sets out its objectives as follows:

> GreenSpec is the UK construction industry's definitive guide to sustainable construction. Inside GreenSpec you will find a wealth of information aimed at helping you to design more energy and resource efficient buildings using materials and technologies that minimise damage to people and the environment.

The site provides:

- a directory of available sustainable products
- a guide to sustainable traditional and new materials
- a checklist to guide specifiers towards aspects of construction where sustainable construction is appropriate.

Another useful resource is the Centre for Alternative Technology, where live experiments have been carried on for many years and from which good and up-to-date material can be sourced.

In-house specifications

Practices commonly build up useful libraries of standard details, and in parallel, where they may have found particular specification clauses effective, it is of course normal for them to reserve them for reuse in comparable circumstances. This can be a valuable practice, especially in the case of an office that has built up expertise in a specialised area of work, such as licensed premises or health centres. The occasion for reuse is likely to recur, and where the wording of a clause describing the surface of a bar or the level of artificial lighting in an examination suite has proved successful, it could be a waste of time to insist on regular reassessment.

Gradually, whole specification documents grow up and practitioners need to be warned against relying on these too heavily. Once dog-eared   20.4

documents used to shame the desks of drawing-board-bound designers, being used and reused uncritically time and again. Nowadays, the material remains pristine on the CD, and it is all too easy to reuse it without appreciating that it may be outdated or otherwise inappropriate.

No doubt it is inevitable that in the pressure of modern office life such repetitions will occur, time should be set aside to review what clauses are being relied on before that inevitable day when one proves no longer apposite.

Chapter **21**

Format

Prescriptive specification

Procedure

As in the case of all written work, it is essential that the task should be approached systematically. It is always likely that preparation will occupy more time than compilation, but the hours spent in research and organisation can be minimised if they are approached methodically.

Writing

It is an easy path to adopt standard specifications uncritically and may initially appear to save on office time, but it is a path to be followed only in extreme situations. Every designer should understand how and why specifications are composed and have acquired the skill to prepare them. It is only on this basis that informed selections from banks of prepared clauses can successfully be made.

It is undesirable for the actual compilation of the document to be delegated, and the writer should:

- Understand the underlying imperatives of the project, preferably as part of the initial design team.
- Not feel that the document is constrained by a word limit. However, it should be borne in mind that long specifications may be taken to imply excessively meticulous supervision and so might tend to lead to higher pricing.
- Use clear simple English, keeping sentences on the short side. Jargon is to be avoided, and language should be used precisely. However, though this is a legal document in the sense that it

21.1

forms part of a contract, clarity must always take precedence. It is not necessary to eschew punctuation.

- Where there is a short word and a long one that means the same, choose the short one.
- Use the spell checker (make sure it is switched to UK, not US English).
- Use a header to include a brief title and date and a footer to put the initials of the writer and page number on each page.

Analysis

As is the case when setting out to solve any problem, the first step in preparing any clause is to ensure that its purpose is clear. It can generally be assumed that a clause is to be included to avoid a potential problem that might be anticipated or to establish what procedure should be adopted should one arise.

To take a simple case, it may be the attention that the brick bonding is to form a simple diaper pattern, similar to that seen in Tudor walls. In this case, particular attention needs to be drawn both to the importance of maintaining truly vertical perpends and to the setting out of the brickwork from arrises. The contractor must be alerted because particular care will be needed, and he or she may wish to set his or her price higher. If his or her attention is **not** drawn to the requirement, he or she will undoubtedly ask for an extra when he or she discovers it on site.

A clause on the lines of that which follows to be included in the trade preambles for brickwork might be composed.

> Brick bonding. The visual impact of the brick bonding to the external leaf of cavity walls is considered to be of particular importance. The courses are to be set out precisely as shown on the drawings, with the relationships to arrises and openings strictly followed, and perpends are to be vertical in all cases.

The nearest relevant clause to this which might be found in the NBS is as follows (Clause 500) and would clearly be inadequate as it stands.

> Lay bricks/blocks on a full bed of mortar: do not furrow. Fill all cross joints and collar joints; do not tip and tail. Build walls in stretching half lap bond when not specified otherwise. Plumb perpends of facework at every third or fifth cross joint and even out the joint widths in between.

It should be noted that in the case of a Contract let on BoQ only, particular care is needed when exceptional levels of quality will be required on site, and there are no drawings at tender stage to point this out.

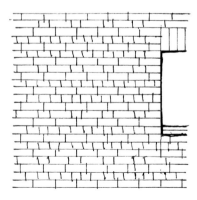

21.2

Preparation

The **preliminary clauses** should follow a systematic order, explaining the nature of the project as clearly as possible. A reasonable sequence, based on the CAWS, would be:

- name of project, position of site and access to it, and contact details of employer and designers
- list of drawings and other documents
- description of the site including necessary clearance, services, results of site investigation and easements
- scope of the work
- the contract
- tendering procedure
- instructions
- control of the site
- inspection, standards and criteria
- safety
- constraints
- temporary works
- maintenance period.

Within the **trade preambles**, trades are as far as possible listed in the order in which they will become involved in construction. The first stage of preparation will be to list these, consulting the drawings to ensure that nothing has been missed.

The list for a simple job might look like this:

- Site:
  - clearance
  - demolition
  - fencing
  - services.
- Groundwork:
  - excavation
  - underpinning.
- Concrete:
  - in situ
  - formwork
  - reinforcement
  - precast.
- Masonry:
  - brick
  - block
  - stone.
- Structures:
  - timber
  - steel.

- Joinery:
  - windows
  - doors
  - accessories.
- Roof covering:
  - sarking
  - tiles
  - flashings
  - eaves and verges.
- Finishes:
  - floor finishes;
    - tiles
    - carpet
    - boards.
  - plaster
  - paint
  - wall tiling.
- Services:
  - drainage
  - plumbing
  - gas
  - heating
  - electrical.
- Landscaping:
  - paving
  - fencing
  - planting.

Notice that in this list the components have been named. It is quite common practice to use the names of the tradespeople instead (Concretor, Bricklayer) as has been done in the longer example in Chapter 22.

In addition, and generally collected together rather than scattered through the trades, a list of the necessary **schedules** should be added. These might include schedules of:

- doors
- windows
- sanitary fittings
- IT equipment
- finishes and so on depending on the job.

The schedules should have been developed during the detail design period alongside the detail drawings, but it must be established by whom they are being prepared, and a cut-off date for their receipt be set.

Next, all PC and provisional sums should be listed. The specification has to include information not only on the sums but also on relevant profit and attendances. Again, some procedure must be arranged to ensure that the material is available from the responsible people by the cut off date.

Development

Within each trade, it is now possible to note all the considerations that must be covered and to arrange these in a logical order. For example, under brickwork, clauses might be needed to cover:

- quality and size of common bricks
- selection of facings
- damp proof course
- coursing
- mortar
- cavities
- ties depending on the job.

It should then be relatively straightforward to compose a simple clause to cover each of these considerations in turn. There are traps that are to be avoided.

Please note that the 'Common Arrangement of Work Sections' code, referred to above, is considerably more detailed than the simplified schedules above.

Compatibility – great care is needed to ensure compatible terminology between drawings and specification, and different sections of the specification. For example, what is described as 'sarking' on the drawings should not be referred to as 'under felt' in the relevant clauses.

Ambiguity – it is important to remember that if a sentence can be mis-read it will be. Each sentence should be read several times to make sure yours does not suffer from this fault. It is good practice to have an objective reader run through the document at draft stage to discover clauses with double meanings so that they can be amended.

One clause like this read as follows:

> All floor screeds are to be a minimum of 30 mm allowing for the thickness of the floor finish.

Does that mean 30 mm PLUS the thickness of the tile, carpet and so on or 30 mm LESS the thickness of the finish? It would be necessary to check a detail drawing to be sure.

Contradiction – it is vital that there is no clash between different clauses, so that conformity with one leads to inevitable failure over another. If in one place the specification requires that a trench does not exceed 500 mm in depth but elsewhere asks for the concrete to be placed at least 750 mm below ground level to avoid the danger of frost penetration, what standard will be acceptable?

Careless composition – be careful about the use of punctuation too. Consider the difference in meaning between 'This does not meet the required standard however you do it' and 'This does not meet the required standard. However, you do it!'

Address – it is best to decide at the outset whether 'The Contractor will…' or a straightforward 'Provide and fix…' format is to be adopted so as to preserve consistency. One common form is to use the first of these in the first clause under each section of the specification, using the second in the following clauses.

Performance specification

Performance specifications, as mentioned previously, vary considerably in scope. At one extreme, the briefing process leads to a direct approach to a number of potential contractors who are invited to propose the means of meeting the brief along with their tender price.

The performance specification passes the responsibility for problem-solving to the contractor unless special considerations, discussed later, apply. The requirements given to a proposed contractor must make it possible for all the competing tenderers to know that they are aiming at comparable outcomes and would generally contain more than the simple design brief. They might include conditions regarding expected life time, life-cycle costs, the possibility of remodelling and so on where these were important to the client.

The document is, accordingly, far more extensive than the normal design brief, because there is no scope for discussion during the development of the design. It needs to be composed systematically so as to be fully comprehensive and leave no room for doubt. In addition to being the basis of the accepted tender, it will (as in the case of the prescriptive specification) provide a yardstick for measuring the success of the project.

It may be set out purely in terms of the experience of the users, regarding space, temperature and a whole range of other attributes. This leaves every detail of planning and appearance to the discretion of the contractor, who is therefore likely to employ his own designers, the whole becoming in effect a design and build contract. In the case of competitive tendering, this implies that a number of competing design teams will be commissioned, which is neither economic nor a good use of scarce design skills.

In many cases, a more satisfactory process, for both the client and the builder, is for planning, massing and the main aspects of appearance to be settled between the client and his or her professional advisers, so that tenderers are provided with small-scale plans and elevations, supported by a brief describing the expected performance and left to make their own assumptions as to which materials and systems will best fulfil these requirements economically. They do not have the responsibility for making either ergonomic or aesthetic judgments, since space planning and architectural effect are predetermined. They are therefore not competing in these areas, which is difficult to describe in sufficient detail to ensure uniformity of outcome.

It is important also to bear in mind that the duty of the designer is to the commissioning body, and therefore in such a case to the contractor rather than the eventual building owner.

Beyond this, it is possible to identify a range of degrees of prescription, down to the condition where most parts of the project are specified conventionally but particular systems, such as the heating or IT installations, are based on performance criteria.

In the construction industry, this has hitherto been the commonest use of the performance specification in the building. However, experience in other sections of industry, such as those where the economy of very large programmes demands the rapid application of research-based advances results in economic use of resources (such as road building), have seen successful uses over whole projects. This may suggest that the process will become common within construction.

The preparation of a successful performance specification depends on extremely careful analysis of the client's requirements.

Design briefing is dealt with in detail in Volume 1 of this series, but in summary it consists of a dialogue between the client and designer from which a document describing the client's needs in meticulous detail emerges. Some of these requirements regarding accommodation may be summarised in the form of a briefing chart, as shown in the illustration. In addition, there will be limitations on the eventual design due to the nature of the site, any planning or other statutory requirements and so on. Cost, and sometimes also time, constraints will also be part of the package.

It is important that the client is encouraged to analyse **needs** rather than state **wants** or preferences. The developed brief sets a problem, which is the designers' role to solve.

A performance specification, at whichever level, is a much more extensive and intensively considered document than the usual run of design briefs. It has been suggested that its preparation falls conveniently into four stages:

- The **commission** that states quite simply, and in the usual way, what type of building is required and usually where it is to be constructed and the financial (and sometimes time) limits.

JOB NO ABC	BRIEFING CHART House in Brindlewood													
Activity	**Arrangement**				**Shape**			**Features**						**Remarks**
	share with	next to	near to	level	aspect	size	equip-ment	light	hum-idity	temp-erature	power	floor surface	wall surface	
Access		sit cook sleep	bath	GF	road	4 people				*		soft		
Sit	eat music	outdoor sit	bath	GF	SE/SW			*						
Eat	sit			GF										
Music	sit			GF			piano		*					
Cook	laundry	outdoor sit		GF								wash wash	wash	extraction
Laundry	cook			GF										
Sleep		bath			SE	1 person						soft		
Bath			access sleep									wash		extraction
Outdoor sit					SE/SW	4 people								shelter

21.3

- A **management** brief that sets out the responsibilities of the parties, which indicates not only which parties will undertake which parts of the development work but where the legal responsibility will lie.
- The **design** brief analogous to that used in a conventional design process but often set out in greater detail.
- The detailed **performance specification** against which tenders will be obtained.

It should be noted that the use of a performance specification is not a way of speeding up the process of commissioning a building. The process is necessarily meticulous and therefore time consuming.

Legal considerations

It is always hoped that specifications will be sufficiently well drafted to avoid problems but contentions do arise. No one should rely on what follows in a particular case. The notes are included for rule of thumb guidance only, and legal advice should always be sought in case of dispute.

In general:

- A professional designer is only held responsible for exercising reasonable professional skill.
- The person who designs and constructs something that turns out to be faulty is held responsible for the failure and its consequence. Some forms of contract expressly limit this level of responsibility, so the specification and contract need to be consistent;
- There is usually a stated time limit for the period during which the specified performance must be maintained, and this needs to be tied to a properly set out maintenance schedule.

In addition, the point raised earlier, that designers' responsibility is to the commissioning body, must not be overlooked. Volume 4 discusses this issue.

Preparation

The considerations mentioned above, in the case of prescriptive specifications, regarding compatibility, ambiguity, contradiction, composition and address will of course apply equally in the case of a the performance specification. There are additional factors that need to be considered.

The brief will be developed between the designers and the client in the conventional manner (see Volume 1) and may be taken to the circulation diagram stage. At this point, it has reached the stage at which designers can begin to consider and evaluate alternative solutions.

Derivation of performance standards

The standards adopted should be objective and measurable, so that there can be no question of subjective judgements coming into play if both the tendering process and the assessment of work on site is to be equitable. In particular, the level of site supervision and the enforcement of standards where the means of satisfying them has been identified by the contractor rather than the design team need to be carefully covered.

For example, a range of appropriate temperatures or a number of air changes per hour should be specified rather than using some vague phrase like 'comfort'. Equally, the load that a joist or beam must be capable of carrying and the deflection permitted should be specified rather than including a statement that it is to be of 'adequate' strength for its position. The numeric values given should be realistic and should

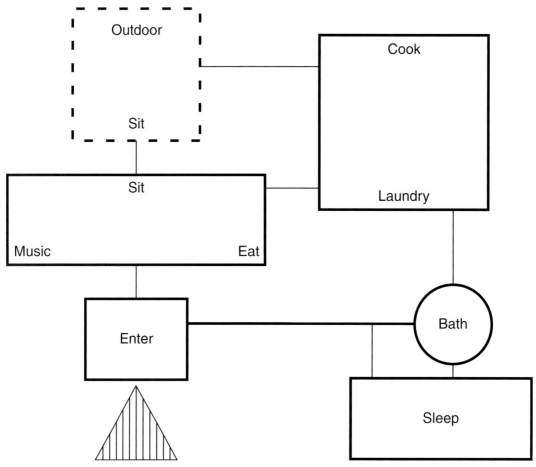

21.4

include acceptable tolerance allowances. Wherever possible, national standards should be invoked.

Clearly, this results in the design responsibility being shared, since determining what level of temperature or of strength is required is a normal part of the design function.

The Unified Classification for the Construction Industry (Uniclass) classification lists sets out a range of performance attributes that may be considered. Adopting the Uniclass hierarchy of criteria referred to above, a parallel specification for brickwork written in performance terms might include the following selected clauses:

U1   Descriptive attributes
           Composition
           Method of manufacture
           Accessories
           Shape, size and tolerance
           Mass (weight) density
           Appearance.
U3   Performance attributes
           Structural
           Thermal.
U4   Applications and activities
           Proper use
           Suitability, efficiency and effectiveness
           Consumption, waste and conservation
           Failure.
U6   Working attributes
           Storage.
U9   Other attributes

In each case, relevant British Standard (BS), equivalent European Standard (BS-EN) or other industry standards would be invoked in detail.

National Building Specification

A specification created by selection of clauses from the NBS is not an easy option. Though careful study of the clauses will show that most circumstances have been covered, this will not invariably be the case.

Parts of a specification for brickwork, drawing on the NBS intermediate version, could look something like this:

[These clauses refer to brick masonry and can be compared with the analogous clauses in the Case Study in Chapter 22. Where spaces are left in NBS for completion in relation to the specific project, a change of font has been used to indicate the material added.

When using the NBS, clauses are selected as required for the particular project. It is frequently necessary to choose between them or sometimes to modify them and it will be appreciated that only selected clauses are included here.]

F10   BRICK/BLOCK WALLING

To be read with preliminary/general conditions.

110   CLAY FACING BRICKWORK   Exterior

Manufacturer and reference:	Messrs . . . .
	(Address) . . . . . .
Mortar	Mix 1 : 1 : 6, lime : cement : sand
Bond	Stretcher
Joints	Struck
Features	True perpends

310   COMMON BRICKWORK

Bricks	to BS EN 771
Minimum average comp. strength	5 N/mm^2
Mortar	As above
Mix	As above
Bond	Stretcher

WORKMANSHIP GENERALLY

420   SITE STORAGE:

- Store bricks/blocks in stable stacks clear of the ground and clearly identified by type strength grade, etc.
- Protect from adverse weather and keep clean and dry.

500   LAYING GENERALLY

- Lay bricks/blocks on a full bed of mortar: do not furrow. Fill all cross joints and collar joints, do not tip and tail.
- Build walls in stretching half lap bond when not specified otherwise.
- Plumb perpends of facework at every third or fifth cross joint and even out the joint widths in between.

535   HEIGHT OF LIFTS

- Rack back when raising quoins or other advanced work. Do not use toothing.
- Raise no portion of the work more than 1.2 m above another at any time.
- In facework, complete each lift in one period of operation.
- Do not carry any one leaf more than 1.5 m in one day unless permitted by the clerk of works.

690   ADVERSE WEATHER

- Do not use frozen materials.
- Do not lay bricks when the air temperature is at or below 3 °C. Do not lay mortar on frozen surfaces.
- Maintain the temperature of the work above freezing until the mortar has fully hardened.

- Rake out and replace mortar damaged by frost. When instructed, rebuild damaged work.
- Protect newly erected walling against rain and snow when precipitation occurs and at all times when the work is not proceeding.

760   APPEARANCE

- Keep brickwork evenly spaced using gauge rods.
- Protect facework against damage and disfigurement during the course of the works, particularly arrises of openings and corners.

790   PUTLOG SCAFFOLDING to facework will not be permitted.

830   CLEANLINESS:

- Keep facework clean during construction and thereafter until Practical Completion.
- Turn back scaffold boards at night and during heavy rain.
- If, despite precautions, mortar marks are deposited on the face of masonry units, leave to dry and then remove with a stiff brush.
- Rubbing to remove marks or stains will not be permitted.

Chapter 22

Case study

A single small house for a private client

This house was unconventional in design, as it was required for use by a single retired person who hoped never to need to move from it. It incorporated a number of features to make it useable by a disabled person, even though the client had no disabling conditions when it was built. It was tendered for by a number of well-recommended medium-sized builders against detailed drawings and specification.

The kitchen appliances and fittings were the subject of a PC sum and were carried out by a nominated subcontractor, following a detailed layout prepared by the architect.

The house was completed satisfactorily, and no problems arose from the documents.

Identifying features, including the location, have been removed to protect the identity of the designer and client. Any similarity of names or locations to actual places or persons is entirely coincidental.

Note: the clauses in this case study are not proposed as ideal models. They are offered as an example of ones used satisfactorily in practice.

After many of the clauses explanatory comments are included in italics. These are, of course, for the benefit of readers of this book and would never be included with such a document in use!

Part 1 Preliminary clauses

Generally

This specification refers to the construction of a single storey house and detached garage with associated landscaping work in ...... The

22.1 The specification is a part of modern drawings

proposed work is described in the drawings which accompany the specification.

If the work were unconventional (e.g. if a prefabricated structure was required), it might be desirable to mention this here.

Parties to the project

Employer   . . . .

. . . .

. . . .

Architect/Architectural Technologist

. . . .

. . . .

. . . .

Telephone:

Fax:

E-mail:

Drawings

The contract drawings are as follows:
Plans sections and elevations to 1:50 scale *(listed)*.
Site and service plans to 1:100 scale *(listed)*.
Constructional details to 1:10 and FS *(listed)*.

These drawings may from time to time be amplified and/or modified by the issue of details.

In the case of conflict between the drawings and the specification or the Contract, or in the case of conflict between the contract documents and the Building Regulations, the matter is to be referred to the Architect/ Architectural Technologist.

One problem the writer faces is to determine the extent to which conditions of the proposed contract should be duplicated in the specification. A sensible rule is to ensure that any matter which might relate peculiarly to the particular project is described but in any case that the potentiality of conflict is brought up and a means of resolution described.

Site

The site forms part of the garden of a house at ...... It is accessible by public transport, and has direct access from a public road. On obtaining possession of the site, the Contractor is to open up a separate road access in accordance with the drawings, and is to fence the site off from the garden of . . . . . . He is at all times to use this new access and to avoid disturbance to the occupants of . . . . . .

The Contractor will be assumed to have visited the site before submitting his tender and to have made himself familiar with all conditions of the site which might reasonably be known from inspection and from the tender documents.

This is an important clause as it guards against the Contractor relying on some feature of the site as a basis for a claim for extras. If the site were subject to any easements such as the right of an adjoining owner to drive cattle across it, this should be mentioned.

Scope of the work

The work to be included in the contract is clearly indicated on the drawings attached to this specification and briefly includes:

- clearance of rubbish from the site at the commencement and at the end of the contract
- erection of a single storey brick house, including the provision of services
- erection of a detached single storey brick garage
- fencing to the site to the south and east site boundaries
- provision of a pavement crossing and a new opening in the existing drystone wall to the north site boundary
- Site works and landscaping.

Contract

The Contract will be the Joint Contracts Tribunal Intermediate Building Form (IC), a copy of which can be obtained from the RIBA 66 Portland Place London W1 N 4AD

It should be assumed that any firm tendering will be familiar with the standard forms of contract or will have easy access to them. They have been adopted by the industry so that the legal force of every clause is (or can be) tested by the courts, and therefore they are treated as unambiguous. It is not necessary to spell out any variations between the form chosen and any other form. The JCT does not itself sell copies.

Variations

Where conditions encountered during construction cause a variation from the work shown in the contract documents the contract sum shall be varied by agreement between the Architect/Architectural Technologist and the Contractor, and an Architect/Architectural Technologist's Instruction will be issued. After the tender is accepted, the Contractor will submit a Schedule of Rates to be used as a basis for pricing variations to the Contract.

The schedule is necessary where there is no BoQ, as otherwise there would be no fair basis for pricing variations. In the case of a Contract based on a BoQ, the successful Contractor will normally be required to submit a priced bill to fulfil this function.

Person in charge

The Contractor shall notify the Architect/Architectural Technologist at the commencement of the works of the name of the person in charge of the contract and his/her telephone number.

Materials

The materials shall be of the specified quality and in those cases where no quality is specified shall be in accordance with the latest British or European Standard Specification, or where no document has been issued shall be of the best quality and to the reasonable satisfaction of the Architect/Architectural Technologist.

'Reasonable satisfaction' is not entirely satisfactory: the Contractors interpretation will depend on how well he or she knows the Architect/ Architectural Technologist 'According to normal good practice' might be preferred. See Security, below.

Craftsmanship

The normal standard to be expected will be that of competent and experienced craftspeople. Unskilled operatives will be used only for labouring.

Building regulations

The current Building Regulations will apply. All notices to the Local Authority are to be given, all legally demanded fees are to be paid, and work is to be left open for inspection by the Local Authority as required.

Statutory approvals

Approvals under the Building Regulations and Town Planning Legislation have been applied for, and there is no reason to expect a delay in the granting of approvals. Work is not to commence before approvals are received.

BS, BS-EN and BSCP

All relevant European and British Standards and Codes of Practice are to apply, subject to specific references in the Contract Documents.

Manufacturers' guidance

The Contractor is to ensure that the manufacturer's instructions and recommendations in respect of handling, storing, preparation and fixing of all products are followed. The Architect/Architectural Technologist is to be informed if there is any conflict between such instructions and recommendations and any other specified requirement.

Security

The security of the site is the sole responsibility of the Contractor, who is to protect all existing fences, trees and services from damage from any cause whatsoever, and to reinstate any damages items to a reasonably acceptable standard.

If, for example, the trees were subject to preservation orders this should be spelled out here.

As in the case of 'reasonable satisfaction' *(referred to under Materials, above),* 'To the entire satisfaction of the Architect/Architectural Technologist' *is a very common phrase in specifications, which might have been used rather than the wording chosen – but it can be highly contentious and is best avoided as has been done here.*

Allow for safeguarding the works and providing temporary security fencing with warning notices. Watching and lighting is to be provided for the security of the public and the works, to protect all materials and plant against any damage, theft or contamination and to prevent trespass. The Employer is to be indemnified against all claims.

All public and private services, roads, pathways fences and existing planting and structures above and below ground are to be properly protected, upheld and maintained. No public service or private property is to be interfered with in any way without the express permission of the service authorities or private owners or the Architect/Architectural Technologist as appropriate.

Claims

In the case of an occurrence arising which may lead to a claim against the Contractor or the Employer or otherwise, the Contractor shall immediately and in any case within three working days, give written notice of each occurrence to the Employer. The Employer shall not be liable to any claim or expense arising from failure to provide such notice.

The Contractor shall similarly give notice to the Employer of any loss or damage which occurs and is at the sole risk of the Employer.

No remedial work shall be put in hand until authority has been received from the insurer and the Employer.

Huts

The Contractor is to provide all necessary huts and latrines, to maintain these in acceptable condition at his own expense and to remove and make good at the completion of the works.

Name boards

The Contractor is permitted to obtain the necessary approval for, and provide and maintain for the period of the works, a suitable and approved name board to identify the project, the Contractor, and the Architect/Architectural Technologist.

*In some cases, he might be **required** to do this.*

Advertisements

The display of advertisements on the site, apart from the name board, will not be permitted.

Plant

The Contractor must include for the provision of all necessary scaffolding, plant, tools equipment and the like and for all facilities reasonably required for the completion of the works, and for vehicles and costs of transport of materials and workpeople necessary to carry out the works.

Electricity

The Contractor is responsible for the provision of the necessary electricity supply for the works.

Water

The Contractor must arrange for an adequate supply of clean water to the works.

Telephone

The Contractor is to arrange for a landline or mobile telephone service, dedicated to the works, and to inform the Architect/Architectural Technologist of the number. Messages are to be diverted to an answering service when the handset cannot be answered.

All the above services, and the contracts for them with the suppliers, must always be the Contractor's responsibility, and this wording makes this clear.

Progress

The Contractor will provide and agree a programme for the completion of the works, indicating starting and completion dates. On obtaining possession of the site, the work will proceed smoothly and continuously to completion in accordance with the agreed programme. It is expected that the work will be completed in a single phase, but there are circumstances in which the work may be passed as shown below. The Contractor should include with his tender what the breakdown in price would be between these two phases, and the premium required should the work be phased.

Phase I	House including internal and main services
	Fencing
	Provision of pavement crossing,
	Entrance space in wall
	Tarmacadam drive
Phase 2	Garage
	Remaining site works

Nuisance

The works are to be carried out in such a manner as to minimize nuisance from dust, fumes, smoke, noise, rubbish or other causes.

Note the term 'minimise'. *It is recognised that some level of disturbance is inevitable.*

Disbursement

The Contractor will be assumed to have included in his tender for all necessary disbursements, profit, holidays with pay, National Insurance and other employers compulsory contributions, and for all attendances of one trade on another.

Sometimes in such clauses, the reference is to the 'Tenderer', *but this is undesirable. The Contractor should be referred to by a single term throughout the document, whether actions referred to occur before or after the Contract is entered into.*

Insurance

It is the responsibility of the Contractor to ensure that all necessary insurances are taken out and kept up to date for the period of the works to practical completion.

Before work commences, the Contractor is to submit to the Architect/ Architectural Technologist documentary proof that the necessary insurances are in force.

It is fairly common for the 'necessary' insurances to be listed. This, however, can mean a heavy burden on the specification writer if something is missed! At practical completion, insurances become the responsibility of the building owner.

Storage of materials

It is the responsibility of the Contractor to ensure that all materials and components delivered to the site are properly protected so that no deterioration of any kind takes place. Any material which deteriorates after delivery to the site will be rejected.

Inclement weather

The Contractor will be assumed to have included in his tender for normal weather conditions at the site. The works are to be protected from inclement weather conditions, and no work is to be undertaken in unsuitable conditions.

Exceptional conditions (e.g. prolonged lying snow) would be accepted as a reason for delay.

Supervision

Inspection of the work may be delegated by the Architect/Architectural Technologist to a professionally qualified assistant, who may be assisted by a Clerk of works.

The legal responsibility for supervision will still be that of the Architect/ Architectural Technologist.

Contractor's obligations

The Contractor is to allow for the obligations, liabilities and services described in the form of contract referred to above, subject to the following conditions:

Stage payments

Monthly stage payments equal to the proportion for the work completed according to progress judged against the programme provided by the Contractor will be certified.

This is bound to be a matter for agreement between the parties: there is no objective measure in the absence of a BoQ.

Retention fund

All stage payments will be subject to a retention fund of 10%.

The Contract says how the fund will be handled, so it is not necessary to detail that here.

Practical completion

At practical completion the site and works are to be left in a clean and orderly condition. All rubbish, temporary huts, temporary services and other matter not part of the completed works are to be removed. All damage howsoever caused is to be made good.

Practical completion will be certified when the building is fit for occupation to the satisfaction of the Architect/Architectural Technologist, whereupon half the retention fund will be released. Should the work be phased as described above, practical completion will be certified for each phase.

Maintenance period

The Contractor will complete all outstanding items of work and correct any defects arising from faulty materials or workmanship discovered during a period of TWELVE months from practical completion in the case of the heating installation and landscape works and SIX months in the case of other works.

The remainder of the retention fund in respect of all items other than heating and landscaping will be released when all relevant works have been completed, and the Final Certificate will be issued and the whole of the retention find released when those referring to heating and land-scaping have also been dealt with to the satisfaction of the Architect/ Architectural Technologist.

*In this case, it is appropriate to use the final phrase. Note that the work is **not** to be done to the satisfaction of the Employer!*

Subcontractors

The Contractor will be responsible for the work of all subcontractors, whether Nominated or otherwise, and is to provide for all necessary attendances and facilities.

Tender

The tender is to be upon a Lump Sum Fixed Price basis, and is remain open for acceptance for a period of THREE MONTHS from the tender date.

Tenders should include a statement of the period required for completion of the work, which may be taken into account in selecting the successful tender.

'Should', not 'are to': *the implication is that tenders will not be discarded because they do not include this statement.*

The Employer does not undertake necessarily to accept the lowest or any tender.

Documents

The copyright of all documents belongs to the Architect/Architectural Technologist. Two copies will be issued free of charge to the Contractor, and additional copies will be available on request but may be charged for. The documents enclosed with the invitation to tender are to be returned to the Architect/Architectural Technologist on notifications of the result of the tender round.

Queries

Any queries arising from these conditions should be addressed in writing to the Architect/Architectural Technologist by the date stated in the covering letter. Answers to all queries received by that date will be sent in writing to all firms tendering.

Omissions

This specification is indicative. The omission from this specification of any material or labour clearly required for the completion of the works is not to be construed as implying that that element is to be omitted from the Contract.
Date . . . . . .
Signature . . . . . .

Part 2 Preambles to trades

Only selected sections of this part of the specification are reproduced as examples of what is appropriate.

Site clearance

Rubbish

On obtaining possession of the site, the Contractor is to clear all rubbish and weeds from the site, and protect all shrubs and trees indicated on the site plan as to remain.

It is necessary to indicate which are weeds and which are to be protected! Who is to be responsible for this?

Topsoil

Remove vegetable soil to a designated spoil heap and reduce levels.

The topsoil is valuable, will be needed and must be protected.

Spoil

Excavated material other than vegetable soil is to be reserved on site for backfill as required and the unused residue removed from the site at the completion of the works.

Access

Make opening 3000 mm wide in the existing 750 mm high dry stone boundary wall at back of pavement, making good as necessary. Materials are to be reserved on site for use in landscaping and are on no account to be used in hardcore.

'As necessary' allows for the skill of the stonemason but may be difficult to enforce.

Bricklayer

Materials

Facing bricks

Where facing bricks are specified, the bricks are to be ...... bricks as selected, in accordance with the sample available for inspection at the office of the Architect/Architectural Technologist, obtained from Messrs ...... *(address)* set in mortar selected to match the bricks in density and colour. The whole of the bricks required is to be obtained in a single delivery in order to ensure consistency.

A particular brick has been selected and agreed with the client and the local Authority. No alternative is permissible. In the case of other materials, note that some clauses indicate similarly definite choices but others allow for different degrees of variation.

Common bricks

The common bricks are to be in accordance with BS EN 771 (FN) properly burnt and well shaped.

Any brick that meets the standard will be acceptable.

Blocks

Insulation blocks are to be 140 mm solid type ...... blocks from Messrs ...... *(address)*.

The calculations have been based on these particular blocks, so no other can be used. Note that although units are not be used in dimensions on drawings, they are included in the specification to ensure clarity.

Lightweight blocks are to be similar to ...... blocks obtained from Messrs ...... *(address).*

Any block that is demonstrably similar to that mentioned can be used (almost always when a phrase of this kind is included, the mentioned material or component will be used).

Mortar

All mortars are to be freshly mixed from clean materials as previously described under concrete and immediately used. No old mortar is to be knocked down for re-use.

This describes normal good practice.

DPC

The Damp Proof Course is to be similar to ...... obtainable from Messrs ...... *(address).*

DPM

The Damp Proof Membrane is to be similar to ...... obtainable from Messrs ...... *(address).*

Lintels

All lintels are to be ...... Lintels obtained from Messrs ...... *(address)* provided in accordance with the Schedule and to be in every case provided with a minimum bearing of 450 mm at each end.

Again, a particular product is required because the Building Regulation approval depends on calculations based upon its characteristics.

Insulation

The cavity wall insulation is to be similar to 100 mm ...... cavity wall insulation obtainable from Messrs ...... *(address).*

Ties

The cavity ties are to be integrated wall ties and clips to hold insulation in position.

It is not clear why no particular product or BS has been mentioned in this case!

Workmanship

Brickwork

All brickwork is to be laid in accordance with BS EN 771. Joints are to be filled and frogs (where present) laid upwards.

The bricks mentioned are perforated rather than frogged, but this allows for an alternative to be offered. Frogs facing up are more naturally filled with mortar than those laid downwards.

DPC

Damp proof courses as specified are to be laid on a full even bed of mortar in a continuous strip with 150 mm laps at joints and full laps at angles. Joints containing DPCs are to be finished to normal thickness. DPCs are to be neatly trimmed on face to an agreed small dimension, dressed down to form a drip and not pointed.

In the course immediately above the DPC, perpends are to be left clear at 900 mm centres.

Cavities

All cavities are to be kept strictly clear throughout construction. Where cavities are closed at openings, full width DPCs are to be inserted between the leaves and lapped at corners and with the lintel.

It is quite difficult to keep the cavity clear, and it is a point for checking during site visit.

Cavity ties

Ties as specified are to be inserted between the leaves at not less than 900 mm centres vertically and horizontally and bedded not less than 50 mm into each leaf. Additional ties are to be positioned at not more than 300 mm centres at openings. All ties are to be kept strictly clear of mortar droppings.

Junctions

All junctions between blockwork and brickwork are to be properly block bonded.

'Properly' is a difficult word, and a better phrase such as 'in accordance with good practice' *might be preferred.*

Chases

Where required, chases are not to affect the stability of blockwork or brickwork.

These will have been detailed. The clause guards against them having been made too deep.

Scaffolding

All scaffolding must be self supporting or braced. Putlog scaffolding will not be permitted.

Putlog scaffolding (built into the masonry) causes damage that is hard to correct.

Faced work

All fairfaced and facings brickwork is to have cleanly struck and true perpends.

All faced and fairfaced work is to be kept clean during construction and until practical completion. No mortar is to be allowed to encroach on the face during laying, scaffold boards are to be turned back at night and during heavy rain. Rubbing or chemical treatment to remove stains will not be permitted.

To protect the work as far as reasonably possible from accidental damage.

Decorator

Materials

Paints

The paints used for the works, including primers, undercoats and other coatings are to be obtained from Messrs ...... *(address)* or other approved supplier.

In this case, it appears that the nomination is simply for guidance.

Auxiliary materials

Other materials, including paint strippers, abrasive papers and blocks, cleaning agents, etching solutions, mould inhibitors, size, stripping, stopping and knotting are to be of types recommended by their manufacturers for the purposes for which they are to be used.

This has all the air of a standard clause. Are all these materials to be used in a simple house?

Workmanship

Defects

Before decoration all defects, such as holes, cracks, defective joints and others in surfaces to be prepared for decoration are made good as previously described, so that the defects are not visible when the decorative work is complete.

This is covered under the preambles to Carpenter and Joiner.

Before decoration, all timber and plaster surfaces must have a smooth even finish, with arrises eased.

Preparation

All surfaces are to be prepared in accordance with the recommendations of the manufacturer of the relevant decorative coating.

All surface as are to be allowed to dry out thoroughly before decoration.

Stopping

All nail and screw holes and similar depressions are to be stopped after priming with stopping pressed well in to a flush surface.

All pore and grain irregularities are to be filled after priming, sealing and stopping with filler, brush or knife applied, remove surplus and left with a smooth even surface.

This does not duplicate a previous requirement – new irregularities are liable to appear when the material is wetted.

Knotting

Resinous exudations are to be removed from all timber and knotting is to be applied to such timber and to all knots, and allowed to dry.

Ironmongery

Where appropriate, all ironmongery is to be removed and refitted as previously specified

This, too, is covered under the preambles to Carpenter and Joiner.

Recommendation

All materials are to be used only as recommended by their manufacturers, taking particular account of the conditions of exposure. The Architect/ Architectural Technologist is to be informed of any discrepancy and written instructions obtained before proceeding with the work.

Colours

All colours to be used will be selected from the BS4800 colour chart and must be strictly adhered to.

Timing

Decorations are to be carried out towards the end of the works after necessary making good has been completed, so that the chances of damage to following works in minimized.

Protection

All completed decorations are to be protected from damage.

Cover

It is the responsibility of the Contractor to ensure that a suitable primer and undercoat are used and that sufficient coats are applied, and rubbed down between coats to give complete obscuration and a final opaque evenly coloured surface.

Specifications used to include clauses to say that there must be ...... number of coats, each with a different colour, to ensure that the number of coats applied could be checked. This clause allows for the improvement in modern paint systems, but is more in the nature of a performance specification.

Part 3 Schedules

The specification included schedules of:

- landscaping, covering pavings and planting
- sanitary fittings
- windows and doors, including lintels and furniture
- external finishes.

and internal finishes as follows:

Schedule of internal finishes

Porch
Floor	Black quarry tiles
Walls	2 coats plaster, painted matt
Ceiling	Wood strip (see detail), painted gloss

Entrance hall
Floor	Black quarry tiles
Walls	2 coats plaster, painted matt
Ceiling	Wood strip (see detail), painted gloss

Bathroom
Floor	Black quarry tiles
Walls	Black ceramic tiles
Ceiling	Plasterboard and skim painted, steam resistant gloss

Kitchen
Floor	Black quarry tiles
Walls	Grey ceramic tiles
Ceiling	Plasterboard and skim, painted matt

Workshop
Floor	Black quarry tiles
Walls	Fairfaced blocks, painted matt
Ceiling	Plasterboard and skim, painted matt

Living room
Floor	Bonded carpet
External walls	Fairfaced blocks, painted matt

Internal walls	2 coats plaster, painted matt
Ceiling	Plasterboard and skim, painted matt

Study

Floor	Bonded carpet
External walls	Fairfaced blocks, painted matt
Internal walls	2 coats plaster, painted matt
Ceiling	Plasterboard and skim, painted matt

Bedroom

Floor	Bonded carpet
External walls	Fairfaced blocks, painted matt
Internal walls	2 coats plaster, painted matt
Ceiling	Plasterboard and skim, painted matt
Internal door linings	Softwood, painted
Internal doors	Hardwood, stained and varnished
Cupboard doors and frames	Painted to match wall
Timber skirtings, cornice and wainscot rails	Softwood, painted.

SUMMARY

This section of the book has:

- examined the objectives of the specification
- considered the alternative forms the document may take
- proposed methods of composing successful documents and
- provided a sample specification with commentary on selected clauses.

Part 5

Bibliography

Anderson, J., Shiers, D. and Sinclair, M. (2002) *Green Guide to Specification*. Oxford: Blackwell.

Bowyer, J. (1985). *Practical Specification Writing for Architects and Surveyors*. London: Hutchinson.

BS 8900 Guidance for Managing Sustainable Development (2006) London: British Standards Institute.

Construction (Design and Management) Regulations (1994) London: Stationery Office.

Construction Project Information: A Code of Procedure for the Construction Industry (2003) London: CPIC.

National Building Specification (1972) London: National Building Specification.

Rosen, H.J. and Regener, J. (2004) *Construction Specification Writing, Principles and Procedures*. New York: John Wiley and Sons.

Stellakis, M. and Lupton, S. (2000) *Performance Specification Report*. London: RIBA Publishing.

Willis, C.J. and Willis, J. Andrew (1997) *Specification Writing for Architects and Surveyors*. Oxford: Blackwell Science.

Webliography

British Standards Institute, www.bsi-global.com

Centre for Alternative Technology, www.cat.org.uk

Construction (Design and Management) Regulations 1994, www.opsi.gov.uk/SI/si1994/Uksi_19943140_en_1.htm

Construction Project Information Committee (CPIC), www.productioninformation.org

Joint Contracts Tribunal, www.jctltd.co.uk

National Building Specification, www.thenbs.com

National Green Specification, www.greenspec.co.uk

Index